THE GRACE IN LIVING

THE GRACE IN LIVING

Recognize It, Trust It, Abide in It

Kathleen Dowling Singh

Wisdom Publications
199 Elm Street
Somerville, MA 02144 USA
wisdompubs.org

Library of Congress Cataloging-in-Publication Data
Names: Singh, Kathleen Dowling, author.
Title: The grace in living : recognize it, trust it, abide in it / Kathleen
Dowling Singh.
Description: Somerville, MA : Wisdom Publications, 2016.
Identifiers: LCCN 2016012203 (print) | LCCN 2016027892 (ebook) | ISBN
9781614292852 (pbk. : alk. paper) | ISBN 161429285X | ISBN 9781614293095 () |
ISBN 1614293090 ()
Subjects: LCSH: Spiritual life. | Spiritual biography.
Classification: LCC BL624 .S5425 2016 (print) | LCC BL624 (ebook) |
DDC 204/.4--dc23
LC record available at https://lccn.loc.gov/2016012203

ISBN 978-1-61429-285-2   ebook ISBN 978-1-61429-309-5

20 19 18 17 16   5 4 3 2 1

Photo of Cynthia Bourgeault on page 277 is by Michael Ambery.

Cover and interior design by Gopa & Ted2, Inc.
Set in Dante MT Std. 11.5/15.3

Wisdom Publications' books are printed on acid-free paper and meet the guidelines for permanence and durability of the Production Guidelines for Book Longevity of the Council on Library Resources.

🌸 This book was produced with environmental mindfulness.
For more information, please visit wisdompubs.org/wisdom-environment.

Printed in the United States of America.

Please visit fscus.org.

Table of Contents

———— ❦ ————

PART THREE: RECOGNIZING GRACE IN YOUR LIFE

Grace will appear
in both sweet and fierce forms . . .
sent from beyond
to open us
to the radiant fullness of being.
—MATT LICATA

An Invitation

—— ⌘ ——

AWAKENING IS FAR MORE ORDINARY and more accessible than we think. In fact, the way we think about awakening can actually be our obstruction to it. Awakening is not a single Technicolor event for most people, but an ongoing, radiant stance—simple, sane, an ever-deepening dance with grace.

The Grace in Living is offered to evoke, encourage, and support that stance—to invite your entry into the illumined and peaceful spaciousness of an awakening relationship with life. I have written before about the grace in dying—the spiritual transformations that occur for all of us at the end of life. Another book takes a look at the grace in aging—how we can nurture those same transformations as we age and awaken as we grow older. Here, in this book, is an opportunity for us to learn to recognize grace, to trust it, and to embrace grace as our own true nature in every moment of our lives.

The Grace in Living offers an exercise in spiritual biography, a wiser and more encouraging view of our lives than the ordinary view that ego maintains. It is a heartening lens through which to recognize that our own life is already a journey of awakening.

Spiritual biography is an exercise of recollection, a contemplative remembrance of the transformative experiences that have taken place, often unnoticed, throughout our lives. It offers a real and meaningful opportunity to grow in recognition of the ever-presence of grace, a recognition that helps develop our faith and our confidence. With that recognition, we can begin to trust grace's unerring guidance.

The first part of this book offers insight into the nature of the spiritual journey and an overview of the purpose and method of spiritual biography. The second part of the book consists of stories of awakening, shared by spiritual teachers and sincere practitioners and offered for encouragement. The third part is yours to create—an opportunity to recognize the grace that is now and always has been present in your life.

I suggest you spend some time with the first part, that you read it contemplatively. It provides a context for understanding the progression of a spiritual journey and, perhaps, some new ways of looking at the ordinariness and accessibility of awakening. It is not written for forward movement—point building upon point. It's written for deeper movement, into our own longing, our own essence. Reading it contemplatively will allow you to notice where your own depths resonate.

The second part of the book, the awakening stories of others, offers a rarely shared intimacy with the inner experiences of waking up. In conversations with me, deeply respected spiritual teachers and longtime practitioners shared their reflections of their own journeys, the transformative shifts they recognize as part of their own awakening. I felt privileged to participate in such meaningful conversations. Their sharings are filled with wisdom and offer a great many moments worthy of pause and reflection.

Rodney Smith is a Buddhist teacher, renowned for his presence. Stunning insights pour forth from his wisdom and humility. Cynthia Bourgeault is a Christian contemplative. She shares from the depth of her own awakening view. Llewellyn Vaughan-Lee is one of the living hearts of Sufism, Islam's inner mystery school. His story offers not only his struggles but the engaged and compassionate wisdom he has gained. Sherry Ruth Anderson is a teacher within the Diamond Approach, as is Prakash Mackay. Ellen Kympton is a quiet practitioner whose life enriched those around her.

Each speaks to the discouragement so common among spiritual journeyers, with a generous intention to encourage us. Each would be happy to dispel the confusing myths and misunderstandings around "awakening," "enlightenment," "nondual awareness"—all of the spiritual buzzwords. These are the intimate sharings of ordinary beings waking up from a deep sleep. The great spiritual teacher Ram Dass reminds us that when we read other people's stories of their meditative lives, we get a sense of the possibilities of our own.

These recollections illustrate the depth at which it is most helpful to look at our own journeys, the view from which grace can be recognized. Each person shared the transformative shifts in his or her life in the hope of stirring your memories of transformative shifts, the milestones along your own path. The stories reveal a view of both the dazzling diversity of paths and the unshakable concurrence of realized awareness.

Each of the awakening stories proceeds in a stunningly unique way—some dramatic, some slow and gradual. Indeed, every precious awakening, including our own, is utterly individual. The sharings—taken together—also highlight the remarkably similar progressions and realizations that arise in the process of spiritual growth. As the Sufi mystic Rumi points out, "There are a hundred ways to kneel and kiss the ground."

As I've said, each awakening story is a fascinating read—and the wisdom offered is deep and rich. The hard-earned insights each practitioner shares are gifts of great value—if we allow ourselves to percolate and shift with whatever expressions of truth resonate with us. Yet, and still, the greatest benefit of the whole notion of spiritual biography comes when we engage in the exploration of our own path of awakening.

The third part of the book offers full instructions for the process of spiritual biography. It includes contemplative questions designed to evoke your memories of the transformative moments and chapters in your life. It also includes directions for making a time line representing your own spiritual journey. Each memory that arises in response to the questions can be charted along that time line in the form of a single-word notation that represents the moment and serves to recall it.

For example, in response to a question about moments of deepening in my own life, recollections of a profoundly transformative chapter—working in hospice—flooded me. Being with people at the end of their lives taught me—over and over—the power of love and the beauty of opened hearts. So, on my own time line is a little notation of that immense transformation—like this:

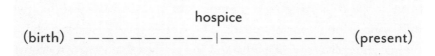

The contemplative questions offered in the book's third part call forth recollections. The experience of recollection is the primary benefit of the exercise. The experience of recollection allows us to recognize grace, to trust it, to finally allow ourselves to abide in it. The charting we do serves both as reminder and as graphic.

By way of illustration, let's use "★" to represent a single-word notation you might use to call to mind a pivotal moment or chapter in your life. At the end of your exploration of your own spiritual biography, your time line with all of your charted notations might look something like this:

★ ★★ ★ ★★ ★★ ★★★   ★ ★★ ★ ★

(birth) — — —|—||—|—||—||—|||— —|—||—|—|— (present)

Each "★" will indicate a significant moment of healing, realization, or transformative shift. With these notations, we create a visual chronicle of our life as an awakening journey. We see a constellation charting grace's presence on our path.

Some people write out the memory called forth by a particular question. That can be helpful, although not at all necessary. The point of the exercise is to recollect. Recollection is, in itself, a spiritual practice. It is an ingathered and focused mind that allows distractions to drop away and attention to touch the ground of our being.

I've worked with many people who have used this exercise. Its effect is revelatory. We see and appreciate and understand our lives in a whole new way. The power of spiritual biography lies in the capacity of our recollections to help us recognize that grace has *always* been present.

Through your own active exploration of contemplative questions, the third part of the book becomes wholly and only yours. *The Grace in Living* was not written for a quick read-through; it is, deliberately, a different kind of book. Its value to you, in real measure, relies upon your participation.

Spiritual biography is an exercise undertaken over time. It's an extended project, a thoughtful and contemplative exploration of your own depths. With that in mind, I urge you to use this book in the ways that work best for you. Begin the exercise of spiritual biography whenever you wish. If you want to go through the three parts of the book in order—reading the awakening stories of others before you begin exploring your own spiritual biography—that's great. If you want to read the first part of the book and then jump ahead to the instructions and the exercise itself in the third part, that's great, too. If you choose to jump ahead to part three, you can read the second part—the spiritual biographies of others—as you're drawn to the inspiration, encouragement, and wisdom they offer. Trust yourself and your capacity to discern what works best for you.

Use this book for your benefit—to bring your recollections into awareness and to deepen your recognition of grace. In the exercise of spiritual biography, we discover and discern the "grace points" in our lives—both in our epiphanies and in our wounds. We come to recognize grace in both its "sweet and fierce forms," as Matt Licata put it.

Llewellyn Vaughan-Lee notes, "The real pilgrim is not the one whose story is told." In that spirit, the process is called spiritual "biography" intentionally. It's not an "autobiography"—that would be of *self*. This process goes beyond ego. It's a biography of growing illumination. In a simple, charted form, you're tracing the awakening of your own essential nature as it comes to know itself as grace.

MY INTENTION throughout is to use language that can communicate with practitioners of any of the noble wisdom traditions. Translate for yourself if need be. Use the words offered here lightly for inspiration and use the words of your own tradition precisely for progress.

Among the words I frequently use are "grace," "self," "Being," "heart," "practice," and "spiritual path." The meaning of each word will unfold throughout the book but, for now, here are some brief definitions:

- *Grace* is a simple, ecumenical word. By *grace*, I mean the sacred, replete with all its noble qualities, the beatitudes. Grace, itself formless, gives rise to form and is inseparable from form. It is Spirit, the alpha and omega of all that arises. Many call it the Godhead, Spirit, the ground of being, the Great Mystery, the Tao. In Christianity, it is often called Christ consciousness. In Buddhism, it is called *dharmakaya*. Grace has a thousand names and is rich with a sense of beauty and goodness and love freely given. We benefit from grace as we align our actions and intentions within it.

- By *self*, I refer very specifically to the "I" we believe ourselves to be, with all of its unexamined thoughts, assumptions, and reactive emotions. Although we deeply believe in its inherent existence, grasping at it and cherishing it, upon deeper examination we see it is a mere construction. Commonly called *ego*, it is a fragile fabrication thrown over an abyss. We don't need to wage war with it. We simply need to know it for what it is. As we mature spiritually, the enchantment of ego begins to diminish.

As used here, *self* does not refer to our precious individual potential to function in the world as a particular manifestation of grace. That individual essence—"soul" or "buddha nature"—is the abode of a liberated life. In some traditions, *Self* with a capital *S* is used in the same sense as essential nature. In this book, *self* means "small self" or ego. From the vantage point of essential nature, we increasingly recognize the small egoic self as limited, confused, and illusory. Surrendering our attachment to it becomes a joy.

- *Being* is a word used throughout this book as well, often interchangeably with *grace* or *Spirit*. Being is the ground of our individual yet interdependent manifestations. It is the dynamism of grace as it endlessly unfolds its exuberant exploration of potentiality. It is dynamic awareness, beyond self.

- *Heart* refers to our innate nonconceptual capacity for knowing. In Eastern traditions, it is referred to as *chitta*, derived from a root word that means "to be conscious." It does not refer to the physical heart organ but to a subtle energy center within the physical body, a gathering place for stillness and clarity—and all of the beautiful qualities that co-arise with stillness and clarity.

- *Practice* is mentioned often, since it aligns us with grace and is an essential aspect of awakening. It is at the core of every authentic wisdom tradition. Practice refers to any transformative discipline— meditation, contemplation, prayer, prostrations, *sadhanas, lectio divina*, and chanting, for example—undertaken in service to awakening. Practice attunes us to our intention and to Spirit. A person practicing a transformative discipline is called a *practitioner*.

- *Spiritual path* refers to the mindful living of our life in resonance with our deepest longing. Our spiritual path includes all of the causes and conditions—the actions of grace—that lead us to intentionally adopt a mindful way of life.

As you explore your spiritual biography, you will most likely discover that the story of your awakening has been one of growing illumination, a merging into grace. The exploration yields benefit in equal measure to the sincerity and depth of your intention and contemplation.

Exploring my own spiritual biography has led to an increase in gratitude, humility, clarity, and faith. I'll share some of my own recollections throughout the book, as it seems helpful. My hope is that the unique recollections that arise for you will help you recognize the grace that is and always has been your own essential being.

PART ONE
Life as Pilgrimage

———————— ✦ ————————

Let's discover together,
underneath all the mess and disappointment
of this bittersweet human experience,
your timeless perfection,
. . . your Home.

—JEFF FOSTER

The Burden of Mistaken Beliefs

Only God could say
what this new spirit
gradually forming within you
will be.

—PIERRE TEILHARD DE CHARDIN

HUNDREDS OF THOUSANDS of people in the West are engaged in serious contemplative or meditative practice. Of the many gifts of our fortunate circumstances, this is among the greatest.

Over years of traveling and speaking, I have been privileged to meet many sincere practitioners. I have deep respect for their steadfastness and their commitment, the earnestness of their practice. Earnestness is a quality that has little cachet in popular culture. It is certainly, though, one of the most transformative of qualities in inner culture.

In encounters with these practitioners, I have been deeply touched to hear of their heartfelt spiritual longing. That hunger, that thirst for more than only self, more than only form, more than only the institutions and dogma of religion, has emerged and is emerging among people in all wisdom traditions. It manifests in sincere and steadfast practice and intention. From the recent determination of the newest practitioner to the old and familiar commitment of longtime meditators, each of these many thousands of personal dedications to awakening is worthy of deep respect.

I have also been moved to hear from so many spiritual journeyers that, in spite of their longing and their commitment, they find in themselves a real measure of discouragement. It is to those sincere yet sometimes disheartened practitioners who struggle with confusion and self-doubt that these words are addressed.

It should come as no surprise that the habit patterns of ego, such as confusion and self-doubt—patterns that have plagued many of us for much of our lives—should follow along with us as we enter a spiritual path. They've frustrated us in our relationships and in our work lives, blocked our relaxation and peace of mind. They've kept us in unease and a real measure of suffering. On a spiritual journey, they are obstructions to waking up. We'll explore these habits both directly and indirectly throughout the book so that their power to obscure our recognition of the ever-presence of grace will begin to dissipate.

The Grace in Living is offered to demystify the confusion around awakening and assist in the acknowledgment of ourselves as awakening beings. As one who romanticized "enlightenment" throughout many years of practice, I feel that I can contribute something in this regard. The book also addresses, with genuine compassion and a deep sense of understanding, the self-doubt and discouragement that can dishearten many spiritual practitioners. I am intimately acquainted with both of those gnawing impediments.

THE CONFUSION ARISING with our idealized expectations of the spiritual path, our "spiritual goals," is widespread, as is the imputed perfection we place upon the very words *awakening* and *enlightenment*.

I've heard a hundred versions of "I've meditated for twenty years and still find myself afraid or angry or prideful." Listening closely to the assumptions behind such admissions, it becomes clear how powerfully our mistaken beliefs hold us in their grip. We judge ourselves and our "spiritual progress" as though we know what we are talking about when we use such words. We mistakenly assume our mental images of perfection accurately define an awakened perspective.

Many of us misconceive the span and purpose of the spiritual journey—often naively believing it to consist of conditioned "highs" requiring rarified atmospheres. Many people have shared their dismay when, after loving the experience of retreat, they go back into the world and still have a hard time relating to family or coworkers or friends.

Clear understanding of the nature of the spiritual journey comes with some maturity. Before that maturity, our misunderstanding can keep us frustratingly trapped in confusion, self-doubt, and discouragement. In essence, the spiritual path is a journey of diminishing the distance between our transformative insights and the moment-by-moment consciousness in which we live with our families and coworkers and friends. We diminish that distance by applying what we know to be true.

The spiritual journey is a process of embodying—acting from, sharing from, living from—what we know in our own direct experience. It is not a question of posturing our insights, trying to prop them up and sustain them, or trying to recreate the causes and conditions that allowed their revelation. The spiritual path is a path of actualizing our realizations. It is in actualization that our insights are integrated and sustained. As sixteenth-century Christian mystic Teresa of Ávila noted, "The demand of the spiritual favors granted us is that they be embodied."

It is common for practitioners to imagine a separation between their "spiritual" life—as we may have come to think of spiritual reading or retreat or formal practice—and all that we typically think of as our "ordinary" life (perhaps even holding that ordinary life as our "real" life). When my children were little, for example, I would often try to bask in the quiet of meditation behind my closed door and then come out and yell at the poor kids for making noise while I was meditating. It took years for me to realize the folly of attempting to keep a closed door between what I perceived to be my two separate lives.

As our practice matures, that imagined distance between our spiritual life and the rest of our life diminishes and awakening embraces our daily presence in relationships, traffic, the office, and an unpredictable body.

It is wise to name our entire life, including all its messy circumstances, as "spiritual practice." Other than in our own misconceptions, our mistaken beliefs, there is no moment outside of our spiritual path. There is no arising separate from Being.

Confused images and mistaken expectations about the spiritual journey abound. Each can land any of us squarely in discouragement.

There often seems to be confusion about what awakening is. Awakening is often sensationalized or romanticized. Within any spiritual tradition, there can be rose-colored idealism about the goals and rewards of the path. We ourselves carry them into the sanctuary or meditation hall with us. Sometimes the confusion about awakening is added to unintentionally from unskillful teaching or from the distortions of teachers with egoic agendas—whether financial, sexual, or the desire to feel superior.

"Spiritual" words are often spoken in hushed tones, emphasizing misunderstood notions. A lofty "endpoint" is held as not present now but as bliss attainable in the future, if you work hard enough and meet the stringent criteria. The imparted idealism mixes with our unexamined ignorance.

Each of us begins our spiritual journey with our conceptual mind holding sovereignty. It is inevitable that confusion will abound as we begin to interface with views beyond conceptuality's grasp.

Likewise, when we begin a spiritual journey, unexamined mental and emotional habits that have been left to their own devices for decades follow in our wake. We bring these beliefs and habit patterns, like tattered luggage weighted with ignorance, along on our pilgrimage. Burdened by who we believe we are—an illusion carried forward from the past—we forfeit who we actually are in each new present moment.

There is much confusion about "perfection," effort, and worthiness. There's confusion about spiritual goals, and—certainly—about the self that is seeking enlightenment. We bring a heavy burden of mistaken beliefs with us.

Even some longtime practitioners feel they have to "try harder"—

perhaps do more prostrations, sit for more periods of meditation, or pray more each day—in order to "achieve" the imagined spiritual goal. Many of us hold awakening as though it were an addition task, an attainment that will be ours when we've accumulated "enough." Many mistakenly believe that awakening depends upon reaching some elusive magical number that will set off all the bells and whistles, like a game at a carnival. "I need to do more work" and "I have a long way to go" are oft-heard refrains.

We keep ourselves trapped in our believed separation from grace in countless ways.

Many practitioners are stuck in the mistaken belief that awakening will occur when they have "perfected" their meditative or contemplative practice. Every authentic tradition offers a practice at its core. Knowing the *hows* of our chosen practice is important, certainly, but we don't want to focus on technique alone, hoping it will bring us as if by conveyer belt to the land of enlightenment. The technicalities of practice pale in comparison with the power of our intention, our heart's longing for the sacred. That power is matched only by the longing of the sacred for our wandering attention to return home to it. As Basil Pennington, the contemplative Christian teacher, noted, "Every prayer is a response to a movement of grace, whether we are aware of it or not, whether we consciously experience the movement, the call, the attraction or not. We are missing reality if we think otherwise."

Within our foggy confusion, clear and grateful recognition that we are *already* awakening beings is utterly precluded. Caught within that confusion, we're unaware that, from the clear perspective of grace, we're already "preapproved," "prequalified," and have been since beginningless time.

We mystify awakening as though it were a thing, existing somewhere other than here, at some time other than now, for someone other than ourselves.

We even mystify the "Great Mystery," mistakenly thinking that living within it is some far-off attainment, beyond our comprehension or capacity. Holding to this belief, we miss the sacred mystery surrounding, permeating, and giving rise to every moment. This recognition is beyond the conceptual mind's grasp, to be sure, but it is perpetually available to the heart's recognition. The *mysterium tremendum* reveals itself to us as we open to it and as we can bear it.

Whatever is so in this moment—the appearance of the objects in the room, the fact that we breathe in the oxygen that plants breathe out, that we exist in a world with other beings who are in truth not Other, that there is a vast cosmos in which who we think we are is less than a microscopic speck, that entire civilizations exist within this body that we think is ours, that there is suffering and joy and every conceptual contradiction and the ineffable majesty of the sacred—this is *it*. This *is* the Great Mystery. It could not be otherwise. We are already living it—inextricably.

Mystery is expressing itself in every moment through the boundless interbeing of our precious individualities. We might as well allow ourselves to live it gratefully, with deepening awe. Our spiritual task is to grow in our acknowledgment of mystery, to open, to surrender into it, to allow it.

Contemplating a spiritual biography, whether one of others or our own, can help dissolve the distorted views that idealize awakening, forever holding it as some magical, mystical thing that we do not presently "have." Ego likes nouns, believing they are graspable.

Spiritual biography is a way of looking at our life from the perspective of more than only self, more than only form, far beyond belief. It brings us to the truth of our life's meaning—a wondrous, beginningless, and endless verb. Engaging in the exercise of spiritual biography offers us a fresh view. It offers the wisdom that dispels confusion.

IN ADDITION to confusion, discouragement and self-doubt can also burden us on our spiritual path. They have quite a few insidious, erosive consequences. Discouragement and self-doubt can stall us in our growing illumination, leaving us feeling "stuck"—an experience that only adds more "evidence" to justify our discouragement and self-doubt.

These two energy systems—discouragement and self-doubt—can keep us forever seeking, always reinforcing the notion of unworthiness. And they can keep us from owning spiritual authority at the level of our own hearts. They preclude discernment and gratitude.

It is possible, with a slight shift in view, to learn to use the arising of both self-doubt and discouragement skillfully. Such skill recognizes the need for the tender mercy of compassion. The application of compassion to the confusion, to the sense of unworthiness, allows healing. Healing dissolves our obstructions and allows further illumination to continue unimpeded.

Let's look at the common doubts. If you recognize some of them as among your own old acquaintances, know that they highlight painful places in need of the healing attention of compassion. Nothing more. No judgment, no condemnation—only compassion. Let's look at how self-doubt and judgment can impede our recognition of grace, trap us in seeking, and block our capacity to live from the authority of our essential nature.

Many practitioners are convinced that spiritual ripening is beyond their reach. Some seekers, doubting their worth, share the delaying thought, "I haven't 'purified' myself enough yet," as if opening into grace depends upon what our conceptions construe to be "good" or "pure." Many practitioners who hold to seeking and striving and all of ego's strategizing efforts to achieve an idealized goal speak of frustration and confide, "I must be doing something wrong." Sadly, some are so convinced of their exclusion from grace—for whatever fantasized reason—that they wonder if they're wasting their time.

Disillusioned or dismayed by the seeming difficulty that arises when harsh self-judgment meets idealized goals, some practitioners have all but given up.

It is certainly the case that some people approaching the path, still flirting with it, have not yet developed a sincere, steadfast practice or cultivated a strong intention. Others, for periods, allow laziness or procrastination to hold sway. And, it is so that others mistakenly assume their own enlightenment after a few teachings, a few retreats—as soon as they are able to mouth the words. Life itself will bring reckoning and a new determination to dig deeper. Honest self-reflection then becomes necessary to address what needs to be addressed.

I am speaking here to contemplatives and meditators within all traditions who have an already established commitment to awaken and yet remain discouraged, plagued by self-doubt. A fairly pervasive belief, when we are honest, is that enlightenment or awakening must be something for others who are perhaps more "spiritually gifted" or "more worthy" or who "try harder" or who are, in any way, *other* than who we are.

For many practitioners, realizing the potential of their own essential nature—abiding in grace—feels beyond their grasp. Our own natural state can't be discovered in conceptual mind. It's not surprising that we think it's hard to locate. If we walk through a meditation hall, we can observe many an outwardly still and silent meditator, never guessing the agitation of unworthiness, egoic effort, and discouragement churning inside them. There's a great deal of unease about simply resting in the ease of natural great peace.

Acknowledging and working through the unease—whether we think the unease is about self or about circumstances—is a large part of the spiritual journey. It's where we start.

When unease is present, it often means we are caught in self's small view. This recognition alone has the power to pull us beyond self and into more wisdom. And wisdom always co-arises with the tender compassion necessary for healing the seen and acknowledged wounds of "unworthiness."

Discouragement with ourselves as "unworthy" practitioners, idealizing the goals of practice, and striving all arise from confusion. Many of us hold mistaken yet deeply believed images about so many things we mentally categorize in a cubbyhole marked "spiritual." We have another, perhaps even more stuffed, cubbyhole marked "self," crammed with self-concept and all of its old notes of both pride and condemnation. It is wise to examine the contents of both cubbyholes. Such inquiry holds great benefit.

Although self-doubt is common, our expression of it is always unique—and we are the only one for whom our unique variation is an obstruction. Feelings of inadequacy blind us to our intrinsic worth and value. They keep us without gratitude for, or recognition of, the grace we experience and the grace we are.

Many of us grant discouragement the power to lead our attention away from here, away from now, away from the resonance of our own heart's wisdom. Engaging in spiritual biography can help us fathom our own depth, with its inherent goodness and worth. Our recollections allow us to take heart and grow in confidence that grace has always held us, embraces us in this moment, and will always lead us home.

We can use the presence of gnawing self-doubt, as it arises, as a call to open into more spacious awareness. We can look more deeply at the beliefs that give rise to the self-doubt and ask ourselves if we really want to continue investing these presumed inadequacies with our mind's capacity to endow belief.

It would be a mistake to turn to the confused mind of ego for reliable guidance on our spiritual path. Discouragement and a sense of unworthiness interfere with the always already available experience of Being and its wisdom. They obstruct the work of grace upon and within us. This is true of any aspect of egoic identification.

Self-doubting arises from a lack of understanding, of both ourselves and the teachings. Its very arising indicates that ignorance is present. It is grace to be able to recognize ignorance and it is grace to let it go upon recognition.

We hold so many beliefs, including unworthiness, without examining them. When we do mindfully examine them, we see their insubstantiality and their deception. Beliefs can arise only with lack of mindfulness—they thrive in unmindfulness. And beliefs lead us nowhere.

The heart—simple, sane, mindful awareness—has no beliefs. In the exercise of spiritual biography, we look at our lives through the lens of awakening. From the clarity of that perspective, the self-doubts and the discouragement begin to dissolve. We simply see them as they are: burdensome words placed on ingrained and patterned neural firings that have neither substance nor authority. Surrendering identification with them, we allow that liberated energy to fall into the clarity of our own heart.

Without mindful attention, self-doubt and confusion can lead *directly* to discouragement. *Indirectly*, they can also lead to egoic striving—the grim determination of the self to choreograph enlightenment—as well as endless seeking.

Too many of us, it seems, have trapped ourselves in seeking—with its goals and its sometime-in-the-future orientation. We've trapped ourselves in unease, without peace. The belief that awakening depends upon learning more and striving harder is widespread. Endless seeking arises from discouragement and self-doubt—and can strengthen both of them.

We judge ourselves as not doing well on the spiritual path and go out in search of the one more book, one more teaching, or one more retreat that will ease the unease and lead us, finally, to that "last missing piece of the puzzle." Books, teachings, and retreats have their place and benefit, no doubt. But that benefit is amplified by orders of magnitude when we actually begin to practice with trust and authority, aligning our intention within the grace that is already present at the level of the heart.

Searching is appropriate when we are exploring, looking for a tradition or a practice with which we resonate, or wishing to amplify our own understanding with another view. Searching becomes an impediment when we engage in it out of idle curiosity or for distraction, novelty, the fulfillment of idealized "goals," or the filling of a nonexistent deficit in our being.

We need to see how our own minds create obstructions to awakening, even when awakening is our fervent yearning, even when awakening is the awareness in which we sit in this moment. Our conceptual minds like being involved in searching and seeking and sometimes prolong it, slyly keeping ego alive and kicking in the process, hoping for its own "enlightenment."

The strong and sincere intention to awaken beyond self is nothing other than grace calling to us. We want to quiet the mind through practice and, within that stillness, hear the call of our heart. Our heart's true intention arises, like a polestar, from the grace in which we live and move and have our being.

Discouragement can indicate the level of maturity (or immaturity) of our faith and confidence. This is not to judge or chastise ourselves when we find ourselves discouraged—that only strengthens the unhealthy pattern. It is more helpful to learn to gratefully accept the presence of discouragement, viewing it as a nudge to observe the obstruction and its dynamics—and cultivate a willingness to surrender identification with it.

Investigation allows us to recognize whether the spiritual journey is an experienced reality for us or whether we have confined it to the merely conceptual. We need to discern whether our words remain on the level of belief, wishful thinking, magical incantation, or even ego inflation. I, for example, used to assuage the fears and financial panic of single motherhood and the inevitable envious comparisons with those whose lives seemed easier with the thinly smug thought, "Well, at least I'm spiritual."

We need to question whether we are just following those who are led by the polestars with which *they* resonate. If we believe in our inadequacy and unworthiness, we often blindly follow others. We miss the one path among seven billion that is calling our name, the only path *we* can take. How foolish it would be to leave it unclaimed— like the last lonely child in the orphanage.

Our spiritual understanding remains conceptual until we authentically *own* our unique path and begin to embody it. Until then, we are stuck, like a car spinning its wheels in the spring mud. Transformation needs traction. Authenticity provides that traction. If we recognize that our spiritual path remains only conceptualized, it's time to let go of all the splattering mud of our spiritual beliefs, transformational ideologies, and convictions of unworthiness. It's time to begin to pay mindful attention to where we're at in each moment. Owning our path means living within it, moment by moment, guided by the resonance of our own hearts.

As our mindfulness grows, we come to recognize the difference between the shakiness of a belief and the stability of a realization. We become increasingly willing to question and surrender the merely believed, putting our full faith and trust in grace's revelations.

To be a Christian or a Buddhist conceptually, for example, has little meaning or transformative effect. Moment-by-moment lived practice nurtures the essential. It allows us to embody the living essence of Christianity or Buddhism in our hearts. Wisdom, compassion, and loving-kindness arise beyond the labels of lineages. We all meet together in grace when beliefs no longer divide.

We can ascertain whether we are living the path or merely thinking it by asking ourselves exploratory questions:

- Are there active, wholehearted inner gestures—subtle, energetic interior shifts—that accompany the words of our "spiritual thoughts"?
- Are our lives coming more into active alignment with the meanings that words can only point to?
- Have we begun to incorporate our insights into our actions large and small, open and hidden, throughout the day?
- How present are we in our moments?
- Have we begun to move beyond the lifeless thinking of a conceptualized spirituality to intimate and transformative, holy inner work?

The exercise of spiritual biography—in particular, the recollection it evokes—helps us tease out the realizations and longings already known to our heart. We recognize the heart's voice as deeper, more resonant, more empowered than the lifeless words of the intellect. The voice of the heart is grace speaking.

The heart resonates with that which we already know to be true. When we are open and attentive to it, resonance guides us, like channel markers at night, and leads us surely to harbor. Listening to the resonance at the level of our hearts, we no longer disenfranchise ourselves with confusion and mistaken beliefs about our singular unworthiness.

Faith and confidence arise when we do more than simply posture being on a spiritual path. When we actually and actively make our own path real—lived, not conceptualized—we move from second-hand information and begin to experience, firsthand, the great release of transformative shifts. We recognize that transformation only occurs in our heart's direct experience and begin to have faith in the authority of the realizations grace grants us. We open into encouragement as we come to intimately know, trust, and allow awakening's unfolding.

Spiritual Biography

— ⌘ —

Live like a river flows,
carried by the surprise
of its own unfolding.
—JOHN O'DONOHUE

ANYONE WHO HAS ever taken a long and arduous hike through a woods or a city or a hillside knows how welcome the sight of a bench can be. Spiritual biography offers such a bench, a chance to sit and rest in the midst of our journey and take stock of what our life has been about. It's an opportunity to look back down the path, noting how far we've come and the conducive and the challenging conditions that we've met along the way.

It's an opportunity to gratefully acknowledge the grace from which we have only imagined ourselves to be separate. As you engage in exploring your own spiritual biography, you'll come to see that you have already glimpsed grace many times, felt its sustaining and healing brush against and within you, known the transformative and liberative power of its movement in and through and *as* you.

Grace has enabled whatever healing we've experienced thus far, whatever degree of inner peace and freedom we feel in this moment. We can gratefully acknowledge the grace of our heart's yearning that led us to begin a spiritual journey in the first place.

Contemplative questions are presented in the third section of the book. They open a perspective on our own awakening journey that most of us have probably not explored before. Directing us to

25

probe the depth and breadth of our experience, the questions point us toward a beneficial shift in the way we view and hold the unique movement of grace in our own precious lives. These questions evoke recollections of significant moments in our spiritual journey.

Looking at our lives through the lens of awakening allows us to recognize that we already embody a certain measure of wisdom that benefits us daily. Recognizing this, realizations that have already arisen will deepen and their imprints become more fully integrated.

Remembering our transformative moments—and all the causes and conditions that allowed them—helps us see our life more clearly as an ever-awakening path. We begin to see a pattern in what seemed like chaos, a pattern of transformative progression that clears our confusions, belies our doubts, and smiles compassionately at our discouragement.

We come to feel respect and appreciation for the grace that has called to us and led us and shaped the unique path we are following into our own essential nature. The heart offers clarity. As we go more deeply into the understanding that clear view offers—a silent place where the obscuring chatter of self-judgment cannot reach—we are moved to bow, to genuflect, to fall in love.

In spiritual biography, we are not looking at the narrative of personality, of self. We're simply looking at the trajectory of our essential nature's illumination. As a result, our perspective becomes increasingly awakened—more grateful, more clear, more focused, more awed.

Spiritual biography removes all the narratives that have nothing to do with awakening. We let go of our color commentary and embellishment. With inessentials and confusions cleared away, what remains is a trajectory of flickering light leading to steady radiance. It's like watching a greenwood log, sufficiently kindled, gradually catch flame.

As we chart our recollections on the time line of our life, we see the footsteps of our own path of spiritual growth and evolution, our maturation and ripening. We see the emergence—however nascent—of

our noblest qualities as we increasingly and with greater thoroughness release self-reference. On the deepest and most meaningful level,
this view of our own growing illumination is the gift of spiritual biography, revealing what our lives have always been about.

Exploring our life from the perspective of its transformative shifts
can evoke and nurture courage and inspiration—even delight. We
begin to trust and have confidence in the exquisite, indestructible
attraction of our love for the sacred and the sacred's love for us. Awakening is a love story, the ultimate tantra.

Our confidence deepens as we own our experience as that of an
awakening being—no matter how fumbling it may appear to our own
judgmental mind, no matter how different from our glorified image
of awakening. Recognizing this, discouragement and self-doubt
begin to dissolve. We shed what is inessential as our essential nature
emerges, each distillation bringing us closer to truth.

As we contemplate the questions of spiritual biography for ourselves, we will find grace's affirmation of our emergence, an affirmation that the separate sense of self can never give.

True faith—clear-seeing and wise—arises from such confidence.
Faith and confidence strengthen our fidelity, the steadfastness of our
intention. Faith, confidence, and fidelity have deep connection with
each other, not only etymologically. They co-arise and amplify each
other. The recognition that we can trust Being's embrace is rich nurturance for our spiritual growth.

My hope is that those who choose to look at their lives through the
lens of awakening will deepen in their recognition that the "Divine
Indwelling," a "Buddha seed," rests within each of us—always and
necessarily. Grace is an integral aspect of each and every one of us.
When realized, we know it to have always and already been ever-
present. It is the Heart Jewel, the Sacred Heart. Thomas Merton, the
great Christian mystic, called it "a point of pure truth . . . like a pure
diamond blazing." There is no other "God particle" to be found.

Reflecting upon our journey, we shift into wiser view and begin to
recognize the ongoing movement of our reaching toward Spirit—and

of Spirit reaching toward us. The grace of our reaching and the grace
we are reaching for merge in deep and intimate interpenetration. Our
recollections, as we engage in spiritual biography, reveal this.

We can drop every idealized image we have of awakening. It has
nothing to do with our notions of "perfection." It is not a thing; it's
neither graspable nor attainable. Awakening is an undefended opening, an allowing, a stance far more stable and sane than the stance
of self-reference. It is not a future goal. It is available, accessible, and
livable only in each present moment.

We are all awakening beings. Regardless of whether it is painful,
joyful, messy, radiant, or foggy—*this* is how awakening is *for us*. We
can let go of the way that we believed awakening would or should be.
We're ordinary human beings, always and already living within the
sacred. It could not be otherwise. Spiritual biography can open our
eyes to this recognition.

WE COULD LOOK at our lives in dozens of different ways, through a
dozen different lenses. We could describe our passage through the
years with any number of different emphases. Each emphasis, each
angle of inquiry taken, is governed by its own set of beliefs. Each
has a different narrative and a different understanding of both self
and world. We probably wouldn't even notice the contradictions, the
inconsistencies, so blind and grasping is the self's impulse to claim
domain.

We could look through the lens of ordinary autobiography, noting
names and dates and places, chronologically charting our comings
and goings, our meetings and partings, like the carefully penned notes
that people used to keep in their family Bibles. If we were to write an
ordinary autobiography, we would be looking at the actions of an
individual—"me"—whose separate sense of self, although engaged
in a variety of activities and relationships and employing different fac-
ets of our being in each, still feels relatively consistent through the
changing chapters.

Résumés are another way to look at our life. They carry a compact list of our work history—all those endless hours and weeks and years in the office or the factory or the store, reduced to a page or two. Our résumés summarize the ways in which we've earned a living and some of the ways we've used our gifts in the world. Even stylistically, something of our sense of self is portrayed and on display. Our résumés hold our prides and our accomplishments, our slight distortions of facts in service not only of marketability but often of self-aggrandizement. They reveal our hopes for public worth and our private shame or preening.

Or, we could look at all the moments in our lives of sorrow or pain or despair and pen the story of our sadness and disappointments. We could write a history of grief and loss, the tragedies and traumas that we've endured, tear-stained narratives recounting our sad and heavy thoughts. We might be able to do this so convincingly that you'd think we never laughed or danced in the night, never knew a "glory day" at all.

We could chronicle our family life over the years, describing the nature of our connection with parents and siblings, with children, with aunts, uncles, and cousins. We could retell the family yarns and laugh in memories we've shared or shudder with memories we've dared not utter. There would be tales of function and dysfunction, nurturing and neglect, chaos and stability, significant others present and long gone.

We might chronicle our familial legacies of attitudes and emotions, our spoon-fed beliefs and allegiances—as influential as genes. Our unexamined cradle paradigms and inclinations bear witness to the tree the bent twig became.

We could write tales of victory or defeat, pride or shame, appreciation or bitterness. Perhaps we've told ourselves all of these narratives already. In the very telling of the stories, we strengthen belief in the self who is the stories' teller.

Each of these would be an *autobiography* in the ordinary sense of the word, written within the context of the way we ordinarily view ourselves and the world.

Each different narrative would showcase a different aspect of our experience. We highlight certain events and then string them together to establish a coherent and convincing story. From a million other moments, we pluck particular moments that cumulatively seem to constitute "evidence," proof of our beliefs and imputations. They appear to justify the conclusions of our assumptions and judgments, and substantiate the sense of self.

Each of these ways of viewing our lives ends up with a distinct flavor. Stories of betrayal and disappointment carry the flavor of bitterness or the cringe of learned helplessness. Documents of accomplishments and achievements carry the smug flavor of pride or the secret, furtive hope to justify our existence. Family and other interpersonal chronicles carry the flavor of trust or mistrust, of attachment or avoidance, the leaning toward inclination or the inclination to lean away.

Whenever we feel the sense of self defined so distinctly—so "flavored"—we can be sure that a measure of distortion is at play.

The saints and sages of every wisdom tradition recognize that the ground of being is of "one taste." When we mindlessly allow attention to be fueled by desire or aversion, no matter how subtle, we sense the self with a distinctive flavor in that moment. The engines of self rev up, gunning for the expression of that particular flavor of reactivity. In doing so, we psychologically remove ourselves from the truth. We separate ourselves from the sacred, the "one taste" of nonduality.

In ordinary autobiography distortion comes into play. That which fits consistently with the tenets of our paradigm is emphasized and reinforced. All that does not fit our familiar storyline and our habitually felt sense of self is ignored. We push it into unconsciousness.

To ignore is to remain in ignorance. No wisdom will be forthcoming. No love will come to fruition. Such stories do not serve awakening. They lull us back to sleep, imagining some comfort deep in the dream of self.

SPIRITUAL BIOGRAPHY works at an altogether different level, serving an entirely different purpose. Although we look at memories and movements of mind, our emphasis is beyond self. Our lens is the lens of awakening. We are looking at the footprints of grace.

We engage in spiritual biography to gain some clarity on three things:

- our essential nature,
- the ever-presence of the sacred, and
- the transformative movement that allows our imagined separation from the sacred to dissolve.

It is a process undertaken in service to waking up.

Spiritual biography is an activity of recollection, of noting the many moments in our lives when grace—in both its sweet and fierce forms—made its presence known. Engaging in this process, we begin to view our life in a new way—as spiritual journey, as pilgrimage. We notice the flickers of the sacred that have already broken through, illuminating, however momentarily, the foggy mindlessness in which we ordinarily live. Through our recollections, we notice the flickerings becoming more frequent. We notice our desire to abide in its light becoming both more fervent and more authentic.

We begin to recognize that form, the universe of self, has never for a moment been separate from the sacred formless. Only our conceptions view them as separate. That they could be separate is impossible. Grace has always been present—even in the moments when we felt bereft of it, even in the moments when we so forgot it that we didn't even know we were feeling bereft of it.

Engaging in spiritual biography, we can discover deep wells of encouragement. It is sweetly empowering to realize our inseparability from the sacred. With this encouragement, we can tenderly assuage our self-doubting and minister to it with less denial, less judgment, and infinitely more compassion. Recognizing that we are already in the divine flow—and always have been—confidence grows.

With confidence grows courage. With courage grows the wish and the readiness to see clearly. That wish and that readiness enable us to face our shadow, to want to face our shadow of self-doubt, with tender mercy and, even, with the lightness of a quarter-smile, such as we see upon the face of Buddha. We see that a doubt is simply a believed thought. We are no different from everyone else who has suffered and does and will suffer under the influence of mistaken beliefs—and certainly no more "unworthy."

We begin to recognize ourselves as ordinary human beings—a profoundly liberative recognition. We accept ourselves just as we are in each moment. We are awakening. We surrender any further need for judgment or pretense.

When we look at our lives as the story of an awakening process that has been taking place in each and every moment, we move out of conceptual mind's *either/or* mentality, a mentality that mistakenly separates our humanity and the sacred. We gradually develop a view that allows the heart to rest in *and*. That *and* view allows us to acknowledge our still-wounded selves, our at times still reactive selves, as awakening beings—engaged in the process of integrating our buddha nature with our human nature.

From the new perspective that we cultivate as we explore our own spiritual biography, we can see our lapses into self-doubt and discouragement as simply part of the journey of awakening. They no longer function as indictments of our unworthiness or lack of spiritual potential. They serve instead as indicators of where to look next, where to trim the sail of mindfulness, where to lean into grace's wind of sweet and healing compassion—no more and no less.

Engaging in this process can free us from our myopic perspective and offer more of an aerial view. We begin to recognize that all the moments of our life are now, and always have been, steps in our dance of awakening. Since we first reached out to a path, to a practice, through maturing and ripening, each step has followed—however falteringly—our heart's intention.

And, truly and deeply, it is not even "our" intention. It is Being's longing for expression through us, Being's love for its own expression *as* us.

We see that love is the ground of our being and that who we are essentially is not other than that. A spiritual biography is not an auto-biography of fill-in-your-name. It's an affirmation of awakening into Being—far beyond anything we believe ourselves to be. It's the story of love awakening to itself.

Nothing that could be written in our obituary or our curriculum vitae appears in this exercise. It has nothing to do with the public sphere. We're not looking at the life anchored in self. Looking at our lives through the lens of awakening is not undertaken to impress, val-idate, explain, or substantiate our sense of self. Instead, we note atten-tion's growing release from self's moorings.

Spiritual biography invites us into the wider view available beyond self. We simply look at the arc of illumination. The exercise of spiri-tual biography demands that we begin to look *from* illumination, let-ting go of our exclusive identification with only self, only form. When we do so, new freedom and clarity arise.

As we go more deeply into the exploration of our journey, our rec-ollections lead us to recognize the operation of grace in our lives. The initial tendency to engage from the perspective of self, the view of conceptual mind, is replaced by greater clarity and more wisdom. It's a process. As the enchantment of egoic self wanes, we begin to rest in essence. Reliance upon conceptuality relaxes, unworthiness begins to dissipate, and awe and understanding arise, fresh and alive.

In our recollections, we recognize the confluence of form and formlessness at many times in our lives. We discover a "zero point" at the intersection of form and formlessness in more of the moments of our days. We begin to recognize that our life occurs in this intersection—not only in form nor only in formlessness, not only immanent nor only transcendent, but in the dance of their interplay. This zero point is awareness—the Absolute and the partic-ular, the sacred and the mundane, resting in conscious, simultaneous balance in each present moment, a living truth beyond the grasp of conceptual mind.

Resting at the zero point, we add nothing to any moment, recognizing "just this." We subtract nothing from any moment, acknowledging "this, too." Like the symbol that represents it—"0"—the zero point simply is, with nothing embellished and nothing denied.

Twentieth-century Tibetan teacher Nyoshul Khen Rinpoche spoke of it this way:

> Profound and tranquil, free from complexity,
> Uncompounded luminous clarity,
> Beyond the mind of conceptual ideas.
> . . . In this there is not a thing to be removed,
> Nor anything that needs to be added.
> It is merely the immaculate,
> Looking naturally at itself.

In the ingathered attention of a meditative, contemplative state, duality no longer determines the vantage point and a nondual perspective arises. Such interior silence allows clear vision and insight into grace both as figure and ground. This is the zero point where paradox dissolves in the heart's understanding. That understanding experiences the sacred in all things, in all moments.

In the exercise of spiritual biography, we are looking at past experiences of presence that have nothing to do with the presence of this moment—except, of course, for the presence of the memory. This may seem paradoxical, but paradox, it has been said, is how truth appears to the conceptual mind.

The glimpses of past transformative shifts offer the view of an alternative mode of living. The only valid and beneficial purpose of remembering them is to more deeply imprint the power and majesty of presence in our hearts. We want to live more stably in presence in each and every hallowed moment, in remembrance of grace.

What emerges in this exercise is nothing less than a new way of viewing the moments in our lives. We're looking at shifts in identity, in perception, in ways of knowing, in the faculties and capacities we employ in the experience of living. By training our mind to look at the "past" in terms of transformative shifts, we begin to see moments that are arising in the present through this same lens. We recognize each moment as further and deeper awakening, a moment in an endless evolution.

It behooves us to hold what appear to be the two "sides" of a paradox lightly. We can, for example, begin to recognize the mark of grace in our wounds and their healing instead of viewing our wounds only as deficits, as our "not-worthy" barriers to grace. We can also remain mindful of the essentially fabricated nature of the separate sense of self and, at the same time, honor and humbly cherish the utterly unique being who is awakening.

Paradox brings us directly to the limitations of conceptual mind. We bump right into the end of its capacity. At the very edge of conceptual mind's reach, we can finally let go of our dependence upon conceptuality alone. We can, with some trepidation but also some joy, leap into the great and freeing wonder of living in the mystery. From that moment of surrender on, a measure of attention is released from within the orbit of ego. The spiritual journey ceases to be a journey of striving and becomes increasingly one of simply being. We move our center of gravity beyond conceptuality's self-reference, to the level of the heart.

The heart leads us forward with less obstruction and more sanity. The heart is the only container spacious enough to hold both the overwhelming suffering of the world and the almost unbearable joy of grace.

The Simplicity of Being

The spiritual journey
is a process that happens to us.
We don't do it.
The Mystery simply unfolds of itself.

—THOMAS KEATING

MANY OF US make our spiritual journey far more complicated than it needs to be. We place idealized expectations on both the path and on ourselves, unmindful of how these mistaken conceptions preclude every present-moment opportunity to step into grace. The self tends to do that. To the degree this tendency still operates in us, it is wise to acknowledge, explore, and release it. We want to cease dishonoring our own experience.

Within any spiritual path, we can encounter an immense number of teachings. Multiple practices may be necessary to release our tightly grasped beliefs, to assist us as we begin to loosen and relax enough to explore our own minds. These various encounters enable us to find transformative disciplines and perspectives with which we resonate. They serve our intention to grow into greater depth, wisdom, and compassion.

The dizzying array of teachings available can, though, sometimes lead to a sense of overload, a sense that awakening is a very complicated thing. "This just seems too hard," "I'll go nuts with one more new practice," and "This is overwhelming" are phrases often uttered by those who, discouraged, back away from their own heart's yearning.

The sense that the spiritual path is complex can also lead to confusion and strategizing. Self puts forth great effort in its attempt to "figure it all out," as if enlightenment were a puzzle the ego could solve—and is failing if it cannot.

I think, also, that we imagine the spiritual path to be far more complicated than it actually is because we just can't believe that an awakened relationship with each new moment is so accessible, that our *natural* state is sacred.

We've been searching so hard and trying for so long. It's difficult to accept that what we've been searching for is right at hand, "hidden in plain view," as the Jesuits remark. Buddhism speaks of "the four faults" that preclude our recognition of our own essential nature. That recognition, from the faulty view of self, is too close, too profound, too easy, and too wonderful. The notion that we cannot recognize our own essential nature because it is "too wonderful" is a poignant one. That the very ground of being is calling our name, endlessly offering openings, is beyond our conceptual comprehension.

Conceptualization complicates. It lands itself in confusion, especially in the face of truth that is beyond its grasp. The conceptual mind has its place, but its place is limited. One of the gifts of embarking on a spiritual journey is learning to live more at the level of the heart. The heart spontaneously resonates with what is true and good and beautiful. The very longing in our heart is none other than that love for which we long. It isn't complicated.

We can keep our exploration of our own spiritual journey simple, removing the distortions of self's mistaken beliefs. The process itself draws us to the heart, where the perspective leads to clarity, as well as to gratitude and respect for our own journey.

In spiritual biography, we work with a time line upon which we can simply note the spiritually significant moments in our lives, our moments of depth and transformation. The third section of this book contains simple instructions for creating a time line for yourself.

Our ordinary conception of the time line of our life is that it is continuous, like this:

(past) ———————————————————————— (future)

The continuous time line, as we ordinarily conceive of it, appears to progress chronologically from a past "then" to a future "then," moving through a "present" that we typically hold with no more regard than a piece of tape that connects past and future together. The present is a moment that we often occupy unmindfully. We often use it to simply bridge the gap between our memories and our hopes.

However much we might think of it and experience it as if it were, the time line of our life is not continuous. What we call our life is a series of freshly arising moments in which a new self is continuously reborn, re-created. We believe in a constant and consistent "me," but, upon closer examination, we see that there is no such thing.

Typically, we conceive of our lives as occurring *within* a continuous time line. We believe our life takes place within the headlong rush of our passing years. We think of the time line as holding "me"—as though the "me" of the past, the "me" in the present, and the "me" in the future are the same. It is only the wish to impute "me" upon an ever-changing but somehow familiar pattern that is constant and consistent.

As we engage in the exercise of spiritual biography, we come to a clearer understanding of the self. The separate, egoic sense of self is illusory, a product of mind and sensations, a deeply ingrained habit pattern. It serves a purpose and it seems real, but it is an illusion that profoundly limits our experience of life and blinds us to the profundity of grace.

We human beings are here for two functions: to survive and to awaken to our own uniquely expressed essential nature, to claim our birthright in the ground of being. We come equipped for both functions: surviving and Being.

In this precious gift of a human life, we each have received two stunningly sophisticated modes of operating: an operating system for survival (a survival mode) and an operating system for Being (a Being mode).

Spiritual biography invites us, among other things, to look at the moments in our lives when Being held our attention. These are our moments of acknowledged grace, the moments of our transformation shifts. Each taste we've had of the Being mode is a recognized blessing. It is a taste for which we hunger. Both the taste and the hunger are from grace and serve as the impetus for ever-deepening realizations.

OUR ORDINARY CONCEPTIONS of the time line of our life are full of self-reference, just as our spiritual journey, as we begin it, is filled with self-reference. Let's return to the solid time line, the way we ordinarily conceive of our life:

(birth) ————————————————————— (present)

When our attention is trapped in survival mode, we live and experience exclusively *within* this very narrow bandwidth. The seeming solidity of the bandwidth, a limited level of consciousness, convinces us that the sense of self with which we unmindfully identify is *separate* from Being. Being is like the whiteness of the page on which the line is drawn, the ever-present ground.

This sacred awareness—Being—is a transpersonal mode of functioning. It is represented two-dimensionally here by the white blankness *surrounding* and *allowing* the appearance of the seemingly solid line of "my life." It is awareness vastly expanded beyond survival mode, yet holding within itself the capacities and functions of the survival operating system.

The survival mode attends only to the seemingly separate self in

a world imputed as form only. Its purpose is its own continued existence. Attention, in this mode, is utterly trapped within needs and
desires, the reactivities and assumptions of the separate sense of self.
Over millennia as a species and over decades as an individual, we've
become entrenched in the survival mode.

Although the circumstances of human existence have changed over
the millennia, the survival imperative has become deeply ingrained.
At this point, much of its functioning is to our own limitation and
harm, to the harm of others, and to the harm of the planet.

We've taken the powerful instincts that optimize the survival of
the physical organism and placed them in service to the sense of self
that arises as a byproduct of survival's operating system.

The survival mode, represented as the solid line, is aware only of its
own desires and sufferings. It doesn't even notice the whiteness of the
page that upholds it and allows it to be. Without mindfulness of more
than only self, we hold the survival mode's time line as all there is and
act as if the whiteness, the ground, weren't there or had no meaning or consequence. We allow the survival function to fill the screen
of our attention. It becomes a congested, obstructive interference to
clarity and to peace, to all that lies beyond self.

Spaciousness, Buddha reminds us, is the home of the awakened
mind. The composition of the universe is 99.99999 percent space.
Within the survival mode of form only, we limit our experience of
existence to 0.00001 percent of all that is available, of all that is wide
open, welcoming and awaiting us. All that is awaiting us is beyond
mere survival's imagining.

Ordinarily, we live within the dynamics and confines of the survival
operating system—the ordinary mind and the understandings with
which we engage in our daily functioning. We can compare living
our life exclusively within the survival mode to having a smartphone
that we perpetually keep on the airplane setting. It's an immeasurable
waste.

With the phone on the airplane setting, we have endless access to
mindless games, old downloads, and past messages but no capacity

to connect with the vast and greater world outside of survival's pro-grammed contents—the vast, radiant refuge of Being, beyond only self.

We stay stuck in and stuck with the same old thoughts, strategies, and reruns. Survival mode is a closed system—not open at all. It is infinitesimally contracted from the vastness of Being, collapsed into smallness. Lost. Far from fearlessness or beauty.

We could say that the solid-line view that we would typically use to represent our life illustrates the "blinders" of survival mode. The blinders of survival mode leave us with such a limited view of the vastness of existence, holding only the contracted universe of the self. It is a universe marked by ignorance of anything beyond the line.

When we unmindfully allow the experience of our lives to remain like a smartphone on the airplane setting, we have no access to new input, no capacity to receive—or even suspect the existence of—the endless grace that holds and surrounds us, the grace we are.

THE SURVIVAL operating system does not have the capacity to observe its own ingrained, patterned dynamics, known in Buddhism as "karmic formations." The dynamics of survival mode can only be observed from attention that is freed into clear awareness by both strong intention and blessing.

This clear awareness is Being mode. It not only observes the con-fused machinations of self and survival, it can hold and heal and release them in compassion. The operating system of Being mode is the formless awareness of grace.

Attention, freed from self, lands in Being. We free our attention through mindfulness, through willing surrender of our attachment to the limitations of self, or through any of the practices of authentic wisdom traditions. The liberation of attention trapped in only form, only self, is the purpose of every authentic practice. Using any of these means to pull anchor from our fixation in survival mode, we move into the great ocean of Being.

No longer blinded within the effort and confusion of survival mode alone, we start to view our journey from the clear and undistorted perspective of Being. From Being, we see the thought "I" as a mental phenomenon, our most frequently arising mental phenomenon. The exercise of spiritual biography can aid in this shift to expanded understanding. It is only from the perspective of Being that we know our journey as one of awakening. Self is incapable of this knowing.

The practice of mindful attention reveals survival mode's dynamics. Survival mode's programming relies upon sensory input processed through conceptuality. It posits and employs form, time, duality, boundaries, narratives, beliefs, memory, and habitual thoughts manifesting through well-nourished neural pathways, continuously churning out desire, contraction, unease, and assorted other knee-jerk emotions.

Together, the aspects of the programming give rise to the separate sense of self, the "I" of the mental ego. The separate sense of self is a byproduct of the survival operating system. Sanskrit has a word for the dynamics of survival mode's functioning: "the 'I'-maker."

The very dynamics of the survival operating system, deeply devoted as they are to dualism, create and sustain the mental ego, the "I" sense that we hold as the sum total of our being. Within many traditions, it is called the false self.

The "falsity" lies in the fact that the truth of the egoic self's *constructed* nature is allowed to go unnoticed. The truth of the fabrication of ego is ordinarily hidden away in ignorance. Ignorance is simply the willing tendency to ignore the truth.

The self-sense arises as a harmonic, as Rodney Smith describes it. The harmonic is the production of the inner workings of the survival mode. The egoic sense of "I" arises feeling very defined, delineated, and boundaried. A great deal of mental energy and trapped attention—all our survival imperative—goes into supporting that feeling of "me."

Survival mode has a negative bias. We live in fear when we posit a separate self: every boundary must be defended.

The survival imperative needs a self to protect. It functions as though anything that self does not want or finds uncomfortable is a matter of life and death—as though momentary pain or loss or humiliation or disappointment were threats that could kill us.

Buddha described human life in survival mode as a set of impersonal, ever-changing causes and conditions. Among the countless causes and conditions are processes of physicality, feeling, memory, cognition, and reaction.

These all arise within a consciousness that is "enactive," that has a strong meaning-making, paradigm-creating tendency. That tendency is one of "cohering," the inclination to make sense of, always wishing for order and comprehension. This enactive mental tendency is willing to engage in many a sleight of hand to create the illusion of self and order and comprehension.

IF WE WERE to magnify the seemingly solid time line of "my life," the bandwidth of the survival mode, we can imagine that, within the apparent single, one-plane line, it is quite crowded, quite cramped. If we were to examine the mechanics of the system, it would look something like this:

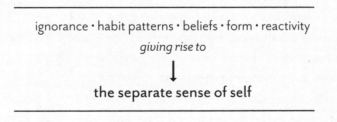

ignorance · habit patterns · beliefs · form · reactivity

giving rise to

↓

the separate sense of self

Buddhist practitioners will recognize that the survival operating system contains the congested dynamics of dependent co-arising, the dynamics that create self and its suffering world. These are the conditions that give rise to the vulnerabilities of psychic wounds and fractures, to a fabricated, unsatisfying universe, and to a form-only conceptual paradigm that cannot ever *know* the sacred formless.

To the degree that our longing for expansion into Being beyond mere survival is trapped with our attention within this survival mode, we are not free and we do not know our own stunningly precious essential nature. Just surviving, just maintaining form, leaves us with an inarticulate sense of incompleteness and insufficiency, and a deep (and understandable) longing for wholeness and plenitude.

The survival mode's function is limited. We would, for example, never turn to a vacuum cleaner to babysit our children. We clearly understand the vacuum cleaner's functions and its limitations. Analogously, the survival operating system is not capable of satisfying our heart's deepest yearning.

Our real spiritual maturation begins when we recognize this clearly, beyond a shadow of a doubt, and cease our familiar turning to survival mode, to self, for that which it cannot do. We let go and mindfully release this habitual pattern—with a deliberate willingness to surrender it. Surrender is renunciation, a willingness to release all that does not lead to Being. When we recognize that we cannot find authentic refuge within a conceptualized life, we are free to realize reliable refuge in the stillness of the heart, in Being. The exercise of spiritual biography can assist in this liberating shift.

The truth is that the survival mode was doomed from the start. The mission was always impossible. It could never fulfill its function completely. We are mortal beings. At some point, the survival operating system has to admit defeat. It has to confront the unthinkable end of life and, when it does, it will self-destruct. Its byproduct, ego, will dissipate along with it.

Within the confined paradigm of the survival mode of functioning, this is a brutal reckoning. At that point, there will be no option other than to leap into the unknown boundlessness outside of its imagined lines, imagined self. We leap, as Saint Bonaventure described it, into a unity "whose center is everywhere and whose circumference is nowhere." This is the grace that has always beckoned.

We do ourselves great benefit by opening beyond self far before death comes to call. We do ourselves great benefit by resting in the larger perspective and experience of Being far before the cessation of the causes and conditions that gave rise to the fleeting appearance of this mindbody.

As YOU GO THROUGH your own spiritual biography, you will recognize that during the moments in your life when you experienced any transformative shift, you experienced Being. You had hopped out or were popped out—depending upon your perspective—of entrapment in the survival operating system and landed squarely in the sacred, in formless awareness, the operating system of Being. Being is the loving and holy ground of all arisings—never absent, never separate, always holding us in embrace.

The exercise of spiritual biography calls forth the recognition that we have already accessed grace, the mode of Being, many times in our lives. We also recognize that our awareness of the availability of this access is now growing in frequency and intensity. We see the open gate more often and can simply walk through. Our recollections reveal that we have, in fact, in the course of our spiritual journey, become increasingly familiar with the sacred—far beyond belief and far beyond form's concern with mere survival.

Rather than thinking of the time line of our lives as continuous, this seems a more helpful way to represent it:

(birth) — — — — — — — — — — — — — — — — (present)

This line is composed of separate small dashes that represent the millions upon millions of momentary arisings in our life to date, each dash an utterly unique arising. Without meditative attentiveness, memory and the mind's enactive tendency connect these momentary arisings as though in a solid line. The memories that create a sense of self are stored in the survival operating system and preclude the experience of the freshness of each moment. We overlay past images upon present reality. This is karma.

It can be beneficial once in a while, as we engage in the process of spiritual biography, to enlarge the time line of dashes, as though we were seeing through a magnifying glass. This facilitates looking through the lens of awakening. Then, the time line would appear like this:

—— —— —— ——

Each dash represents a moment's arising in our experience of life. Under the magnifying glass of mindfulness, we see the empty space that surrounds each moment. We see the spaciousness, the openness, the lack of solidity of that which had seemed so continuous, encasing, and real. We see the whiteness, representing grace, in every gap.

Looking at the dashes and the spacious whiteness surrounding each of them, we can—if we pause to do so—imaginatively visualize attention's movement into Being, occurring in every direction as a consequence of our longing and intention.

We can picture the energy of freed attention *moving out* through the gaps—toward our eyes as we read, away from our eyes and into and beyond the page, up, down, left, right, in, out, and every limitless direction in between. We can visualize Being simultaneously penetrating attention—*moving in* and doing so from every direction, in every moment. As we long for Being, Being longs also for us. The dynamic trajectories *out* from our longing and *in* from Being are the movement of grace, the ground of everything.

It can be of benefit to take the time to visualize this and to open our minds a bit with the visualization, resting imaginatively in the experience. And it is certainly beneficial to hold this opened view of the time line of our life as we engage in the exercise of spiritual biography—recollecting our wounds and our longing, and grace's responses to them.

Each gap represents a pause of potentiality. Each gap is an opening. The term used in the Tibetan Buddhist tradition is *bodhimandala*, signifying every moment's opportunity to "just step this way" and enter sacred presence.

In every moment, including this one, our life has been shimmering with the simultaneous longing for, and the welcome into, Being. It is a stirring and quivering, an easing and releasing of the tight, congested contraction we experience when we believe survival mode to be the final statement on the breadth and depth of our existence and potential.

Each gap between the dashes is attention's gate out of entrapment in survival mode and into grace, into formless awareness. Survival mode can quickly return and fill the gap with its own agenda. Gradually we develop the capacity to remain unmoved by its need to give form to self and story, memory and desire. We become less likely to return to a form-only world whose illusory solidity blocks the simple experience of Being.

As we hear the call to step out into Being, to allow our attention entry into grace, we realize that the gates to grace abound. The gate can be grief or a flash of wisdom, an experience of oneness, a heart melting in compassion, the taste of water. A gate opens in every single moment of presence. Love and fear, gratitude and sorrow, abandonment and suffering are all gates.

Recognizing the spacious openness of each "now," each moment of presence, we can ask ourselves, along with Rabia al Basri, the seventh-century Sufi poet and mystic, "How long will you keep pounding at an open door?"

WE'VE ALL HAD our moments of self-forgetfulness when letting go lands the energy of our attention in Being. Whether in love, nature, meditation, or contemplation, this has been possible before. We *know* there is other than, more than, simply the survival mode. We've already experienced beyond self; we've already expanded our continuum of functioning. We chart our recollections of these past times of profound figure-ground shifts and integrations as we engage in spiritual biography. Doing so, we can grow confident that it is possible to step beyond self in every present moment.

The work of healing allows us to step through the gate. Acknowledging our wounds with humility and tender compassion releases our attention from each wound and into Being. We heal first our shadow, then the split that survival mode created between mind and body, and, after that, we heal the split survival mode severed between self and other—especially between self and the sacred.

We discern the gaps and slip through them in connection, in solitude, in silence. We find them when we inhabit our body, whether in lovemaking, childbirth, dance, or pain. Our three great teachers— aging, illness, and death—will lead us directly to them.

And we have our practice, long engaged, to train our heart and mind. Our training allows us to *want* to see through our clinging and our illusions. Practice, aligned with grace, develops a perspective that *can* see. It develops our capacity to simply show up in our lives and be present.

We step through the always-open door in such a simple way: by our willingness to be where we are in each never-before, never-again present moment. We *allow* each new arising and *release* it in its dissolution. We remain at the zero point in our simple willingness to be, bare and prop-free, where we are. This is the abode of wonder, an aspect of presence, alive with the realization that we have no idea what will appear in the next moment. There is an innocence, an enlivening, when we are living in grace.

We can notice the tight, exhausting vigilance that survival mode demands and compare it to the relaxed and refreshing vigil of Being— effortless and sacred. The choice becomes choiceless. We just have to coax our reluctant egos until our familiar grasping to them diminishes.

Stepping through the door, the shimmering gap of the *bodhiman-dala*, the perpetual offering of communion, we become "stream-enterers," as it is phrased in Buddhist tradition. The stream we enter is none other than Being, the "divine flow."

Wisdom traditions, when viewed from conceptuality and the sense of self, could be classified as either liberative or salvific. Either we liberate ourselves into sacred awareness or the Sacred saves us. The Being mode notes no distinction between the two. Those are just apparent differences as seen from within the survival mode. The longing for beyond self and the beckoning from beyond self are identical. It is only our perspective within the survival operating system that would have us view them as distinct.

Exploring our own story of awakening, we see that our tense grasping to the survival operating system can be released. We are capable—with practice, intention, and grace—of letting go, of surrender. The recollections that arise when we do spiritual biography help point out that this has already occurred on our own path. We recognize that we've already had tastes of that for which we hunger. Our confidence and willingness to simply allow our own unfolding will grow. We begin to take refuge in our growing realization of the unity of the sacred and what we have thought of as "the mundane," and live from within that ever-deepening recognition.

This confidence allows us to respond to the invitation of each momentary gap more readily, more defenselessly, as our unending journey continues. No longer so trapped in the consuming ups and downs of mere survival, we come to rest more stably in the natural great peace of Being.

We begin to recognize that awakening is simply the shift we are beginning to experience into a new and liberated relationship with each moment. It is a growing shift into functioning from the heart, a mindful awareness that both includes and transcends the capacities of the conceptual mind.

Each of us, no matter how new or old our commitment to the journey, is on a trajectory of spiritual maturation, carried along by grace. As we mature spiritually, we finally begin to open to and experience more of the 99.99999 percent of reality that we've been overlooking for a long time.

Looking with a Different Eye

Take one step away from yourself
—and behold!—
the Path!
—ABU SA'ID

WE VIEW OUR LIVES from the perspective of a deeper understanding when engaged in the recollections of spiritual biography. We look anew at the actions of grace throughout our lives, the beliefs that have impeded our recognition and receipt of grace, and the wounds that needed grace's healing. Recollection is a deep look, a process that helps us grow in wisdom and clarity.

Countless beings have traveled innumerable spiritual paths before us and many have examined their journeys. We can learn from their wisdom and clarity, their experience of the grace in living.

Centuries ago in Tibet, for example, there was a tradition of writing spiritual biographies. Many were apocryphal and written to inspire or to encourage reverence and commitment to the path and, often, to a particular lineage. In much in the same way, "Lives of the Saints" were widely circulated in Catholic parishes in the West, various fearless martyrs and stainless saints serving as the inspiration of many a nun and priest and layperson.

The Tibetan spiritual biographies were called *namtars*. Their internal structure can give us helpful insight as we set about exploring our own spiritual recollections. These *namtars* endeavored to speak at three levels of depth—corresponding to the three levels of the dazzlingly sophisticated Tibetan practices. The intention of these biographies was to reveal the outer, inner, and secret aspects of the journey of awakening.

Likewise, we can look at the outer, inner, and secret aspects of the transformative moments in our own lives. The outer view recounts what we appeared to be doing during a pivotal moment or chapter. The inner view recalls the thoughts, emotions, and insights of the experience of the transformative shift. The secret view recognizes the liberation, the newly freed exaltation of Being.

Saint Bonaventure, a thirteenth-century Christian mystic, also offered helpful insights we can use as we explore our own spiritual biography. He described the "eyes" with which we might look at our own awakening journey. Saint Bonaventure recognized that, within this gift of a human life, we are endowed with three different "eyes." These eyes, in his terminology, are the three tools for knowing the three domains of our experience of life-in-form.

First, each of us possesses the eye of the senses, or of the flesh—for the perceptual/sensory knowing of the world of form. This allows the experience of contact—visual, auditory, tactile, and so on. Second, we are equipped with the eye of the mind, or the intellect—for conceptual knowing, mental operations, mental images, beliefs, thoughts, and emotions. The eye of the mind allows us to know our inner world, the subjective experience of ego. Finally, each of us comes equipped with the eye of contemplation, or the eye of spirit. This apperceives the direct realization of grace. For most of us, this "sacred gaze" of pristine awareness—far beyond the senses and the intellect—is a gift rarely unwrapped.

The first two eyes, of the senses and of the mind, gaze upon sensations and concepts. These are the anchors that, untransformed, unawakened, and not understood, hold us fast to the world of form—the world in which we typically confine ourselves in our ignorance. If we are not mindful, these eyes can both distort and deceive. We often see what we believe without mindfulness.

The eye of the senses and the eye of the intellect do not, in and of themselves, access ever-present formless awareness. The eye of spirit, on the other hand, the contemplative eye, *is* formless awareness. The eye of spirit gazes *from* formless awareness. Formless awareness embraces and encompasses form without getting trapped in form's gravitational pull. It is "the untarnished mirror"—in its clarity, free of distortion; in its lack of self-reference, free of reactivity. It is Being. It is grace.

As we delve more deeply into our own spiritual biography, we recognize that when the eye of the senses and the eye of the mind align in the eye of spirit, we begin to function without distortion or misunderstanding. Exploring our own emergence, we note how the eye of the senses, aligned with the eye of spirit, begins to *see* boundless interbeing and the sacred in all things. The eye of the mind, or the intellect, aligned with the eye of spirit, acts and engages in the world with wisdom and compassion, creativity and sanity. Aligned with and in service to the contemplative eye, the eye of the mind responds spontaneously and appropriately. Everything becomes *darshan*—Being meeting itself—whether we're weeding a garden, taking a shower, sitting on a subway, or sitting with the dying.

When we look at our lives through the lens of awakening, all three ways of seeing are engaged. The questions we reflect upon in the process of spiritual biography focus our contemplation. They show us *where* to look. The Tibetan *namtars* and Saint Bonaventure's insight show us *how* to look, providing a contemplative context for our recollection.

When we look at the *outer* aspects of our lives in a spiritual biography, we look at the transformative moment as though we were the narrator of a documentary about our awakening, bringing as much clarity and objectivity to the task as we can. We observe what is observable to the eye of the senses.

For the *inner* aspects of spiritual biography, we recall the inner dimensions of the activities and practices that we were engaged in during the time we are remembering. We recollect the feeling tone and imagery of the inner experience as well as the mind's articulation of the insight that arose from it. Again, we look as though we were a camera or a narrator reporting, this time looking with the eye of the intellect at the conceptual mind. We examine our mental images and the conceptions we held about the sacred, about the self, and about our spiritual practices and transformation.

Looking with the eye of the mind, we ascertain whether there were thoughts or feelings during or immediately after the experience under reflection and what they were. We look at how we conceived of what was happening and how we felt ourselves to be impacted by the experience.

The *secret* aspects of spiritual biography have to do with the releases, revelations, realizations, and the sudden and startling paradigm shifts from which we emerge transformed. They are "secret" in the sense that they are beyond words' capacity to thoroughly and accurately convey.

When exploring our path of awakening and reflecting upon various moments in our lives, we look at the secret aspects of our deep transformational shifts through the eye of spirit, the eye of contemplation. We're looking at what shifted and what was shed. We're looking at energy liberated from limitation and the emergence of growing radiance. We're looking at our transfiguration. Every spiritual path is a path of increasing illumination.

The eye of spirit is "vision," as Cynthia Bourgeault phrases it, "that can look right through the physical appearance of things and respond directly to their innermost aliveness and quality." We all possess this nonverbal, contemplative eye—we just don't typically employ it.

At the beginning of our spiritual journey, we are relatively unfamiliar—and sometimes even uncomfortable—with abiding in the gaze of the contemplative eye. Our practices, both in formal meditation and in mindful awareness throughout the day, are vehicles to its access. The eye of spirit unveils the truth of the way things are. Understandably, this is unsettling to an ego long familiar with denial and unexamined assumptions. The eye of spirit shatters paradigms and, initially, we can experience suffering with the shattering. As we continue to evolve spiritually, we grow in our recognition that, in fact, the closer we are to truth, the less we suffer. Our relationship with the truth transforms as we awaken.

With our development of the eye of spirit, we come to have greater clarity and deeper understanding about the nature of our spiritual journey. We take heart as we begin to *see* that what we experience as longing is actually grace calling us. We take heart as we recognize that our practice, in itself, is a manifestation of grace.

Our greater clarity and deepening understanding lead to the intensification of sincerity and intention, a growing surrender to the pull toward conscious unity. Clarity, intention, and understanding amplify each other. Each is a quality of Being, facilitating the emergence of the essential.

There is a lovely reassurance in the recognition that long-ago monastics from Tibet and Europe offer us, contemporary non-monastic householders, a context for understanding our work of spiritual biography. We can use the insights of their solitude to deepen our unfolding in the midst of our own busy lives. Looking through the lens of awakening always cultivates the contemplative eye. The eye of spirit calls us to become more familiar with resting, being at ease, within its compassionate clarity.

As we reflect upon the working of grace in our own life, it is the sacred gaze that allows our recollections, our deep understanding of our epiphanies, and our gratitude for them. This gaze allows us to recognize the sacrament of every ordinary moment.

We become devoted to the sacred, growing in our realization, along with the eighteenth-century Zen poet Hakuin, that:

> *This very land is the Pure Land.*
> *This very body, the body of Buddha.*

The Journey

And we are put on earth
a little space,
to learn to bear
the beams of love.
—WILLIAM BLAKE

THE SPIRITUAL JOURNEY goes from love to love. This is a pivotal recognition for each of us, whether we're new on the path or a weath-
ered traveler. It's helpful to practice within this view, even practicing
"as if" we actually realized it while holding the intention that grace
will gift us, sooner or later, with that full realization.

Truly, we live these fleeting lives as an expression of love. Llewellyn
Vaughan-Lee observes that our every breath is love in form. Rodney
Smith shares his recognition that the essence of all form is love, that
love reclaims everything until nothing else remains.

We live formed of love and suspended in love. In fact, love is simply
another word for grace. Our origin, the very ground of our being,
is love. And, as the great Christian contemplative Thomas Merton
noted, love is our destiny. He speaks of "the deep secret pull of the
gravitation of love."

We might be engaging in the process of spiritual biography at a
point in our lives that feels like a detour from love, a roadblock. Still,
the realization of the beautiful symmetry of "from love to love" is
available in this very breath—as is the trust that grace is leading us on
this journey.

We may feel our heart blocked, tied up in old sorrows and disappointments and fears that need our compassionate attention. If we look only from our survival operating system, from self, we experience struggle and suffering. But from the eye of spirit, our Being mode, we see only love in its myriad expressions—both fierce and sweet.

Exploring our own spiritual biography can highlight for us the wounds that may yet need healing, the defensive bindings that keep our heart from softening and knowing its own beauty. Healing is the holy work of the journey.

Growing wisdom and compassion, our gifts of grace, allow us to open to our wounds. As we allow awareness to touch our unhealed habit patterns, we open to where we had been closed, open to that which we once preferred to ignore. And, as we begin to open and look, we see that the congestions of the habit patterns also open. They become wispier, no longer so solid or convincing. We can parse apart their narratives, the conclusions these narratives seem to justify, and the self-beliefs we've clung to as a consequence. Once untangled, once understood and seen clearly, these obstructions can be released, no longer interfering with our experience of Being. It becomes a joy to simply surrender them, to let them go.

When we look at our lives through the lens of awakening, we recognize old assumptions and convictions that we've now shed, like shells that litter the shoreline after a storm. We see that we've already let go of old mistaken beliefs, that we have the capacity to simply let go. The view through the lens of awakening also illuminates what present beliefs we may be investing with our credulity, indeed our identity, thereby keeping ourselves asleep. These, too, can be dropped into the compassionate clarity of the heart and carried off on the tides of impermanence.

The spiritual journey is one of surrender—and of the transformative shifts that follow in surrender's wake.

THERE SEEMS TO BE a natural progression of chapters in a spiritual journey.

The questions in the last section of this book are given in four parts, or "quarters." They follow a sequence of movement into Being. There are landmarks on the way, turning points, as we shed the consuming, shadowed energy of self-reference and begin to abide, radiant and sane, in the grace in living.

The four quarters of a spiritual journey express our expanding liberation from survival mode. They trace an arc of illumination, a continuum of increasing refinement and subtlety. Enlightenment *is* this endlessly growing illumination.

When engaging in the exercise of spiritual biography, it's best to proceed sequentially, going through the questions from quarter one through quarter four—the sequence of awakening. After you've done that once, there is great benefit in sweeping back and forth over the four quarters again several times. Our contemplative eye becomes stronger in the process and a second or third sweep can often highlight what a first sweep might have missed.

As you engage in the exercise, you may also discover that the process of your awakening hasn't yet carried you along to some quarters of the journey. We can take this recognition as an egoic blow or as a revelation of truth pointing out where next to put our attention, recognizing the challenges and opportunities of our experience of the present moment. I'll address this in part three.

THE FIRST QUARTER

THE FIRST QUARTER of our spiritual journey can be described as a movement from "tastes" to "hunger."

It starts with wondering, with curiosity, and moves to our first deliberate explorations in search of an authentic path. This part of the journey encompasses our childhood all the way through to the moment we began actively searching for a wisdom lineage that spoke to us, that held the promise of fulfilling the growing yearning we came to feel.

This first quarter includes whatever moments of wonder, of vastness, and of presence we had as a child. These are our "tastes" of
grace. They get buried for a while for most of us, but they eventually
burst forth again later in a "hunger" for more.

In my own spiritual biography, for example, I recalled a meadow in
my childhood neighborhood that was filled with thousands of violets
in the spring. I remember one spring day just sitting and picking them
for hours with a great, appreciative awareness of the abundance all
around me—old apple trees in bloom, bridal veil bushes, blue sky, so
many violets I could never pick them all. The smell of the gathering
bouquet had incredible sweetness. I heard the quiet drone of a single-
engine plane passing overhead. There were no thoughts, just a very
quiet *hum* around me and inside me. I loved the peace in that meadow
and its soft long grass. I developed a taste for peace, for stillness.

The recollection itself was as powerful as the original experience
and I recorded it like this:

violets

———————————|—————————————

Using one word this way is a touchstone, a reminder that evokes
the full sensorial, spiritual experience.

Many people report these early kinds of "knowing," rarely verified by
the people around them but, nonetheless, leaving a deep and indelible
impression that marks the beginning of their inclination toward Spirit.

Exploring the first part of your own story of awakening, note the
way you held whatever immense and subtle understandings that
impacted and imprinted you, even as a child. Note how you shared
or did not share these experiences, whether or not you found anyone
who could help you make sense of it, and what meaning you gave to
the experience and to yourself as "the experiencer."

I had a recollection of my Catholic upbringing. There was much about the Mass that I loved—the solemnity, the ritual and mystery, the sense of connection with something greater. I often went to daily Mass and loved the feeling of being inside the tiny chapel, with the early-morning light filtering through the stained glass windows and the bell-like Latin chanting. There was no way to talk about this deep response, about the beautiful feeling of profundity that was nurtured there. I just didn't have the words, so I kept it to myself. Many years later, as an adult already on a spiritual path, my mother said to me, "You didn't really need to *believe* all that stuff." I felt sad for her, actually, that she hadn't also felt herself blessed with more than just believing.

In a spiritual biography, we note not only our early deep experiences but the burying of our depths under the pressure to forge an acceptable identity. To be accepted by peers, for example, I hid my attraction to depth. In this exercise, we chronicle both joys and disappointments, the accumulation of wounds and unexamined beliefs, along with transcendent moments—simply noting them all.

My earliest memory, stirred by the exercise of spiritual biography, was of sitting in a room, just being. The light was golden, like honey. I felt golden, like honey, too. There was no questioning of that ease and joy and simplicity of being. There was no awareness that life could be any other way. It was delight.

My mother came into the room. As I watched her coming through the doorway and approaching where I sat, her energy seemed to be a swirling, jagged gray—kind of menacing, kind of disapproving, kind of shaming. I didn't have words for it but I knew I didn't want it near me. I felt a resistance to receiving that sort of energy within my space but I had no defenses. I think my sense of a separate self was formed in that moment, with a sense of defenselessness and a sense of shame and deep sadness. Anger, too.

You will have your own recollections of wounds as well as a deeper understanding of the causes and conditions that gave rise to your desire to awaken.

Our exploration of the first quarter also leads us to recall our moments of meeting with whatever "teachers of goodness" we encountered along the way. It explores the causes and conditions that gave rise to our desire to awaken. Many pivotal memories were stirred for me.

From the time I was twelve until the time I was sixteen, my father went into insulin shock a couple of nights a week. It would happen in the middle of the night and my mother would wake me from sleep. My job was to try to hold him down so that she could get some pineapple juice in him. He was enormously strong and it was very frightening for me. One time he threw me across the room and my mother thought he had killed me. My father would have hated to have known what happened. We never spoke about "the night before" on any next morning.

I was left with a deep uneasiness when the truth is denied. I was also left with a tendency to become anxious when I'm asked to do something I haven't done before, having been asked as a child to do things so much beyond my capacity.

When I was seventeen, my father died. The hospital called around four in the morning to say he had "taken a turn for the worse." He had already died, but they didn't say that. I said the rosary for the whole hour's drive to the hospital, praying he would be okay.

When we got to the hospital, I went into his room with my mother, and although I wanted to stay and say goodbye—it was all just too quick—she didn't want to be in the room. She wanted me to go call my brothers to tell them he had died. While I was walking to the phone, some nurses wheeled his body, covered with a sheet, past me in the narrow hospital hallway. I had to back into the wall to make room for the gurney. I don't know if they would have done that if they had known I was his daughter. In that moment, my heart froze and stayed frozen for many years.

I noted this recollection of a frozen heart on my time line, like this:

Dad

— — — — — — — — — — — | — — — — — — — —

When my father died, the bubble of what I had presumed to be the safety and security of my family simply burst. A few months earlier, Kennedy had been assassinated, and I had felt a similar bubble of what I had presumed to be the safety and security of my country burst. A few months later, in my first week of college, sitting in a Modern European History class, the teacher mentioned that the pope issued the Edict of Infallibility to consolidate the southern German states on his side, rather than with Prussia. In that moment, it was as though my faith in the Church were a brick wall and, in my mind's eye, I watched every brick in the wall tumble down. The presumed safety and security of my religion shattered as well.

When the late sixties and seventies arrived, not much was holding me back from exploring new views that resonated with what I knew to be true and right, but I was shaken and unsettled and adrift.

The biggest influences on my spiritual path at the time were reading *The Duino Elegies*, by Rilke, Hermann Hesse's *Siddhartha*, Carlos Castaneda's books, and Paramhansa Yogananda's *Autobiography of a Yogi*. They spoke to me directly and re-placed me back in the longing for union and presence that I had felt so many times as a kid.

In graduate school, a friend brought me Ram Dass's *Be Here Now*— still in a box, straight from the print shop at the Lama Foundation. I stayed up all night reading it and felt that I had finally found a voice and a view that resonated with me. I was deeply moved, crying with relief. It stirred a deep intention in me to recapture the simple joy of being I had known as a child. It gave me a kind of solace to know that other people wanted it too, and were finding it. I felt like I finally found my tribe.

THESE ARE SOME of my memories of the first quarter of my journey, from tasting to hunger. Some of them had been hidden away for a long time. As I explored my spiritual biography, I simply noted powerful recollections on my time line, using a word that evoked the memory. In that way, I began to trace the presence of grace throughout my journey and the wounds that blocked me from recognizing it.

The first quarter was, for me, a mixture of both grace and wounds. I hope using my stories as illustration gives a sense of that. You will find your own mixture of grace and wounds as recollections arise of your unique path.

THE SECOND QUARTER

THE NEXT NATURAL division, the next quarter, of a spiritual journey encompasses a second period of movement, from seeking to the end of seeking. We begin the Great Search when our longing for beyond only self becomes so strong that we deliberately reach out for a path. And seeking ends when awareness begins to rest in Being, the only reliable refuge.

The end of seeking involves surrender—of self, of self's strategies, of effort, of conceptual reliance, of ignorance. The end of seeking is seeing. Seeing, seeking ceases.

Buddhism, with its twenty-six-hundred-year history of looking at the subtle depths of the spiritual path, names the path of seeing as the game-changing moment(s) of everyone's journey. In this view, the path of seeing is the recognition of the conditioned and illusory nature of all phenomena, including the self.

The path of seeing is preceded by paths of accumulation and preparation, all of the "developing" activities of seeking and practicing. They lead to the moment of seeing. The path of seeing then opens into the endless "discovering" paths of meditation and consummation. Consummation is a beautiful way to describe the conscious merging into grace. These last two stages correspond to those

I am calling maturation and ripening, the third and fourth quarters of a spiritual journey in this schema.

The second quarter, from seeking to the end of seeking, can be a long stage. And it is often a hard stage, not because grace makes it so but because self has blindly accumulated so much "learned ignorance," in Saint Augustine's words, that needs to be discarded. We need to stop *assuming* before we can actually look and see.

This quarter of the path includes the books and teachings that opened our mind, traditions and teachers that we've encountered, our experience of the practices we've engaged in, as well as everyday joys and challenges along the way. It also includes the pivotal recognition of the need to heal the self's wounds and the hard work of the healing itself.

The exercise of spiritual biography can lead us to recognize that our wounds will continue to call us back from further growth until we see and acknowledge them and engage compassionately in their healing. With increasing clarity and honesty, we recognize that our unexamined beliefs and unconscious habit patterns will continue to run our lives until we begin to rest more in Being mode, an abode of awareness clear enough to compassionately witness the patterns of mind from a nonreactive equanimity.

This second natural division is also the story of two of our greatest obstacles—seeking and striving. Endless seeking arises from a restlessness, from a nonacceptance of the way things are, a dissatisfaction with the state and rate of our own awakening. Egoic striving seeks to change the way things are. It operates without trust or confidence in the truth that grace is already at work upon us.

For many, the second quarter can be a frenzy of spiritual practice, arising with a sense of wanting to "storm heaven." It is the time of our greatest exertion of effort, the period where the self thinks it can strategize its way beyond self—relying on its familiar illusions of control. With conflicting intentions, this time period can also witness the machinations of the survival mode as ego resists the end of its dominion.

The movement from seeking to the end of seeking includes, as well, the longing that arises from our brief glimpses into the heart, the resting place of the Being mode. These moments both encourage and allow us to continue with resolve.

As we explore the questions of the second quarter of our spiritual biography, we can see our changing relationship with our "spiritual life." Perhaps we pursued it obsessively for a while, only to see that our very pushing is an obstruction. With that discovery, we relax into trusting and simply allow grace and sincere intention to guide our way. When we come to "the understanding that what is intrinsically here cannot be willfully induced," as Rodney Smith points out, we relax into what is referred to in Buddhist tradition as "wise effort." In wise effort, we continue with committed formal practice and continue to go through our days with mindfulness, alertness, and conscientiousness. Trusting in grace to carry us, we release the rigidity of self and will.

Perhaps, in the early part of the second quarter of our journey, our spiritual path was pursued as mere flirtation, enjoying the identification as spiritual practitioner as another ego inflation. Perhaps, initially, we relegated our spiritual path to the corners of our busy life in the world.

The second quarter of our spiritual biography reveals the movements and shifts in how we hold our spiritual path. We see when our practice moved from a position as an important part of our life to a position as central. As our life itself becomes practice, we own our path authentically—from our heart rather than merely from our mental ego. Allowing grace to have its way with us, we begin to thoroughly and sincerely take responsibility for living the realizations of our direct experience.

The moment when our spiritual path becomes inseparable from our breathing, from our being, we become devout. "Devout" derives from a Latin root that conveys nuances of both "vow" and "offering." The moment our spiritual path and our daily life become indistinguishable, our vow to never abandon it is complete. We spontaneously recognize our being as both an offering from grace and an offering to others.

The second quarter of a spiritual journey is a time of deep psychospiritual growth work and great commitment to the holy work of awakening. It demands steadfast intention and courage as well as tender compassion. In her poem "Sangha," yoga practitioner and poet Danna Faulds comments:

> . . . To take one step is courageous;
> to stay on the path day after day,
> chasing the unknown,
> and facing yet another fear,
> that is nothing short of grace.

Ken Wilber reminds us that the fires of transformation are not a relaxing hot tub. The work of healing can entail great suffering as we allow ourselves to feel, finally, all that we have rejected, ignored, and stuffed deep inside. Many practitioners experience a dark night of the soul during this time. We break open. This state of brokenness is the leaping-off point for surrender. We've exhausted ego's possibilities and have nowhere left to turn.

We stay in survival mode until we've had enough suffering and—surrendering—wish to see through the causes of suffering. Many people, especially those without a practice, stay in survival mode until the very end of life, when there is no choice other than to let go, surrender, and see Reality as it is. May each of us have the grace to die to who we think we are before who we think we are dies.

MANY MEMORIES were recalled from this second quarter as I engaged with my own spiritual biography.

During this time, I quickly had children, went to graduate school, played with the ideas of awakening that were everywhere at the time in the university town where we lived and, within a few years, was divorced.

I had, following a growing longing, already done several Arica train-
ings with Oscar Ichazo. Those were periods of highs that were unsus-
tainable but that left deep imprints of the limitlessness of awareness.
The imprints remained—they were never lost—but they diminished
in the urgency of their call for a while.

The next fifteen years were a bit of a nightmare. The kids and I
tumbled into a poverty that I could not have previously imagined. I
felt I was being punished by the universe somehow but had no idea
what the punishment could possibly be for. Fear really colored those
years.

Although I meditated and prayed repeatedly, the diminishments of
fear and poverty on hope, ease, and self-esteem took their toll. Since
I was using meditation and prayer as ways to try to cancel out the
nightmarish parts of the whole experience and they weren't working,
my confidence in transformative practice—which hadn't yet deepened enough to be authentic—diminished.

For years, I meditated daily, with the hope of easing the fears and
stresses of poverty and single parenthood. Then, for years, I didn't
meditate. Back and forth. Hoping and despairing. My self-esteem
was in shreds. I tried hard to make parenting (which was joyful) and
enduring poverty and hopelessness (which were horrible) into my
spiritual practice.

Many of the teachers I was able to meet were charlatans, and yet I
kept thinking I just hadn't met the one true one who could help me
yet. I had a powerful dream one night. There was an archetypal spiritual teacher who told me he could "cure" me. That's really what I was
looking for—a cure. The wish to return to the simple joy of being was
totally muffled beneath the felt need for a cure, for someone or something to fix the life that seemed to have gone so totally awry.

It wasn't really until most of the kids had gone off to college that
there was even a chance to take stock of myself. I saw that there
was an incredible amount of healing work to do. I was a mess and
utterly worn out. Healing took a long time. And, until I addressed the
wounds that needed to be healed, lip service was all I could give to my

spiritual searching. I still tried to use "but I'm spiritual!" as a balm on my bleeding self-concept, but I didn't really fool myself.

I wondered if the real, genuine longing had died out in the hardship. Antonio Machado wondered the same thing: "I thought the fire was out / and I stirred the ashes. / I burnt my fingers." I was grateful to find the longing still there.

In long stretches with the absence of teachers or community, I read the spiritual classics. I lived off the grid for a long time, really trying to believe my simplicity was voluntary. Upon my return to a more conventional world, I was blown away that there was such an extensive field of new spiritual literature, that so many people had the same hunger. Finding Chögyam Trungpa and Ken Wilber, for example, was a delight. I remember thinking, "Wow. We can really talk about these things now."

I began again to study and practice, for many years practicing the yoga of light and sound from the Surat Shabd tradition. After that, my attraction was to the clarity of Buddhism, and I have spent years working with practices from both the Vajrayana and Theravada Buddhist traditions. I have so much gratitude for the untold number of practitioners who kept the flame of Dharma going—across centuries and across traditions.

It took a long time for me to recognize that courage, strength, love, and compassion had grown in me during all those hard years. It's like they grew under the surface of the stress. As I began to recognize that those qualities really were there and began to be grateful for them, healing began to happen. I had been halfhearted until a critical number of wounds began to heal. Time and circumstance, validation from those I respected, and honoring the qualities that had grown in me helped. Prayer—to the universe, to some unknown, yet hoped-for goodness—helped. I sensed that the hardships had carved out some real space inside me.

Reading was my primary access to teachings and I read widely from many traditions. Some resonated more than others, although almost each and every book contributed, allowing an opening in my mind. Whatever resonated inside me allowed a recognition to plant itself in my heart.

Years later, someone told me that my practice, a practice that had just naturally evolved, was called "the yoga of imagination." I didn't know that name for it at the time I began doing it. I didn't even know it was a practice. It was spontaneous, a natural inclination to be open to insights. The insights were like "seed" thoughts that, with the nurturing of contemplation, gradually took root. When I recognize a view that is beneficial, I imagine what it would be like to experience life in that way and the inner work of aligning with the view begins.

Meditating on the thoughts and realizations from a wide variety of traditions, my mind would shift. I could usually discern the truth. Truth has a simplicity and a power. My faith rekindled, as did my intention to keep opening and going deeper. I was thirsty for all of it.

I received a Christmas card one year that said, "And His love is for all time and His love is for all men." I translated the patriarchal language and removed it from a traditional, theistic framework and something opened in me. There was a deep and piercing realization that Love was also for me. I was not the only human being to be excluded from it. All were included—even me. *That* was powerful.

Many recollections came to me as I explored my spiritual biography. Other powerful experiences affirmed that the flame of my spiritual longing hadn't died out.

One recollection was of walking through the beautiful Sangre de Cristo mountains, deep in a woods that was covered with snow. It was completely silent. Peaceful. Undisturbed. I wondered with each step if any other human being had ever stepped on that spot on earth before. I found a forty- or fifty-foot-long Douglas fir that had fallen to the ground so many years earlier that it had turned to dust, without a single footstep marring it since the moment of its fall.

Walking through the snow and the silence, my mind was filled with my own version of the old Native American prayer:

Above me, beauty.
Below me, beauty.
Before me, beauty.
Behind me, beauty.
Outside me, beauty.
Inside me, beauty.
I, beauty, walk in beauty.

It was a moment of a dramatic shift and a deep understanding of the power of view to determine our experience. It left me breathless, in awe. And changed somehow. I knew something wordless I hadn't known before. And I knew it was a blessing and was grateful.

But, I still felt lost a bit, still searched for a teacher, and was finally forced to rely upon and take refuge in whatever realizations I had and to continue growing with my own heart as guide. In that sense, it dawned on me that maybe I *had* found the perfect teacher. I realized that the seeds that had been planted had already begun to transform my mind and deepen my understanding and intention. There arose a deep new commitment to following my heart's intuition and guidance. Mark Nepo, the Buddhist poet, speaks of the seeking that keeps looking for one more teacher, "only to find that fish learn from the water and birds learn from the sky."

That was a turning point that I can only characterize as trust. I began to go more and more deeply inward, ingathering attention and holding it fast in silence. In that silence, there was no self. It could be trusted. It felt like being in the presence of a holy being. It came to me, deep in meditation, that this was *my* holy being, Spirit shining through this individual soul.

THESE ARE SOME of my recollections of the second long quarter of my journey. I hope they stir up memories of your own as you explore your awakening path. As in the first quarter, I noted these and other memories by simply placing a word or two that evoked the memory on my time line.

This second quarter is a period where discouragement and effort, all the machinations of self, can keep us stuck for quite a while. Movement through it is pivotal. It is a quarter marked by healing and the growing sincerity that gives birth to trust.

THE THIRD QUARTER

THE THIRD NATURAL division of the spiritual journey is one of maturing. Spiritual maturation begins to take place when we reach the outer limits of effort, conceptuality, and *selfing*. It arises at the end of self's effort to seek anything at all. This is truly to surrender. Surrendering—as we do at the end of the second quarter—we let go of our inclination to live a conceptualized life, having seen its limitations and felt its suffocating contractions. Attention, freed, relocates in Being.

In the process, our center of gravity begins to shift. We often sit to practice simply as the natural expression of Being. Formless awareness begins to manifest *in* and *as* us and we more effortlessly live in peace, in grace. Equanimity begins to mature within awareness. This is a spiritual gift of the path. We become more deeply present in our lives and to the world around us, increasingly aware of sacrament in each moment.

Familiar habit patterns, the echoes and detritus of old beliefs and emotional reactivities, and the self who identifies with them, however, continue to arise. Our very being, having become more vast in this transformative process, becomes spacious enough to hold these old habit patterns of mental and emotional formations without being swept away by their rip tides—or at least not swept away for as long as we used to be. We cease judging ourselves as these old patterns arise, since we no longer so blindly identify with them. This sliver of disidentification provides the space through which compassion can shine its healing light.

In this way, we heal into maturity. Healing leads us to increased openness. We simply have fewer snags to get caught on. Opened, we allow. Resting in refuge, we begin to let go with greater ease. We come to prefer to let go.

Letting go is an awakened action, referred to by Cynthia Bourgeault in the lovely phrase "the gesture of surrender." Letting go becomes an ingrained inner gesture, an inner attitude and inclination. As we practice over time, the growing power of our capacity to surrender begins to exceed the energy level of our habit patterns. We simply become more interested in Being than in grasping and hiding and posturing. Old beliefs, assumptions, and identifications drift away, as though they were the fluff of dandelions. Surrendering, we clear out the vast space within us.

We attend to those deeply rutted patterns that are not so easily released with tender mercy—without judgment or discouragement. We simply hold the intention that what can be healed in that moment be healed, that wisdom will continue to allow increasing clarity into the dynamics of the patterns, and that steadfast courage—along with the grace of intention—will allow us to endure the repeated arising of the pattern with compassion for ourselves, for all others who suffer similarly, and for those we harm.

We begin to recognize that letting go, surrender, however easy or difficult, is the very essence of the path of awakening. We come to know surrender as release from entrapment in smallness, as liberation found in the simple stance of allowing, as a jump into ease.

We iron out the remaining snags, the wrinkles of habitual mental/emotional formations. We become less enchanted by temporary gratifications and the seductions of self, much less willing to render the experience of Being over to mere survival, like ransom to a highwayman. This is maturity.

In this stage, we come to know ourselves as awakening beings. We become conscious of our open-eyed entry into grace, into mystery, into reverence. Trust, the essential psychological task for any child's development into a functioning self, reveals itself as essential, also, for our movement into beyond self. With trust, we gratefully and confidently begin to allow our awakening to unfold unimpeded.

The surrendered self allows grace to do its holy work. In deep Christian practice, which views the spiritual journey as one from self to soul to Spirit, this is the movement into soul. Buddhist wisdom calls these levels of awareness the bodhisattva grounds, deeply transformative passageways.

Our movement is into increasing depth, refinement, and illumination and toward the embodiment of that depth, refinement, and illumination. Increasingly, we experience life as Being rather than only as self. Our buddha nature and our human nature increasingly merge.

As grace works its way, Being mode increasingly holds our attention and wonder. Wonder is filled with aliveness, like the ionized air beside a rushing stream. It is compelling. Its absorbing stillness becomes more compelling to us than the dramatic, noisy chatter of the survival mode.

Finally, we begin to live in our own holiness, in the holiness of all that is. We welcome, allow, and let go of each new passing moment. We begin to recognize, with wonder, that each new moment has never arisen before. We begin to recognize, with appreciation, the experience of a moment that will never arise again.

You will recognize these shifts in your own being as you engage in spiritual biography. My own recollections were powerful, reflecting deepening gratitude and growing trust.

ALTHOUGH THERE ARE many, perhaps the biggest challenge that still remains for me is anxiety. It became so deeply ingrained that overwhelm seemed normal. It still arises, sometimes seemingly out of nowhere. I now practice opening to it instead of contracting into it.

Somewhere along the way, I noticed how fear blocks us. For a long time, I felt I couldn't move forward until fear was gone. But there were too many demands—especially those of parenting—to simply stop moving, and I realized there wasn't any choice but to move forward and do what was necessary. Rather than thinking I could only move when I had "conquered" fear, I learned to hold hands with fear and keep going.

Anxiety often comes with the same thought: "I can't do this." In one meditation session, I saw this believed thought not only as an obstruction to grace but also recognized it as *ingratitude* for the grace already working in and through me—allowing me to do much my small egoic self viewed as beyond my capacity. In that moment, gratitude rushed in and filled the space the belief had occupied and I could feel the release of that pattern's heavy weight.

I used to believe the thoughts of the anxiety and identify with them. Now it arises simply as an unpleasant bodily experience of racing heart and clutched throat that I have learned is endurable. Simple breaths, simple kindness to myself, simple compassion for all those who suffer with anxiety.

There is incredible sadness within anxiety, and I'm grateful when tears can flow. Buddha describes us as all having bindings around our heart, like the rings that hold a barrel in place, the knots in the subtle energy systems of our bodies. When I cry, the binders loosen along with the binding sense of self. "I" dissolve in an opened heart. "I" can't be found.

Sometimes crying was how every meditation began and continued—just sadness, just sorrow. There's a lot of sadness in the world. Although, too, sometimes it is joy that squeezes out the tears.

I still judge. Most often, I can just shake my head and let it go. There's also more humility—like, this is what the human mind does, this is what self-cherishing and self-grasping do, and this is how we wake up. There's more of a sense of humor, too. Although the anxiety that occasionally visits has no sense of humor at all.

Discerning wisdom now comes a little more easily, and caring, blessedly, is often authentic and spontaneous. Many ordinary seductions have lost their enchantment. Ego gets slyer and more subtle. I'm stunned sometimes to see it still so hard at work, so quick to hop in.

I think of insights and realizations the way I think of popcorn. You stand there with the lid on tight and wait for a pop. And then there is a pop and then in a little bit another pop. That's how it was for me for quite a few years—great stretches between the "pops." I think we slow the pops down with the fear of letting go. Now the popping has sped up. Insights and realizations seem to come at a faster pace and there is a willingness to align very quickly with that knowing. I feel grateful for all the ways my mind has shifted, all the transformations along the way.

To say that I've come to trust my own heart does not in any way negate my gratitude for the teachings I've received. I remember one moment in particular, as I was engaged in a Tibetan practice, coming upon the sweetness of two lines of question and response: "Dear One, who are you?" "I am a fortunate being, seeking great enlightenment." Those lines led me to trust in the way all this works, even though it was beyond my understanding. They resonated within me deeply and allowed me to finally acknowledge worthiness and a dignity far more real than any negative self-image ever was or could be.

I've come to see that my essential nature is beautiful. When my first child was born, I was reluctant to go, "Oh my God, look at him! Look at how awesome he is!" I was afraid people would think I was bragging. But, after having more kids, it was so easy to say with all the others, "Would you just look at that beautiful baby!" and share the joy of the universal beauty of babies. It's the same with our essential natures—they're all beautiful, and so why not rejoice in it and be grateful for it, holding the intention that it endlessly deepens and that it is endlessly shared.

I HOPE THESE memories of grace's work on me illustrate the process and benefit of exploring the path of your own awakening and remind you of memories of grace's work on you.

THE FOURTH QUARTER

THE FOURTH NATURAL division is the period of our spiritual ripening. Exclusive attention to self has been transcended, its capacities remaining inclusively within soul. Soul begins to move into and merge with

Spirit. You could just as easily say that Spirit begins to move into and merge with soul. They are just words, after all—pointing us toward understanding.

The Being mode becomes fully engaged. Renunciation, the "gesture of surrender," becomes our natural state of being. As Rodney Smith notes, we no longer allow thoughts of self, although they still arise, to take form.

There are many ways to name the movement of our growing illumination. A. H. Almaas (the pen name of A. Hameed Ali, founder of the wisdom-filled Diamond Approach) traces the progression through our spiritual path by noting the sequential emergence of value, presence, and luminosity.

In the first quarter, we get a taste of vast and wondrous new dimensions of being and knowing. The first quarter also includes our movement into ego, into survival mode, and ends when we enter a transformative path. This is the first step of our liberation from entrapment in the survival operating system—the first step in turning off the airplane setting on the smartphone. As we enter a transformative path, our absorption in the shadow cast by self as it blocks radiance begins, albeit slowly, to diminish. Our polestar changes. We begin to turn toward the light of Being. This reorientation allows progression through value to presence to luminosity.

Although challenging circumstances continue, as does reactivity to them, the healing and deepening understanding of the second quarter release us from feelings of insufficiency and unworthiness. We move in our experience of existence into value, into a grateful and humble ownership not only of our own dignity but also of the endearing vulnerabilities of being a person. Value is the integration of shadow and persona in honest acceptance and appreciation. Energy is no longer squandered in denial or pretense.

Entry into the third quarter—marked by surrender and a new sense of the value of our own being and direct experience—brings the end of our incarceration in unworthiness. This liberation allows us to recognize our loving embrace within formless awareness. We realize, as the Tao Te Ching reminds us, "Every being in the universe is an expression of the Tao."

Through a demanding process of seeing and releasing, the third quarter brings us to thorough and open authenticity. Our experience of existence moves into presence—integrated and embodied, here and now. Presence is mindful, easy, and authentic. It is without egoic self-reference and without any illusion that there is an alternative to the present moment. Presence does not confuse conceptualized life with aliveness.

The fourth quarter brings us to luminosity—the embodiment of the Absolute in the particular, in the individual holographic point of existence. No separation, no other—unified and yet an individual manifestation of that unity. We begin to live within the embrace of form and formlessness, resting in the refuge of truth, the refuge of grace and Being. We become humble in the face of the beauty of it all—the suffering, the ineffability, the majesty.

In the ever-deepening last quarter of a spiritual journey, a quarter without end, higher-order capacities emerge. We cease fabricating false ground or relying upon false refuge. Being mode cherishes the unique expression of our individuality as a vehicle for Spirit to shine through. We exchange fabricated ego for our endearingly unique essential nature.

Ripening is a beautiful time. We no longer think of meaning as something to be found but as something to be lived. As we enter deeper levels of Being, meaning exists in each act, thought, and moment of aliveness.

Here are some recollections of this last quarter of the journey that engaging in spiritual biography brought forth for me.

FOR A LONG PERIOD on my spiritual path I felt like a graduate student who never quite finishes the dissertation and gets stuck in school forever. There came a turning point, after meeting yet another teacher who appropriated the dharma for his own ego, when I realized that I had learned enough to leave graduate school and launch my own career, so to speak, on the spiritual path. Deepening awareness stopped being dependent on the condition of finding the perfect teacher.

My understanding was amplified, in some ways immeasurably, by the teachings of others and by shared insights, but I came to a point of trusting intention and the universe. I think of intention and the universe as the two sides of grace—and grace has come to mean everything to me. It is my refuge, and aligning within it is my "all-day" practice, as much as I stay in mindfulness.

I zero in on and resonate with "hints" like the incredible hint of the Heart Sutra: "Form is empty; emptiness is not other than form." I let Buddha's realized understanding point the way. If form is empty and emptiness is not other than form, what does that mean for me, in my practice, in my life? If they are inseparable, I am in ignorance every moment I believe in separation. And—lo and behold—my mind is shifting a little as the realization slowly begins to take hold and deepen and transform even some of my very ordinary thoughts. I'll sometimes look at my hand or the kitchen counter or a fast-moving cloud and know it as yet another beautiful display of grace. These are glimpses of radiant Life behind all the appearances, and "I" disappear in the recognition.

Another thing that is noticeable is the transformed nature of my relationship with *metta* practice—a practice of loving-kindness for self, at first, extending then to others, through the inner merging with the thoughts: "May I (you) be happy. May I (you) be well. May I (you) be safe. May I (you) be peaceful and at ease."

I remember the first few times I sat to do *metta* practice and found powerful resistance in my mind. Imagine that—resistance to offering myself happiness and wellness and peace and ease. The resistance was the belief in my unworthiness, my conviction that I didn't yet deserve to be happy or hadn't yet "earned" being peaceful. It was both sad and stunning to become aware of the resistance of all those deep, damaging, draining beliefs.

And, of course, my kind wishes for others were a bit shallow, not really authentic, when I couldn't even hold them for myself. Gradually I began to rest in a dispassionate place of stillness where there was enough clarity to see the stories that gave rise to those mistaken beliefs and—just observing, just looking—they began to dissipate. After a while, it made me laugh to myself to see how stuck I'd been. *Metta* practice began to happen from a new place—actually resting *in* loving-kindness.

My prayer: "May this space I call *me* be happy, well, safe, peaceful, and at ease." There is a deeper place—closer to essential nature, less filled with ego's thoughts—that holds the intentions and wishes. It is grace. Grace's intentions and wishes for the beat-up little ego that's still around are tender and merciful. *Metta* has become a practice that sweetens me, that lands me right in my own sweetness. And from the sweetness, not really mine but also somehow mine—part of this individual expression of the holy—the wishes for myself and others are real.

During this time in my life, I feel gratitude often. At the Buddhist meditation center Spirit Rock, there is a little building called "the gratitude hut." I think of the little house where I live now as a gratitude hut.

WHEN I WAS A KID, my aunt was a nun. She was in a walled, semi-cloistered convent. She could have visitors periodically, but her vow was never to leave. One time during a visit to the convent, we were walking through the gardens and I saw a whole set of walls inside the convent grounds and asked her what they were. She said that another group of Sisters lived in there, totally cloistered, and that their job each day was to pray for the world.

That really struck me. I could almost see their prayers. I felt that all those women in there who no one else would ever see were really making a difference. So, from my little gratitude hut, I try to send some bit of sweet compassion to the world.

I have a deep yearning to realize and embody Ryokan's intention: "When I think about the sadness of the people of this world, their sadness becomes mine . . . O that my priest's robes were wide enough to gather up all the suffering people in this floating world." I keep it in remembrance and life keeps it in remembrance for me. We live on a sorrowful planet.

This is the richest time in my life. There's no way I could have taken the degree of unconsciousness with which I entered adult life and been able to enter into a spiritual path for real without having to reckon with the truth of what it meant to be a person. Specifically, this person, "me." Seeing myself clearly and with compassion led my experience of life to a new home base. The old stuff still arises—irritation, pride, the wish to control, for example. I just see them a little more quickly—and there are enough dear people in my life who point them out if I don't.

I wish the scared young single mom could have known what was in store. I wish everyone could have a sense of what's in store with this unfolding.

These are some reflections on this last and boundless quarter of my journey. Your recollections will reveal your own unique footprints of grace on this path "from love to love."

In the fourth quarter of a spiritual journey, as we begin to abide more stably in Being, in the soul that mediates between self and Spirit, higher-order capacities emerge in us. These are the fruits of transforming realizations, emerging as we humbly and gratefully recognize grace. The evidence of fruition is abundant.

Attachment gives way to appreciation. Politeness elevates to kindness. Honor elevates to integrity. Believing gives way to awe. Hope gives way to gratitude. Self-consciousness melts in the intimacy of self-forgetfulness. Unworthiness ceases in grateful humility.

Judgment evolves into discernment. Confusion gives way to clarity. Separation begins to dissolve in a growing experience of unity. Contraction-in-self eases into vastness, saturated with Being's spaciousness. Conceptuality gives way to wisdom. Striving relaxes into the simple awareness of natural great peace. Defendedness melts into connection as indifference ceases in compassion. Seeking ends in the discovery of always-already grace, refuge.

There becomes here. Then becomes now.

And love begins to flow.

The journey "from love to love" is complete and, now, simply and endlessly deepens. Meister Eckhart, the great medieval Christian mystic, notes that what a person takes in by contemplation, he or she pours out in love. The greatest fruit of our spiritual ripening is love. We begin to embody the love from which only our ignorance kept us. Ripening, we begin to function in service to compassion and justice. This is how love manifests in the public sphere, as Martin Luther King Jr. noted. It is the realization of interbeing in action, engaged.

No one may notice or label our "ripening," but many will recognize kindness. Many will recognize presence—a force field of Being. Many will be drawn to the love we embody in a peaceful, quiet wisdom and a playful innocence that we freely, spontaneously, and un-self-consciously share. We become an offering. Recognizing that, we can rejoice in the grace that showers us and share it, far and wide, in an ever-expanding circle of love.

For those of you who are going to skip ahead to the instructions in part three and begin your own spiritual biography now, it would be helpful to consult the introduction to each quarter in part two before you begin contemplating the corresponding part of your spiritual journey.

Part Two
Stories of Awakening

— ❦ —

Listen to the silence inside the illusion of the world,
and you will remember the lesson you forgot,
which was taught in immense milky way
soft cloud innumerable words long ago
and not even at all.
It is one vast awakened thing.
It is perfect.

—JACK KEROUAC

THE FIRST QUARTER:
From Tasting to Hunger

Allow, and grace
will carry you to higher ground.
The only safety
lies in letting it all in—

. . . .

practice becomes
simply bearing the truth.
In the choice to let go
of your known way of being,
the whole world is revealed to your new eyes.

—DANNA FAULDS

Introduction

— ⟨∞⟩ —

THE FIRST QUARTER of a spiritual journey often begins with our early senses or glimpses of beyond self. These are our "tastes." This quarter traces movement through to our first deliberate inclination toward a path or a teaching that resonates with our growing longing for that "beyond." This is our hunger.

The first "reaching toward" often arises, as the philosopher William James noted, with the cry "Help!"

It can arise with the validation of those who long similarly or who are similarly "depthed." After lonely years of silently holding the longing in our hearts, the first quarter ends when the longing becomes too strong to hold quiet any longer, when it begins to assert a priority in our lives. Setting out on the Great Search marks the end of the first quarter.

The first quarter is the period in which our attention becomes trapped in survival mode. Through childhood, adolescence, and even some decades of adulthood, most of us lose touch with the eye of spirit, beyond self. We come to rely almost exclusively upon the eye of the senses and the eye of the intellect.

Early in the first quarter, we begin our engagement in the necessary task of survival and the creation of a functioning self—especially a functioning self that can somehow "fit in." We do tend to believe that fitting in, even if we attempt to fit in by standing out, will help to ensure our survival.

The first quarter of our journey is the time spent in the formation

89

of a coherent identity—however healthy or unhealthy that sense of identity might be. In the confluence of the idiosyncrasies of our own survival operating system with the causes, conditions, and circumstances we encounter, mistaken conclusions arise. We endow them with belief.

These mistaken beliefs become imprinted. Habit patterns develop around them and shape the course of our existence. This unconscious shaping of our experience ends when we finally cultivate mindfulness and intention powerful enough to facilitate a leap into freedom from those habitual, emotion-laden thoughts. It's like the velocity needed by an electron to make a quantum leap.

During the first quarter of our spiritual journey, we collect unexamined beliefs as well as the wounds that every "self" experiences. The egoic sense of self is inevitably wounded, as its own ignorance and mistaken importance grate against reality.

The egoic sense of self is permeated by inadequacy. The ego *is* inadequate—it's based on a mistaken belief in its separation from others and from the sacred. Living this far from the truth is like trying to balance on a beach ball. There's no ease.

We attribute our lack of ease to a personal flaw, experiencing the sense of inadequacy in our own personal way. "I'm not good enough, smart enough, attractive enough, competent enough" are among the variations of this theme. We each attempt to hide our sense of inadequacy, blind to the fact that every egoic self-sense feels the same way. We spend much of our lives as the homespun philosopher Anne Lamott describes: "comparing our insides to other people's outsides."

Rodney Smith has said that our very sense of incompletion is the heart's yearning to be heard. It calls for the expression of its wholeness. Growing disenchantment with the small, cramped, and limited world of survival mode only, self only, allows that clarion call to register. Following our heart, we set out on a spiritual quest, hoping to find a tradition, a teacher, a path that resonates with us and appears to understand and respond to our longing.

Questions we ask ourselves about this quarter of our journey have to do with remembering and exploring our early sense of vastness or wonder. They explore circumstances we encountered and the conclusions we came to about the world and ourselves as a consequence of those encounters.

Engaging in your own spiritual biography, you are encouraged to look at the paradigm you created in your mind—a paradigm that circumscribed and may continue to circumscribe your conceptions of self, other, and the sacred. You may well become aware of the ever-presence of grace throughout this quarter, calling to you in multiple and unexpected ways, perhaps not heard at the time but recognized now upon deeper reflection.

FOLLOWING ARE the sharings of respected teachers and other sincere practitioners—both from interviews and other offerings—as they explored the first quarter of their own spiritual biographies, marking outer, inner, and secret experiences.

Gleaned from my conversations with them, these are their explorations of their spiritual biographies. Their stories have the aliveness of thoughtful recollection. Since the single-word notations they might make on their own time lines would have meaning only to them, their sharings are presented as spoken, in narrative form, for our understanding as readers.

These stories of awakening are best read with a quiet, contemplative mind. We can savor and appreciate the working of grace in the awakening of each beloved individual expression of Being.

Let these stories stir your own memories. They are offered as illustrations, not as models against which to compare or judge your individual awakening story. Spiritual biography has nothing to do with the comparisons and judgments that arise only from self, from the perspective of survival mode.

Your spiritual biography traces your own wondrously unique path. We can each add our voice to a grateful chorus.

Rodney Smith

I CAN REMEMBER many times in my childhood when I would be awe-struck, really, by something majestic or beautiful. Perhaps it was just a view from a mountaintop, or it was something as subtle as dew on the grass. I remember holding that gaze and sensing that something was very close, as if I could wake up to what it was that was in front of me.

I remember feeling a little strange in doing so, because mostly my other friends or family weren't as interested in sustaining "the pause" as I was. There was a sense in me—I have no idea where it was coming from—that there was something else that this was communicating besides the visual object I was watching. I can remember getting a feeling that was almost overpowering, as to how it was affecting my body. It was very pleasurable. But I had no idea of the context of what was occurring or had no idea of how or what to do to sustain it.

There was a disposition to feel as if life wasn't as separate as my eyes portrayed it. Even at a very young age, I somehow sensed the power of being still with something. I felt the sense of connection with the object not through thought, but just through the quiet of a pause.

Our hearts respond with complete acknowledgment because the sense of unity touches the part of us that is alive beyond the deception of the self. This was not easy to share with friends or family.

Most people didn't understand what I was talking about or what I was pointing toward, I think. So very quickly you learn at that age that there's something wrong with you or it's not worth speaking about. I did not want to be different.

I didn't understand what was happening at the time, but I felt somehow limited in my consciousness. I felt bound to the way I thought, to what I perceived, to my beliefs, to my opinions—everything. It just felt repetitious and it felt very limiting. This was very disturbing and it lasted a number of years.

Again, there was no adult to whom I could turn and say, "Do you feel limited in your consciousness?" And, of course, my friends didn't really connect with what I was saying either. I was left with this profound sense of alienation within myself, and I had no idea what that was about, except that I knew that I could never get out of myself.

That's what it felt like. I felt like I was trapped within myself, a sense of limitation within confinement. I can remember thinking, "My God, this is the way it's going to be my whole life!" And I felt almost imprisoned. I had no way of dealing with it—it was like a stone in my shoe. I think that's one of the driving forces that led me into a spiritual tradition.

MY SENSE of what life was all about was totally inarticulate. I had no revelations at that age—I know some spiritual teachers do—that showed me my life, that sort of took me out of life, some kind of transforming state. I only had those moments in which I would become engrossed in the awe in front of me. They always felt pleasurable—not because I could make sense of moving beyond my boundaries, but more because I *was* moving beyond my boundaries—but, at the time, I had no sense of what that meant. There were moments when awe—really, *beauty* is how I describe it—would catch me. It wouldn't necessarily be beautiful to the average observer. It was just beautiful to my heart.

In those moments, I would drop down below the level of thought and I would just be present. There would just be presence with it. And that energy would free me from the sense of confinement. I understand the experience at a new level as I recount it. It's being put together now. That freedom of feeling unbound is probably why I appreciated those experiences so much—though "movement from limitation to unboundedness" wasn't in my vocabulary at the time.

You just fall into these moments and you don't know what to make of them. You think that everyone is having them but you find out that isn't so and you think you're crazy.

Related to this, I had a very poor sense of myself. I didn't like myself very much. There was an agitation in me. I just kept myself on an edge that was very high-strung.

There was a lot of sort of acting out and a lot of disturbed energy that I just didn't know what to do with except to run with it. The agitation was in everything. I remember needing my friends' approval in ways that were very unbalanced. I felt hungry for people's attention or recognition. I did that in the classroom, too—hungry for attention. In some ways, I was a very wild child.

WITH ALL THESE CHALLENGES, I did develop some strengths. One of them was risk-taking. It started out as antics and being the one that wanted to prove myself in front of my friends and all that. There was a sense in me of risking, being willing to do what others weren't doing or were afraid to do.

There was also a drive in me to understand what was beyond the edge, what was beyond the immediate knowledge that we had.

I can remember an incident of compassion arising in me, having a friend who was hard of hearing and feeling really sympathetic. The sympathy wasn't only for him. One day, the teacher was yelling at him because he wasn't hearing her. She didn't know about his condition. So I asked to speak with her outside of the classroom and told her. It's that kind of sympathy and caring for someone else that was always a part of me.

Along with that, there was a kind of dogged determination that I was going to do something and prove others wrong when they said I couldn't do something or said I was limited in some way. I just was never able to tolerate that sense of definition very well. Often I wasn't able to prove that I could do it—but I was always willing to try to expand people's definitions.

I also had a sense of independence where somebody would tell me something and I would say, "Let me see. I have to see for myself." It's a very thin line between that and a kind of stubbornness. I was also stubborn.

BOTH MY PARENTS were often unavailable and inconsistent. With my mother, you would do one thing and she would behave toward it in one way and then you would do exactly the same thing the next day and she would react in a completely opposite direction. There was this sense of never being completely settled in the house.

My father just sat there and I had no relationship with him at all. In fact, when he died many years later, I had no feeling about him, which was really interesting. I never grieved him; he was a person I didn't even know.

When I look back on it, my home looks a little insane, but actually it was stable enough for me to get through with some sense of values.

Yet it felt like there was a missing piece. I grieved the fact of not having any kind of mentor or somebody who was of my gender who I could look up to and sort of model myself after. I didn't find that in sports figures or in teachers. Sometimes I found it in one of my friends' parents, but I wasn't around them enough for them to really affect my growth.

I REMEMBER a huge change in high school. It was maybe in my sophomore year or so. I just started feeling from my heart in ways that I'd never felt before. All the civil rights marches and all the bus rides and all of that. That had a tremendous effect on my empathy. It felt really urgent. It really opened me in a way that I can't completely explain. The heart became a central organ in that period of time.

There were so many dynamics going on: the Vietnam War, the Civil Rights movement, people dying. The '60s could create a lot of confusion or they could create a kind of resolve. In me, they raised a kind of resolve of the heart and eventually that would lead me into a spiritual orientation.

I felt I shared my growing resolve and empathy with the music of the times. I just felt so compatible with the music of the times and the times themselves. I felt the songs and demonstrations were speaking to me almost daily. I was very much tied into that whole Zeitgeist of the '60s.

There was a spiritual uplift at that point as well. There was something that was underneath the surface of all the music and all the demonstrations and all of the heart openings and all of the depths. There was an uplift there.

For me it came out in writing. I would just start writing about the nature of God. I remember trying to prove the opposite of what the minister was saying in church or what the particular political wave was saying. I was always kind of taking the other side.

I wasn't a contrarian. It was more that I wanted to get the whole story and I just didn't feel like the whole story was being told. So I would try. And writing and poetry became the medium through which the spirit of the heart could venture forth. I didn't take on a spiritual tradition.

I was raised in the Episcopal church but I never had any connection with it whatsoever. I was a forced acolyte, and all of that stuff was just meaningless to me. But looking back, it was the spirit, it was the sacred. It was interfacing with the sacred.

Those questions, those long dialogues I would have with myself, those papers I would write, that poetry, all of that was the breaking through of the sacred in my life. Although I wasn't going to call it sacred at the time, because for me religion at that point meant the church my family brought me to, and that held no meaning to me.

It was just that the heart was filling. It was coming alive and it was showing me a world that was very different from the world of childhood, the world in which I was just acting out or just acting for attention. It was a world that had a deep and rich meaning, a deep and rich intuitive sense of connectedness. I couldn't verbalize that at the time, but I think that's what was rising in me.

I knew I needed to meditate. It was in the '60s when they had Transcendental Meditation. I wasn't going to pay. It was like a hundred dollars for a mantra and I wasn't about to pay a hundred dollars for a mantra, so I made my own mantra up.

I felt that meditation held something outside of the normal. I was feeling that sense of confinement within my own consciousness and somehow I sensed that meditation would allow some escape from that imprisonment—though again, I didn't verbalize it that way at the time. But I think that's what drove it.

I was just fascinated by meditation. I tried to read Zen Buddhism back then, some D. T. Suzuki, but couldn't understand a thing. It didn't make any sense to me whatsoever. It just sounded like gibberish. But this one thing—meditation—made sense, to just quiet the mind and be able to sort of break away from normalcy. I think that a lot of the early momentum in me was because the spiritual was very deeply within me.

I remember an actual conversation I had with a friend of mine sometime in high school. We were wondering if an alien spaceship came down and offered to give us a ride to another planet but we could never return to this one, would we do it? I said, "Yeah, I would do it." And my friend said he wouldn't. And I thought everybody would want to do that, just break out, break out into a new world. So it was that sense of me, of breaking out, that really was the motivation.

And it was also the heart; my heart was breaking out too.

I DIDN'T HAVE a rigid map of awakening—those can create their own obstacles. Our minds conjure up images of what the path must be like and we attempt to mold our journey around the idea. I think of the path to enlightenment as one of concrete steps. It's like when somebody says, "Okay, here's your potential. You're a human being. Here's what a human being can do." And you think, "Oh, wow, I can go in any direction I want to." So, for me, when I heard statements about my potential, whether it be intellectual or spiritual potential, I always took them as possibilities, as things that I could do. I never put a roadblock on myself in terms of what I was hearing. I wasn't going to stop prematurely and not try.

For whatever reason, self-doubt, although it has plagued me in other ways, never plagued me in relationship to the potentials, especially the spiritual potentials, I would hear about. When I heard about enlightenment, it sounded like something possible, something attainable, something available. And there wasn't an immediate backlash that said, "Oh, you can't do that." I wasn't provided with a sure way of getting there and I knew I had to discover it on my own, but it provided me a potential of what I could be.

The first book that I picked up that I could actually totally understand, and it resonated with me extremely deeply, was Ram Dass's *Be Here Now*.

It's like it had me—I'd start reading and then just cry. I'd just fold up on the couch and I couldn't even pick myself up. It had that effect on me.

So far, there had been some years of yoga, some years of Transcendental Meditation, but not very much of that—and when I was in the army for a while I had some army guy teaching me breath meditation. There were a lot of little inroads I had along the way, a number of people sort of reaching out to me and accessing what I needed to hear. But it didn't ignite into a blaze. But, boy, *Be Here Now* ignited it into a blaze.

I knew, reading it, that reading it wasn't going to be enough, and so I went right to the "cookbook section," the practices he had in the back pages. There were like a hundred practices—and I did every one of them. I was very, very hungry. Something happened from the high-school era to the time of college that baked.

There was something that was baking there. And it was ready to come out.

Cynthia Bourgeault

—— ⚭ ——

THE EARLIEST THING that comes to mind as a clear moment was when I was about three and a half years old. It must have been October because there were pumpkins in the field in Pennsylvania, where I was growing up. I was standing around in the pumpkin patch and there was a sudden rush of "I am here! This is me!" It was breathtaking.

There was also an encounter I had that I remember really clearly, probably at the age of about four and a half or five. We'd moved into a new house in the city and my mother was out shopping or something and my father was playing with my younger brother in the next room. And I suddenly had this horrible sense that just overwhelmed me that I was going to die. I realized that this "I" that I had just discovered was going to be finite, that there would be a day when it wouldn't be.

I went running into the next room in horror and said to my father, "Daddy, Daddy, I'm going to die!" I can still remember this stricken look on his face, just sheer terror. And then you could watch his eyes glaze over and he did the "No, no, you're Daddy's little girl and I'm going to take care of you."

I remember catching the look—and I said something equivalent to a five-year-old's version of "Aw, shit, this is even worse than I thought." I knew not only that I was going to die but people were going to lie to me about it all their lives!

I could see by the look of sheer terror in his eyes that I wasn't alone in the realization of death. But I was trapped in these cordons of denial, masking as love. Everything in his voice changed and I could see that it hit him. His own mother had died when he was eighteen and then death was everywhere, hounding him.

He drew back from it and tried to find some slick, reassuring thing to say that he didn't believe in a bit. But I could see that that was how business was going to be conducted on this planet.

I felt really embattled because it was not just an isolated incident. I could see very, very clearly that adults trapped themselves in this kind of collusion and that real questions were not going to be honored or dealt with. They were going to be shoved down, stuffed under.

The adults had gotten so expert in this kind of self-numbing that there was no way to talk about it. That was my experience right through grade school, right up until I got into high school and found some teachers who knew how to talk about this thing and burst the bubble that had been inside me for, at that point, twelve years or more.

I felt that my spiritual experience far outweighed anything that people would let me talk about, that they would acknowledge, or would direct, or shape—so I just had to keep it to my own self.

YET I WASN'T ALONE—I had a fine time with God. I always knew that there was spiritual presence and I knew that I was connected to the planet in a very deep and compassionate and intentional way, in a way that would eventually bear fruit—I never *didn't* know that—but I realized that I wasn't going to have access to trustworthy adult mentors that would shape me and draw me along in those early years. Yet I was just too rebellious to let that knowledge get lost beneath the surface of conforming to a conventional world.

Nature was vivid to me—natural things, like the ocean. We grew up near the Jersey shore and I very, very quickly fell in love with the ocean, swimming in it and riding the waves. These things—like jumping off the sand dunes and riding my bike and the sort of exultation of the natural world—allowed me to realize that human artifices were a *hassle* but they didn't negate the beauty and the ultimate coherence of everything.

MY SELF-IMAGE was very conflicted. I grew up in the '50s and I was decorated by my mother in the conventional fashions that girls wore then. I never felt at home in them. I felt awkward. I could look at myself in the mirror and say that other people could wear these clothes and be seemingly at ease—but I always felt slightly stupid in them and artificial and like I was going to trip or spill something on myself.

It seems to me that every time they put me into a dress or party shoes, I just felt scrunched up and alienated from myself. I had no option to be female in an alternative, also beautiful, way. In a party dress, I often felt like a little pink eraser—but when I was able to put on shorts and a baseball cap or swimming cap or pants (which were a no-no in my day and culture), I felt much more like myself. I felt like I could dress so that my body could express what was inside me.

When I was in fifth grade, sixth grade, I developed a set of very, very best friends whom I loved dearly. We were together as family. I finally got a set of friends that I could really share intimacy with, which is not something I knew at all in the first ten or eleven years of my life.

I didn't feel any sadness about this because I didn't have any basis for comparison. I knew from the inside that life in my family was edgy and fraught with denials and volatile explosions and a lot of tension. I knew that. But it didn't make me feel sad. It was just the way life was.

It wasn't until I really was able to discover and add some alternatives that I could look back and say, "Boy, that was bizarre." I grew up in a pretty dysfunctional household.

A lot of these habits that arose in me were physiological ones because the dysfunctional household was constructed around my mother's insistence on Christian Science as our path. So there was a whole bunch of shame with being ill. In Christian Science, right spirituality is supposed to reflect in bodily health. When there's a bodily upset, as my mother used to interpret it, it meant that something was wrong with your spirituality. Sickness was an unacceptable claim. There were many, many times of being sick and hiding the remains and going off to school anyway so that nobody knew. There were very shaming and separatist habits around illness, like a cat slinking off to die.

We had shame around all kinds of bodily functions. I didn't dare tell my mother when I got my period, for example. I just figured out how to handle it myself. There was so much embarrassment around talking about anything in the body that we just kept it to ourselves.

Even to this day, I'm really affected with it. I watch some of my friends who get a cancer diagnosis and immediately put it all over the Web and call on the help of all their friends—and there's no way I could do that. I would slink off by myself and talk it over with God and figure out how to come to terms with it, with the least amount of disruption to other people.

Not disrupting other people was very strongly reinforced in our family. Every time you disrupted other people it was like you were pulling hot coals down on your own head.

I HAVE HAD moments of deep intimacy with others, beginning with best friends. But it's only a very one-on-one situation with the one who sees your soul and mirrors your soul and respects your soul and calls your soul into being. It's always been one-on-one with me. I haven't to this day trusted group-think to be able to come up with that kind of deep-seeing intimacy that will hold me in any way that's safe.

There's a wonderful line in a book called *Mount Analogue*, by Rene Daumal, where he notes that "life experienced me as a kind of alien body that it either had to expel or encyst." That sounds like me. I've found in my life that when I get with groups there's almost an instant sense that the group picks up that I'm going to be destabilizing to the group. And there are all these kinds of subtle language mechanisms that go out to contain me, prevent me. My very freedom that was born in self-sufficiency is instinctively picked up on at an intuitive level by groups. They see me as not a team player, but as a destabilizing influence.

It's not so much about being too intense as it is about being too unimpressed by the norms that control either the behavior code or the limits of their inquiry.

The threat is that I'm not willing to be contained within their paradigm. There's an instantaneous realization of that, even while I'm thinking, "I'm fine," and when I've embraced so many group movements in my search for the path toward transformation. There's a repeated pattern that the groups—and it doesn't matter whether they're Gurdjieff groups or Contemplative Outreach groups, Christian Science groups or the Girl Scouts—perceive me as one who is inherently going to tread a little bit too cavalierly with the sacred cows that hold their group together.

And, they're probably right. Right from the time with my father when I was five years old, I have had very little trust in sacred cows. I think they get in the way of the clear light of truth.

THE COURAGE TO BE this way came from the force of freedom. It's a freedom that's not an attitude or a head trip. It really resides intimately in my body, from the time I was a kid swimming or riding my bike.

I know what motion is like and what sensation is like when you move through the world without restrictions. And I know what it's like when the restrictions and constrictions clamp down, including those you apply to yourself through trying to work a program that's not authentic to you.

Staying in the body is a tendency that has deepened and intensified along my path. There were other, early gifts of the Spirit that seem to have been strong and powerful. They always called to me or, I would say even more accurately, they called from me. I think most kids have a strong degree of awareness, just not acknowledged or drawn forth by the people around them.

WHILE I WAS RAISED Christian Scientist and that's where we went on Sunday morning to church, I was sent during the young years of my life to a Friends school, where they had silent meeting for worship as part of the weekly program for kids. It was in those meetings for worship that I was exposed to that other deep current that I knew in my being, the one that was so often unacknowledged by the adults around me. In those meetings, I could see that there were people who honored it and respected it and drew it forth. That form of worship gave me great instruction, silent instruction, in the walk of the Spirit.

I had a different experience when they first sat me down in Christian Science Sunday school when I was three: I instantly knew with all my being that there was something that was wrong in the premise here and that it was simply not true. It was not correctly the way things were with God.

I could look at the faces of the people who were teaching, who had this kind of fixed smile on their faces that was obviously denying all darkness and having to make everything come out the way they had formed it. Again, it was my body's natural sense of freedom that knew that there was constriction there.

I drew deeply on the actual space of encounter that was being taught to me in Quakerism. And there was never really much teaching except that there is the light of God in every person and that, in sitting in silence and stillness, that light will be known to you.

But before that, I tried for a while to work with Christian Science—and I was going in and out of sincere, hard practices. Yet I knew that the way of trying to heal yourself of a stomachache by saying statements of metaphysical principles wasn't the way to go. There was one point—and it was at a very crucial time in my life when I was about eleven—when the father of the family that was living next door was dying of kidney failure. He was only in his late thirties or early forties—very young—and his four kids were my playmates. I tried to do all the Christian Science drill on him, knowing that he was God's perfect expression of love and that this problem with his kidneys was a fallacy.

Then one day, sort of down the home stretch, when he was really in the hospital on his last round, I went to the park across the street from our house and had it out with God. I said, "What's going on? Am I doing something wrong? Are you doing something wrong? How can this be? What's happening here?"

And I felt myself surrounded by this kind of golden light that calmed everything. And this voice, that wasn't an external voice so much as an internal resonating within, just said to me, "Hush. Dan will die and it will be all right." And I went, "Oh!"

It was a shock. Because in Christian Science, death was *not* "all right." It was the ultimate failure of practice. And you had to do everything you could do to fix it and prevent it.

This was the private secret life that went on while, on the surface, I was getting Girl Scout merit badges and trying to sneak onto the Little League team. I felt no disconnect. It all flowed together for me as a single whole.

Where the disconnect came in was in the realization that the secret life that went on inside was really not a topic that could ever be shared anywhere. This meant that the disconnect was not within myself but between myself and that channel of intimacy that I yearned for with the other denizens of the planet.

I WAS GIVEN some good rules and some not-so-good rules for living. Some were kept and some were discarded.

One of the most powerful teachings I ever received was from my father when I was about nine. My dad sat me in the front seat, beside him, as we drove home once from the Jersey shore. He showed me a road map and he showed me how to read it, how to orient—where north and south were and how the red roads were the big roads and the blue roads were the little roads. And he said, "If you have a map with you, you'll never get lost."

It was a profound transmission he gave me that day. I realized he was giving me a skill that was going to carry me through life. And, by God, it did—for over sixty years now.

I saw that he was empowering me and I saw that he saw my yearning for freedom and he was giving me something so that I could actually implement my intelligence. It was such a deep bonding and such a powerful gift of love that it became a powerful life lesson for me.

I got that love of freedom from him, I think. It's almost like he showed me in so many little gestures along the way that, although his own life felt trapped beyond what he could ever get out of, he was giving me a kind of trousseau—the things that he knew would allow me to use freedom in a way that was just really, truly exhilarating and freeing.

It gave me the capacity to look at people very, very different from me and to approach them with strength and respect for their strength. That was powerful in Quakerism. They were a great social witness, a place for compassion and radical justice. And they didn't do it in that kind of demeaning way of so much of Protestant charity that always puts you in the "have" position, the so-superior position that can look at others with "compassion."

These were great gifts. And, of course, the wonderful gift of my own childhood—that my grandchildren only have in small doses—is that we were free. We were kids of the '50s and we were shoved out of the door in the morning and were expected home for dinner.

We had to rely on our own creativity and had the freedom to enjoy play and exploration. It was a fortunate time to grow up.

MY LEGACY from my mother was much more complex. I would say that my relationship with my mother was much more convoluted and conflicted than with my father. From her we got an incredible orientation toward beauty. She loved art, she loved the mysterious. She yearned for that kind of mysterious, grace-filled feeling. She had this great attraction to mystery and the sacred and the beautiful. She was an artist. She had an impeccable sense of color and taste and she was just physically oppressed by the slick and the cheesy and the tawdry. She had a powerful influence on us.

She was desperately there for each one of her kids. She loved us; she supported us fiercely. She saw my own educational potential and my hunger and made sure that I was sent to good schools and had spiritual and intellectual stimulation. She was my champion in her own way out of her own deepest heart and, although we didn't have an easy mesh of personalities, her love for culture, for beauty, and for spiritual becoming was the way she gave nurturance.

Although she felt that she wasn't free to climb out from the walls of her box, she occasionally threw a bright flaming ball of hope over the top of that box and we caught it—all three of her kids.

IN HIGH SCHOOL, I met three teachers who began to give me hope that I could be understood and that there were ways of dealing with what was boiling inside me, my own metaphysical awakening, and my own sense of how the world really was.

One teacher was able to validate for me that what I was feeling and working with so hard was early witnessing presence. He was able to connect me to both the stream of Eastern tradition and also that of Western tradition, which helped give me a context and would affirm that I wasn't just going crazy.

He exposed me to the best in what was going on in our Judeo-Christian traditions and in religious thinking in general. We were required to take religion for a year, studying the Bible, which he taught as literature just beautifully. Then we took a course in contemporary spiritual thought, including the best of Paul Tillich, Reinhold Niebuhr, and Ian Barbour—all the people who were the mostly Protestant geniuses of the post-WWII Christian scene. I was reading Tillich when I was fifteen.

The reading gave me more confidence in what I was doing. I had just thought I was a freak, that I had these funny little thoughts running through my head that nobody else was thinking. I felt like I had to cover it up because it wasn't understood by my friends or fellow students, at least in the beginning. But in this class in high school, that shifted.

I WAS REALLY INTERESTED in something I call "focus in/focus out." I would sit on the bus riding down to school and I would ask myself, "Well, I can do either of two things with this sitting. I can talk to the person next to me on the seat and have a real encounter and get to know people, or I can move back and sort of take in the whole scene and reflect on it and be in my own space." And I thought, "Which is better?"

I couldn't decide, so I kept going with the "focus in/focus out" questions. My teacher framed it to me that what I meant by "focus out" was the threshold to witnessing consciousness. He showed me how to shape it—as best you can teach a seventeen-year-old girl who doesn't have any contemplative meditation under her belt. But at least I was acknowledged and encouraged that questions like that were important questions and that they were part of our becoming fully human.

My other teachers mirrored this back to me too. They reflected that culture is built not just of dull people in books but people who strode out on the threshold and really wrestled with their own conscience and their real understandings and created the world out of their inner life.

Each one of them was living a certain integrity. One teacher was Jewish. She escaped with her husband from Nazi Germany and shared with me from her experience of human tragedy and human resilience. Another teacher showed me the language of beauty in music, showed me music as the original language of the heart. I actually launched my religious conversation because we sang, of course, bits of the great requiem Masses, the Brahms Requiem, Bach cantatas.

I began to learn an alternative to the Christian Science over-intellectualization of religion or the Quaker just dropping all into silence. I began to learn the transformation of the heart in beauty as a real religious pathway. And that drew me into more liturgical forms of Christianity. My eventual path with the Episcopal and Catholic and Benedictine traditions all grew out of that initial exposure to the sacred music of the Christian tradition.

Llewellyn Vaughan-Lee

WE HAVE TO HONOR what it means to be a human being even if we have tasted what it means to be dissolved in love. The journey of the drop back to the ocean is a human story, as we appear to flow here and there, sometimes nearer, sometimes farther, from the ocean to which we are returning.

It is difficult to understand today what it was like growing up in an English middle-class family in the 1950s. It was a very impersonal environment. I was fifth of six children and we had little personal relationship with our parents. I grew up with the saying, "children should be seen and not heard," and, for example, we were not allowed to speak at meals with the adults and there was little emotional input. There was no love, little physical contact, and feelings were never discussed. In this sense, I would describe my childhood as lacking, but I accepted it as quite normal.

When I was very young, I had a series of powerful experiences that were like nightmares. I had the physical experience of being enormously vast and tiny at the same time. I did not even think to share these experiences with anyone—there was no one to talk to anyway—and only many years later did I describe them to a teacher who explained them very simply as an experience of the Self, described in the Upanishads as "smaller than small and vaster than vast."

The experience of being enormously vast and tiny at the same time was my only spiritual experience until I was sixteen—although when I was in my forties and did some regression work, I did remember the first two years of my life waiting for someone to recognize my spiritual nature, to recognize me as a soul, as for example happens in the

Tibetan tradition. But by the time I was two years old, I gave up and just inwardly removed myself.

Despite attending church regularly, which was required in my background, there was no sense of the sacred or even any awareness of any reality beyond the physical world of the senses. I was just a boy attending school, learning Latin and Greek, and playing sports every day, whatever the weather. I did not have thoughts about spirituality and, being English, I certainly had no emotions. I do not think any beneficial qualities emerged in me except possibly a solitary nature, but that had always been with me.

As for crises and difficulties, those only began when I was fifteen and my parents divorced and I had to look after my mother, whom I later discovered was an alcoholic and was manic-depressive—though, of course, that was not spoken about at the time.

One weekend home from school, my mother tried to kill herself and my father could no longer cope. In the course of that weekend, I went from being a child to being a parent. But, again, I do not think I carried any spiritual gifts away from that experience, except maybe an inner sadness. It did mean that I didn't really have an adolescence, as it is understood today. Maybe as a result I developed a certain resilience, certainly a quality of resiliency.

Then, one day when I was sixteen, I was sitting in the tube train in London reading a book about Zen Buddhism that was becoming popular at the time in certain hippie circles. I read this:

> The wild geese
> do not intend to cast their reflection;
> the water
> has no mind to receive the image.

The saying was like a key that opened a door I did not even know existed. There, in the morning tube train, I felt a joy I had never before experienced, a moment of intense exhilaration.

This joy stayed with me for weeks. There was a sense of laughter, a feeling of seeing the joke within creation. A world that had seemed gray sparkled with a hidden light. I laughed at everything I saw. My boarding school was beside a river and there was a beautifully tended garden on the riverbank where one could sit, away from the sports fields and any noise. Those summer afternoons, when school was over, I would come to this garden and watch the river, full of wonder, full of delight.

There was no desire in me to understand the reason for this sudden change. Something in me had awakened and there was just joy and laughter. When this Zen saying opened the inner door, I did not question or even think about it. There was no frame of reference, so my conceptual mind did not even try to understand. It was not as if a question had been answered. I just found myself in an inner world that, looking back, was much more familiar to me than anything about my English upbringing. I felt alive in a way I had never known before.

I borrowed the book on Zen and discovered a simple meditation technique. I practiced this meditation and immediately had inner experiences. The most powerful experience was of being enormously large, spreading into infinite space and at the same time being very small, incredibly dense, with a feeling of great power and compactness.

Outside of space and time the experience was very tangible and intensely real. There was also an exhilaration, the exhilaration of going beyond the limitations of the outer world, for the first time consciously knowing an inner dimension so different from the world around me.

As a child, I was terrified of these experiences of feeling both tiny and vast and told no one. Now, I welcomed it—it was a taste of an inner reality that was very potent and deeply satisfying.

In the evenings, I would sit and meditate and find myself inwardly expanding beyond my physical self. I had no inner or outer context for these experiences. But neither did I question them—they seemed both natural and miraculous. I just knew that I had found something very precious.

There was no one to share these experiences with, but no interest to share them either. Later, when I did share with some school friends, I was ridiculed. I was happy to leave school and traveled in the Far East for a year.

When I returned, a series of events drew me deeper on the spiritual path. It was not so much that I was seeking as I was drawn. In Sufism, there are two ways of journeying. One is called *suluk,* disciplined traveling on the path, and the other is called *jadhba,* divine attraction. Looking back, it was more a process of attraction, although I was very disciplined in my meditation.

I knew I wanted more and wouldn't stop until I found it. I visited with a friend where I unexpectedly found a library of mysticism, Chinese philosophy, and yoga books. Here I discovered *The Secret of the Golden Flower* and *The Tibetan Book of the Dead* and other classics that pointed to a reality beyond the physical.

I would sit on the grass, transported into the mysteries of Taoism, my whole being held in the wonder of this other world. Although my study of Zen had been very solitary, I discovered a spiritual friend and we would discuss esoteric subjects for hours. For the first time in my life, I enjoyed spiritual companionship.

I was introduced to hatha yoga and practiced it with the intensity of a young man, only to experience it awakening my kundalini energy. That, and the fasting that I was practicing at the time, and various psychological problems, began to stretch me tauter and tighter. I was putting pressure on my physical body with an intense inner drive that finally resulted in a neurosis about food and continual stomach problems that were both psychological and physical.

But this drive to *find something,* to reach *somewhere,* could not be diluted, could not be put aside. Somewhere I knew that whatever it cost, whatever it took, I had to seek.

This spiritual drive was an inner compulsion that drove me, without outer logic or reason. I was not seeking answers to questions—I did not have any questions. I just wanted something desperately. I inwardly knew I needed a container, but had no way to find it. I had not yet made physical contact with my spiritual tradition.

Sherry Ruth Anderson

I HAVE MANY FRIENDS who have had those really significant transcendent experiences from the time they were very young—maybe two or three years old—and onward. When I tried to recall experiences of vastness or wonder I had as a child, my first thought was, "No, I don't have any of those." That was not my experience. My first significant experiences really happened when I was about twenty-eight or thirty.

When I was a child, we lived in Atlantic City, New Jersey. The summers were spent on the beach. When I started to have more distinct experiences of waking up later in my life, some of the first things that happened were experiences that reminded me of experiences I had as a child playing down at the ocean with my brother.

My mother would be sitting way far up in the high sand and my brother and I would be right at the water's edge. The light of the sun on the ocean was so beautiful, somehow I think I was able to dissolve into that. I spent just a timeless time with the water and the sunlight, being undisturbed by anything. Later on in my life, when significant waking experiences began, often the first kind of impression was like those early moments at the edge of the water—there would start to be a relaxation of the familiar sense of self.

It was just so real and so *how-things-are* there at the ocean. One other thing I would do as a child involved standing on my toes to look out of the window in my brother's back room, the only window in the house where I could see the ocean. I would go back there when things got hard in my house and I would look out the window at the ocean and think, "There is something else besides what's happening here." If I could only see the ocean, then I'd be connected to it. It was something like that—you don't put those things into words as a child. I would guess I was eight, nine, ten—somewhere around there.

I think my question was "What's real?" Somehow you know there's something that is real. Annie Dillard has a great line in which she talks about what poetry did for her as a child. She said she'd be in school and she'd have a poem or a book of poetry that she could look at and the poems whispered to her behind enemy lines: "There is life. There is another life." It was that kind of feeling.

Around the time I was in latency—eleven or twelve or so, before high school or junior high—I would go down to the recreation room in the basement. There was a doorway down there that went into a part of the house that wasn't finished. You could go through this doorway into a little crawlspace under the house and there was sand—the smooth, cool sand—because we lived just a block from the beach. I would go down into that crawlspace and I can remember the feeling of the sand and I'd just be so lost. I'd put my face on the sand, my head on the sand, and just keep trying to feel: "How do I reach what's real in myself? There must be a way to do this. But I can't find a way." There didn't seem to be any way. Nobody I could talk to seemed to know deep things. How would I have said it then?

I kept wondering. I knew my parents listened to Frank Sinatra. I tried to listen to Frank Sinatra to see if that could take me there. But it couldn't.

THIS LOSTNESS was really vast inside me and it didn't go away. I never heard anybody talk about anything that seemed like it was connected to me. By around my second year in high school, I shut all this down, shut down the *the* feeling of looking and longing. I got very involved with school and friends and dating and parties. I just seemed to forget myself. I was an ordinary kid living the normal life at Atlantic City High School.

But the feeling didn't disappear entirely, it didn't get lost. One time, maybe I was about fourteen or fifteen, I remember reading Gerard Manley Hopkins's poem called "Carrion Comfort." I read the phrases:

"O the mind, mind has mountains; cliffs of fall / frightful, sheer, no-man-fathomed." And I thought, "He knows."

It was the first thing that I ever found—here from a priest who lived a hundred years ago—where I felt someone knew what I was feeling and had words for it. It felt like a miracle.

I remember my first solo Zen retreat years later. I took one book by a ninth-century Zen master and, as I was reading some of his words, I went again, "He knows. How does he know?" I felt like the one who wrote that and me—there's no distance between us. And it was completely thrilling to realize the connection in being that could happen. It was the words at that point, as well as Hopkins's words, that let me feel that connection across centuries. That began my love affair with poetry and maybe with words.

I HAVE A MEMORY of a place I liked to try to get my dates to take me. I went to a women's college outside of Baltimore. There was a beautiful reservoir where the college was and I would love to go there because of the way the light on the water made me feel. That's a thread of connection with what I felt at the ocean as a young girl.

One of the men I dated gave me the gift of Teilhard de Chardin's *The Divine Milieu*. That, also, was awfully important to me. For me, no matter where I was and how people may be not interested and certainly not talking about deeper things, there are books. There have been books for me or words that set a resonance, that said, there is something else than the life you are living now.

I RECALL A TIME after I had gotten my PhD in psychology. I was living with my first husband and his two children, my stepchildren. We lived in Toronto; I was head of my department at a big psychiatric teaching institute, and I had a corner office. I even had my picture taken there, thinking how proud my dad would be of me. I felt I kind of had it all, at least as far as my mind could imagine what that meant, at that point in my life. And then I started wondering, "Is this all there is?"

My husband and I ran into difficulty and we separated. I was living alone and a friend invited me to come hear a talk with her. I wasn't particularly interested in the talk but she got me to come. (She was a true spiritual friend and still is. She and I have been there for each other through our whole lives. She will lead me to a teacher or I'll lead her to a teacher and it goes back and forth.)

So, even though I didn't want to go to the talk, I went. We sat in this medical auditorium, filled with all the people from the medical research institute I was involved with. We were way in the back row. The speaker was Stan Grof and he was talking about his LSD research, which held no interest for me, and besides, I could barely hear him.

But something happened. When he was speaking, my heart opened and I was just astonished: "What's this? What's happening?" He was passing around some flyers and he said that he and his wife, Joan Halifax, were offering a month-long retreat for healers and doctors at Esalen. He said it was about consciousness and that you could just sign up if you were interested.

I took the flyer. At that time, a movie about Esalen had just come out, called *Bob and Carol and Ted and Alice*. Where I worked, all that stuff was a joke. So I was very embarrassed that I wanted to go to Esalen and didn't tell a soul.

But I signed up for it. A month of retreat at Esalen—that seemed to me to be the total end of the world when I was there in Toronto. The location of the retreat felt far away, some place who-knows-where in California. Applying, we had to send in all these credentials of who we were and what we've done and a photograph of ourselves.

I got a call a bit before the retreat was scheduled to start. I was told that all of us who were coming to the retreat with so many credentials were not going to be able to learn anything. They were recommending that we sign up for an extra week with a Zen master before the actual retreat began. It was a seven-day Zen retreat, in silence, with the suggestion that, then, we might be able to learn something.

At that age and at that stage in my life, this was so beyond anything I'd ever done before. I didn't know how to judge whether to go or not—so I just went.

I signed up for the fifth week with the Zen master and flew into San Francisco. A van picked us up and drove along Highway 1 to Big Sur. I was a little bit late, so when I came into the room, everybody was already in silence. I had never sat Zen or anything. And what's more—this is a characteristic that has happened throughout my life—I had a great aversion to everything I'd heard about Zen. It sounded horrible.

As my first introduction to a Zen retreat began, I was sitting along with everyone else, facing the wall. None of us had ever sat Zen before. There were about thirty or forty of us sitting there knowing nothing about meditation. Our knees hurt. We would be standing up, sitting down, standing up, sitting down. I didn't know what to do except that we couldn't talk. I was having these wild sexual fantasies about the guy sitting next to me. It seemed like a pretty good way to pass the time. So that was the beginning of my spiritual practice.

I was actually very scared. I didn't see any way to escape. I didn't know anybody there, I didn't have a car, wasn't sure where exactly we were, and we couldn't talk. What's more, the Zen master did interviews in a room over our head and I could hear him smacking the floor with this big stick he had. And so my fantasies started to go to "If that bastard touches me with his stick, I'm going to punch him." I was really scared. I didn't know what he was doing with the stick and I had heard scary stories.

Finally, it was my turn to go up to see the Zen master. You're supposed to bow and then he bows to you and you sit down and he sits across from you and he says, "Good morning." When he said that, to my great shock, I began to cry. Wild crying. Finally he said that my time was up and I had to leave. Believe me, I had had a reputation for being someone who never cried!

On the second day, it was my turn to go up for the interview again. He was ready for me—he had a roll of toilet paper to use as tissues. Behold, the crying started again and it went on for the whole ten minutes or so of our time together. Around the third or fourth day, I could finally get some words out— and my words were something to do with wondering what my path was. And then I did cry again—crying and crying.

I couldn't even really talk until near the very end of the retreat. I said, "What do I do? How do I keep going with this?" By that time, my mind had begun to quiet a little bit and I began to experience simple awareness. It was such a revelation. I was completely shocked—I had had no idea this was possible.

I remember seeing a moth. And I saw it with the nameless consciousness before the labels. This was a miracle. And so I said to the teacher, "How do I continue?"

He said that every day I should do one hundred and eight prostrations. We had been doing prostrations as part of the retreat. And I said, "I hate those prostrations. Why should I do that?" I remember so clearly that he looked right at me and said, "Doing the prostrations means believing in yourself a hundred percent." I remember thinking, I have no idea what he's talking about, but I wanted that experience of simple awareness to continue.

That was my first experience of really feeling the turning of the soul. I wanted it.

Prakash Mackay

———— ❧ ————

I THINK ONE of the first times I became aware of vastness and wonder was reading Hans Christian Anderson's fairy tales.

My grandmother had taken me to the library and I was reading this book and the illustrations completely transported me, like I had entered a magical dimension, suddenly moving out of a two-dimensional world into a world that was filled with color and wonder and boundlessness. A whole new universe opened up—one in contrast to the church world I had known previously

My grandmother was very Catholic and my father was a Protestant, so she took me to the chapel just to make sure that my soul was saved—but I didn't feel a connection to the Christian logos. My father was told by an elder that I should be in the church and suddenly I found myself going there on a Sunday. And it was very dull and barren. It never really spoke to my soul.

To me, it was grim—dull and dark, no lights, no colors.

I was thirteen when I read *With Mystics and Magicians in Tibet*, by Alexandra David Neel. Reading it, at that tender age, I first became aware of my spiritual longing.

The experience of reading it was of magic and mystery—it was really exciting. I just loved the stories of it. I wanted to find out everything I could about the tradition and about meditation.

Those worlds felt like home to me, and I felt homesick. I searched for anything I could find about Tibet. I read *Born in Tibet*, by Chögyam Trungpa, and then *The Way of the White Clouds* and *The Foundations of Tibetan Mysticism*, by Anagarika Govinda. Reading Aldous Huxley woke up my mind, and he became an intellectual and spiritual mentor to me through his writings. At this time, I also discovered the writings of J. G. Bennett, who introduced me to the ideas of G. I. Gurdjieff and Ouspensky.

The only thing that I could do was read—but then, when I was seventeen, I heard about Samye Ling, the Tibetan meditation center in Scotland. I got myself there and stayed for about three weeks during the summer, meditating with the lamas.

It was something I was longing for and it wasn't anywhere else in the world where I was living.

FOR ME, the deepest experience in the monastery was the silence—I had never been around people who didn't talk before. It took me a while to settle into the silence, because I was wanting to interact with people and they weren't doing that. I was initially uncomfortable and then I was able to relax into it.

While there, the head lama asked me if I wanted to be initiated into Ngondro [the preliminary, foundational practices for more advanced teachings of the Tibetan tradition]. Kalu Rinpoche was going to be coming later that year to give initiation and I would have had to do Ngondro to receive his initiation. And I said no. There was a part of me that knew that that wasn't my path, even though I liked the association and the monastery feel. I knew that I wasn't going to follow a traditional Tibetan path. In a way, that clarity was quite strange.

ALDOUS HUXLEY was very instrumental in waking up some discernment in my mind. It was almost as though before I connected with that, I had felt totally asleep. And suddenly this woke up a longing to find people who were awakening, and for me to be awake and to deepen that experience.

I had had my first LSD experience during the same year and it opened my mind and heart to the experience of love and oneness and that triggered my search for transcendental experiences that weren't drug-induced.

There was a lot that was a cause of suffering for me. From thirteen to sixteen, I was sexually abused by my brother's friend. My brother was at a kind of training college and his friend would stay at our home for weekends. He would wait until people were asleep and then he would sexually molest me. I lived with that secret until I was in my thirties.

It has taken me many, many years to feel worthy and to have healthy relationships. I have done a lot of work on the impact of the abuse.

The habit that came from that was that I wanted to escape from the feelings and so I started using alcohol and drugs, whatever I could get ahold of. I was really quite wild, in a way. But yet, I was good academically. I was able to kind of balance it and not go completely off the rails.

I think I thought of awakening the way Ram Dass described it as "the big ice cream cone in the sky," and longing for enlightenment as the longing to salve the suffering. For years, that was it. I imagined, "This will take away all my pain."

After the retreat at Samye Ling, I returned to university. I thought that I would have an environment of stimulation and like-minded people and I was very disappointed.

While studying psychology there, I created a group for spiritual and psychological discovery. We met twice a week to meditate, explore different paths and spiritual teachings, and work through the exercises in the book *Gestalt Therapy: Excitement and Growth in the Human Personality*, by Fritz Perls, Ralph Hefferline, and Paul Goodman. Also, during that time I was initiated into Transcendental Meditation, and that was my practice for quite a while.

I CHALLENGED EVERYTHING. I learned this practice from my grandmother—who was very fierce in her attitude of having to be yourself— and also from the way that I saw Huxley challenge ideas.

There was this rebellious part but there was also this good young man who would do enough to get by—though in my second year of graduate school, I almost quit. The group that I started, where we were looking at different paths, had an astrologer who was also a physicist, and I told him I was thinking about quitting school. And he said to me, "If you do that, you'll never finish anything in your life. Even though you don't like it, just finish it." So I did, I just buckled down and finished the degree.

Even so, I had run from my family, and I was very much a hippie, and I did a lot of acid and hashish. When I was about nineteen, I met a guy who actually taught me to use LSD as an ally. Rather than just taking it and letting it take me wherever it would, he taught me to program it, to use it to enter meditative states, to deepen the experience. Around that time was also when I came across *The Center of the Cyclone*, John Lilly's book about Oscar Ichazo's work, and I was very excited about that. I was introduced to a whole group of other experimenters, explorers, by a friend from the original group I had started.

The woundedness was still there in me—and there was also another deep wounding that occurred in my relationship with that friend. It sent me into a period where I kind of lost my faith. That was when I felt that I just had to go back into the world. So I started teaching school kids, feeling too young to be a practicing psychologist.

After a couple of years, one day I was just standing looking out a window and I heard a "calling." I heard a voice in my head say, "Okay, you've been in school since you were five. It's time to get out. It's time to be in the world." I felt the rightness of it. And so I did. I quit and bought an airplane ticket.

I just started being a wanderer and looking for my soul again.

Ellen Kympton

─────────────── ⸎ ───────────────

I DIDN'T HAVE "great spiritual moments" as a child. I would have to say—and I don't know how to describe this other than in a way I've seen said—I sort of felt "cast out of Eden."

As a child, I was so busy taking care of myself that I'm not sure I was able to really experience anything beyond just that. I have to honestly say that for a long time, spirituality was closed to me. As I got older, I eventually reached out for something. I felt a need to connect with something much deeper and bigger than who I was. But as a child, I didn't have a sense of something deeper and bigger.

Although I didn't have to take care of myself in terms of the basic wants of life—I was very well provided for and I wasn't in a harsh environment—I just knew that I was on my own from early on. I realized that my parents were doing the best they could, but nonetheless I didn't feel protected or nurtured—so, maybe in a way, I cast myself out of Eden.

There was a real sadness at feeling so separate, feeling like somehow I didn't belong. And yet I had a sense of determination, a sense of strength, because I knew I could take care of myself. I knew that in some ways my mother needed me to do that, because she just couldn't do it all. I'm the oldest of four—so there I was: competent, able to take care of myself.

When you're cast out of Eden, that's what you have to do. It's sink or swim. My situation was certainly not severe. There are people who have horrible situations—mine was not.

I remember one of my own children telling me of the wonder she felt when she was little, just looking down into the grass—her wonder at nature. It took me a long time to connect with nature. I don't think I did that as a child. I just felt separate and apart.

It took me a long, long time to unravel the feelings of my child-hood and to understand them. I think some people are able to explore their spirituality in a deeper way earlier than I was. I don't feel like a "victim," I really don't. But I feel like my struggle to get out of the cast-out-of-Eden feeling I had since I was seven or so took me a while. It took me later in my life to go deeper into my spirituality, to figure out how I might connect.

The desire to connect grew in middle school and high school. I remember there was a sense of being very attracted to "religion" because there was a certain sense of loving connectedness to it. I began to do things like pray—knowing I was praying, asking for help or guidance.

I guess because I felt alone, I didn't look to my parents for that sort of depth of meaning and connection. I looked outside of the family. I didn't look within it.

We were a "churchgoing family," even though it was a very social churchgoing. But I became very active in church. We went together when I was young but as I got older, I did things on my own like youth group and that sort of thing. It wasn't so much that the wish for con-nection, for something bigger and deeper, came from anything my parents said or did, but just from being exposed to a church commu-nity. I was raised in an Episcopal church that was not always so vocal about what it believed, but that sense of something more was there.

It was good to connect with other kids at the church but it was more about the thoughts, the ideas, and values there. I remember having one good friend when I was in high school who was sort of like that, too. We talked about God and we talked about praying.

At that time, my thoughts of God and prayer were very institu-tional. I felt that God was always available but, at first, God and spir-ituality and all that were definitely something external. It took me a long time to think of God as both external *and* internal.

I had a yearning for depth and meaning and connection with

people who also were yearning. I liked being in a community where those things were valued, and since I went to a church school, I was often surrounded with religious language I found beautiful, something that I cared about and liked.

I liked going to church, and went to a college that was also church-related. During my junior year abroad, I went to church every Sunday all by myself.

All this nurtured a sense of the holy and the transcendent—something deeply meaningful. But at that point in my life I thought of it always as beyond me, not within me. I felt that it was more something that was outside of me, something I needed to search for and look for, in church and in books.

On my own, I would read devotional books—what we would now call meditation books—where you would read a meditation for the day and spend some time quietly with it. I don't remember reading anything earth-shattering. I did this on my own, though at college, I also chose to take religion classes because I liked that sort of thing. In those classes, I was introduced to critical thinking in Christianity, as well as theology and historical biblical criticism.

My meditations weren't the kind of meditative practice that I think of today. I'd read something and then say prayers for people. I didn't sit in silence in any way looking for anything deeper within me. I was asking outward—which is fine, which is a part of growing and learning in a sense. That felt good to me at that stage of my life.

I have a different perspective now. Everything back then was the product of very dualistic thinking: this is right and that is wrong. That was pretty clearly imprinted: this behavior is right and that behavior is wrong; this belief is better than that belief. And amid this dualistic thinking, I always tried to choose the one I thought was better. I began relying on my own intuitive sense for a lot of it.

I feel like most of my real growth, spiritually, came so much later in my life.

Of course, I was preparing for it all along.

Reflections on the First Quarter

—— ⟨∞⟩ ——

RODNEY URGES ALL of us "to look at the topography of the journey from beginning to end, the multiple ways we undermine the very growth we seek, the shift that does occur, and the life that arises out of that shift." This is the benefit of engaging in spiritual biography, in deep reflection upon the many transformative shifts in our lives.

We can see patterns in the first part of all of these awakening stories. You will see them again when you engage in your own exercise of spiritual biography.

What emerges is a sense of the perfection in our lives, hardly noticed before when viewed from self's perspective. But through the lens of awakening, we begin to see that our journey could not have been other than it was, cannot be other than it is, and that grace has been working upon us and within us all along the way. We begin to see the turning points, the "watering holes," as Cynthia calls them, that have fueled and refreshed our path.

The stories reveal the tellers' accounting of the outer, inner, and secret events in their journeys. They make use of the eyes of the senses, intellect, and spirit.

We see intimations of beyond self, rarely verified by the world around us. We see the experience of Being that so many of us knew as a child.

For Rodney, Being was expressed in a sense of presence in "the pause"—a sense of more than just physical manifestation. Cynthia lived with a sense of the ever-present sacred and a love of freedom.

Llewellyn was catapulted into subtle dimensions by the evocative words of a Zen koan. Sherry yearned to know what is real. Prakash was introduced to "beyond" by his grandmother—and was drawn to it. Ellen knew somehow that there *was* an Eden. Feeling cast from it, she longed for reconnection.

They share a sense that the transpersonal was hushed not only by their reluctance to speak of any reality beyond the conventional but also by our culture's spiritual immaturity—its lack of understanding, ease, or even language with which to speak of depth.

Some had a sense of being different from others and a sense of the necessity of covering up what they knew or yearned for. I think anyone who has been touched by depth and becomes intent upon opening to it already leaves conventional company, in some ways. The deeper we go or even wish to go, the smaller and smaller the percentage of others who are similarly engaged. Traversing the first quarter can be tricky. Although we long for depth, there is a pressure to fit in, to find a place of security. It's an imperative of the survival operating system.

In our earlier years, we create a sense of self that is, hopefully, healthy enough to navigate the world and, in some senses, healthy enough to integrate the powerful transformations of spiritual practice. Yet the ego, created as a byproduct of the survival operating system, is a wound magnet. In uniquely different ways, we each begin our spiritual journeys with the suffering of egoic wounds. Perhaps the cry for help is our homing device, calling us back to what we know and most deeply yearn for. We begin to follow our own resonance and move—with our wounds—where grace calls us.

Rodney notes the unique way each of us uses the wounds of self to name the continuum of our own longing. It might be simply "from suffering to the end of suffering," as Buddha framed the transformative views and practices he offered. Or we might name it "from separation to union," "from ignorance to wisdom," "from the smallness of self to the vastness of Being." Our pilgrimages have many names, many paths, many ways in which grace might beckon. All are healing journeys.

Survival mode can hold our attention within its confines indefinitely, regardless of our longing and intuitive knowing. Only when we begin to reach toward the transformative energy of an authentic practice does the first quarter of our pilgrimage come to a close.

During the first quarter, we accumulate habit patterns and self-concepts, the dynamics of the survival operating system. Most of us usually jump into our spiritual journey assuming these habits and beliefs are intrinsic aspects of who we are.

In the second quarter, we crash into those very habits and beliefs. They are revealed as obstructions that block the light from shining in and through us and out to others. With a growing inner insistence to move toward Spirit, wounds suffered in the survival mode are highlighted, as is the need to wisely and compassionately attend to them. They keep us trapped in self, in the strategies of survival, causing further suffering and blocking further illumination. These are our imprints of ignorance.

It is a blessing that early transpersonal experiences leave deep imprints as well. They remain as karmic formations beneath the veneer of acculturation and the residue of wounds. The grace of those early experiences—even Ellen's painful experience of feeling cast from Eden—marked each of these practitioners and set the beginning of their lifelong inclination, a tropism, toward the great expansiveness of Being, toward grace.

The knowing that there's "more," the yearning for increasing illumination, is in all of us. It flickers, seemingly dimmer at times, but it always has and always will lead us. Cynthia commented that "even the times of letting it be fallow are times of turning to it, as any good gardener will know." We move inexorably, even if slowly, with grace's yearning in our heart.

Once imprinted, we move like sunflowers toward the sun. It is this tropism that we trace in our own story of awakening.

THE SECOND QUARTER:
From Seeking to the End of Seeking

As swimmers dare
to lie face to the sky
and water bears them,
as hawks rest upon the air
and air sustains them,
so would I learn to attain
freefall, and float
into Creator Spirit's deep embrace,
knowing no effort earns
that all-surrounding grace.

—DENISE LEVERTOV

Introduction

As WE LOOK through the lens of awakening, we recognize the pivotal significance of the second quarter of our spiritual journey. It begins when the longing for the end of meaninglessness, unease, and alienation becomes so strong that we actively reach out for an authentic path to lead us beyond only self, beyond suffering. The longing is a growing inner urgency.

We might begin our search with books, teachings, or various lineage groups—looking for ones that seem to hold promise, ones that resonate with a truth that our longing can discern. Exploring our own spiritual biography, we begin to see that central casting has sent many teachers along our way, some in the guise of friends, some in the guise of difficult people, some in the guise of warnings or challenges, sorrow or depression.

As we begin the Great Search in earnest, we can call ourselves seeker, marking our entry into the second quarter. As seekers, we try on different views for size and fit. Since we still believe deeply in "self," we continue to act from self's patterns and ploys. We often find ourselves conforming to the norms of the group in whose circle we've landed. Others of us despair in not being able to find a group where landing even feels possible. In either case, wherever we go, at this point in our journey we carry the burden of self and its habits.

As a beginning practitioner, we strive and strategize. The ego wishes for enlightenment. The second quarter of the journey eventually reflects this fact—and its absurdity—back to us with humbling clarity, like a startling view in a mirror.

Much of the second quarter leads us—again and again—into our own ignorance, resistance, attachment, doubt, and self-judgment. For many, the stress of that ignorance—that cramped and uncomfortable experience of living only within the survival operating system—is what propelled us toward the spiritual path to begin with. The need for healing is pronounced.

Healing work can be painful. To move through the second quarter, however, we cannot turn away from it. Healing is essential to spiritual growth and is a necessary task through much of our spiritual journey. This is the muck, as Buddhist teacher Thich Nhat Hanh reminds us, in which the lotus is born. We heal through intention, inquiry, compassion, wisdom, and grace.

For most people, the second quarter goes on for a long period of time. We uncover the believed thoughts that leave us feeling flawed and insufficient—unworthy. Every mental ego has, at bottom, a sense of second-class citizenship. The insufficiency we feel is not caused by a personal deficiency, although we operate for a long time under that assumption. The sense of insufficiency arises almost like the phantom limb syndrome: we know something is missing. We feel wounded and cut off from wholeness when trapped in survival mode. The second quarter is marked by a gradual expansion of attention out beyond mere survival. In that wiser view, we can release the woundedness and judgment that arise within self's paradigm.

Surrender requires the ultimate letting go of anything the self thinks it can "achieve" spiritually. We need to let go of whatever concepts of perfection we impute on enlightenment, "mystical union," nondual awareness. The ego loves labels—especially *I*, *me*, and *mine*. It is wise to surrender them all, allowing the divine flow of grace to dissolve all labels, to carry us along with nothing but clear intention as rudder.

As we practice, our intention to free ourselves from mistaken views grows. Liberation follows intention that is in alignment with grace.

Our perspective begins to shift. We recognize the futility of thinking that the conceptual mind can ever touch the sacred, or that the self's strategies will ever lead to awakening. We witness wisdom's growing discernment.

The second quarter of our spiritual journey ends when we see through the illusion of the seeker and the fantasy of the search. We let go of both. Seeking becomes seeing, the simple willingness to remain mindful and open.

Surrender is a tumble into undefendedness, a thorough and complete "allowing." It begins with gradual, intermittent letting go and becomes a stable willingness to surrender all that is illusory, all that is not of essence. Surrender is key—it's pivotal. It leads us directly into powerful transformative fields of Being.

Surrender appears frightening at first—even terrifying—to our sense of self. Self has no footing in *beyond self*. *Beyond self* is formless awareness, Being. It contains none of the props and conditions that sustain ego. It only supports our essential nature, a beautifully unique expression of interdependence. In Being, attachment and attraction to self begin to dissolve, as naturally as early morning fog dissolves in the midmorning sun.

In surrender, trust increasingly becomes an embodied realization. We begin to trust the grace that is calling us and working through us, giving rise to our sincerity. Even if our path is one of "guru yoga," devotion to a guru as a divine being, we can still cease looking to an authority to guide us at every turn and start to trust the unfolding of our own direct experience.

We begin to own our heart's path. Confidence grows as we come to recognize, with deep appreciation, that we are, in the words of the Gospel of John, "grafted to the Vine."

Knowing our own value, in humility, we become increasingly present to, and accountable within, the path of our own awakening. Self-reference and forced effort transform into a purity of intention that wishes only to abide in grace. Our love and compassion increase and we begin to spontaneously wish that all beings be free from suffering, that all beings consciously live in grace. We begin to genuinely care about each other.

The questions of spiritual biography during this quarter ask us to explore the teachings with which we've resonated. We look at our struggles, challenges, and discouragements. We look at our obstructions and the movements of grace lifting and shifting us. And we explore the authentic realizations that took root in our heart and transformed our experience of being on every level.

Rodney

READING *Be Here Now*, a transmission occurred. It was literally night and day. I changed my lifestyle. Overnight I became a vegetarian. I turned my back on socializing. It was really a moment in which the transcendent formless realm shined through my everyday existence.

Something became apparent to me that had never been apparent before—and I couldn't turn away from it. It was very consuming. I just became hungrier, reading everything I could get my hands on, attending every lecture I could find—though there weren't that many back then. I found various teachers who would make different promises, none of which fed the hunger.

I found one teacher who was promising that if I shut my eyes and wished for something that I wanted in my life, over and over again, it would appear. That was the meditation he taught. And after the first session, I realized that this just isn't the way I wanted to go—having more of what I had become despairing of was not going to move me forward.

I had to go through many different teachers and books to find resonance.

I got hold of some very early tapes by Joseph Goldstein from Naropa University, around 1974. He was teaching mindfulness meditation and there was something in the word "mindfulness" and how he described it that activated a recall system in me. I saw that much of the fear I had of myself could be countered with a simple willingness to see it for what it was. And that, I felt, gave me a firm footing to move forward.

Psychologically, I was very damaged. When I look back at those times, there was a lot of despair in me. It wasn't just the despair of being in my twenties and not having a set goal or direction, but it was a despair of what life could offer me. How people were describing the meaning and purpose of their life just didn't feel like it was going to ever be completely satisfying to me. There was a deep yearning to see what else life had to offer, but I had no idea what that was. That yearning set me up for the experience, the "transmission," of *Be Here Now*.

IT WAS SUCH a radical shift that my friends and family didn't know what to make of it. They just knew I was changing. And I would do things that were so extreme. I remember one time I spent the entire weekend in a closet because I wanted to really face myself, but had no real practice through which to do that. Staying in the closet was extreme, but there was also something there that was being activated, a voice that needed to be heard. But I didn't have the practice in order to direct that voice in a sane way, and so I floundered.

There is a point in the path where many of us attempt to *will* our way through. I was aware that that was what I was trying to do but it was the only way I knew to get there, through my own diligence and my own determination and, by God, I had those things. I came to recognize that ego's efforts and ego's strategizing have limited return. I came to see them as "counterinfluences" on our journey of awakening. They circle us back toward self and suffering rather than toward beyond self and the end of suffering.

I felt like my deepest desires and my conventional life as I was living it at the time were a rough fit. Something wasn't right—something wasn't right about me. That's sort of the way it goes when what isn't right for you seems to be right for everyone else. So I tried to cover up the depths of what I was feeling—but you can't cover it up.

Once I was exposed to a direction in which what I thought wasn't right about me *was* right, then it all kind of straightened out. When that happened, when conventional life really became secondary, the deepest despair in me had a way forward. And I really changed. It was literally lights-out on the conventional world.

That extreme, of course, can't be carried forever. And so as I settled more comfortably into the routine of spiritual life, the conventional life came back in with it—which it has to do. I had to move to a location in which I had *sangha*, a spiritual community, around me. I had to have other people who were also hungry and applying themselves in a particular practice.

There were deep psychological issues in me. I had a very disturbing self-assumption that there was something wrong with me. But I felt, at the same time, that there was a limitation on what Western psychology, as it was practiced back then, could do to move me forward.

Through encountering *mindfulness*, I realized that bearing witness to your own mind was itself a healing—and then the world opened up for me. I wasn't as afraid of being the mistake I thought I was when I could see that mistake and correct it through the bare attention of my observation. Before that, my definition of enlightenment had been defined by my aversion to the person I thought I was. I wanted to live free of myself.

ALTHOUGH THERE was a huge shift at first, the rest has occurred in stages. The first stage I perceived was that sort of spiritual exuberance that settles down, of course, when you feel the potential within you. But then you've got to come back to the conventional way that you've assumed yourself to be prior to that exuberance, a feeling of being tied in knots.

You still realize the exuberance, know it's there, that something is calling you—but you realize that you're in the way of the direction it's calling you toward. At least, I felt that. And so for me the next stage of my journey was the stage of self-dislike, because I was in the way of something I knew to be true. I just didn't know how to sidestep myself or get over myself to pursue this richness I had just experienced.

I realized that deeply embedded within our psyche, almost by the nature of the way we live our lives in the West, is this unworthiness that is really a product of the way we live, the evaluations, the comparisons, the market economy of *us*.

But we have to deal with our limitations—and many people, because of the nature of their self-dislike, have set themselves up to spiritually bypass that area. We often select practices that do just that—that move us beyond our pain and put us in a kind of intermediate step where we can feel the loveliness of ourselves but not have to deal with the painful issues that still exist.

Those painful issues don't go away—and when we drop our guard, they arise again in abundance through the assumptions we hold. I'm seeing now that you can go sometimes decades and not deal with these self-assumptions, but they will come up. At some point, when there is a relaxation of tension, the repressed issues arise. They arise with such conviction that they pull us back into day one, to where that self-assumption first arose. Whatever age we were or whatever the circumstances were, that's where it pulls us back to. That was true for me. I couldn't get rid of it.

AROUND THIS TIME, Krishnamurti, who was another very influential person early on in my practice, would talk so clearly about dealing with what was in front of you without bypassing anything and never offsetting anything with a "skillful means." He was not given to skillful means. He was given to just seeing *what was there*. This teaching drew out my honesty. I knew that I had a lot of inward work to do and that I was being blocked by how I felt about myself—and I wasn't about to pretend that it wasn't there. That just seemed like fantasy.

I knew I had to face this lifelong pain or I'd only be able to abide in the sacred for a few moments. Because what takes us out of the formless, what takes us away from the transcendent, is our belief systems. As soon as a condition arises in which that belief system about myself is activated, then I'm full of reactivity. I'm yelling at my wife, I'm throwing things—or whatever I'm given to do. That's what comes from those circumstances as long as that assumption is believed and not perceived as it is, as empty.

The hardest part of the spiritual journey is going into the pain of our own self-assumptions—because it is in those pains that we really believe that's who we are. It's not like this is just fanciful memory, nothing as simple as "Oh, my mother told me that I'm that way but I know I'm not." These self-assumptions are what we *really believe* our identity is. If there was a gun to my head and a person said, "What do you believe you are?" It's *that place* that we would have to admit.

This is where absolute independence needs to occur, because when we're facing the kind of pain I'm speaking about here, we're looking for ways to get out of the pain. We very rarely, no matter how sincere we are, want to go into it. We want to bypass this thing.

IN MY MINDFULNESS TRAINING, I experienced a period with a lot of judgments. I would go to the teacher and say, "I'm just full of judgment." He said, "Well, just be aware that you're judging." Still, I was judging all day long and nothing was affecting the judgment and I thought to myself, "Something else is going on here. I have to do this alone. I don't think my teacher has the wisdom now to take me where I need to go within myself."

I started asking myself, "What's behind the judgment? What is motivating the judgment?" And I saw that what was motivating the judgment, when I didn't look out to confirm the judgment, was that my own sense of self-inadequacy was judging to put others' heads down so my head could be raised. When I saw that, then I knew that judgment would never cease as long as that feeling of inadequacy stayed so poignantly clear and true to me. So I said to myself, "Okay, so now I need to go into this inadequacy, because I realize that life is going to be bound by my judgment unless I do."

At that point I had no one telling me how to do this, but I had a sense, a strong conviction, that what was inside of me had been conditioned in me from a lot of different sources: family of origin, teachers, and so on. But it was *conditioned*. It was conditioned in me. So I had to let that conditioning out. I had to extinguish that conditioning.

I would look for opportunities for that pain to be accessed. When I was judging, instead of focusing on the person I was judging, I would focus on the inadequacy behind judgment itself and then I would walk with it. I would let it tell me what it was saying inside of me, verbalizing it. I really looked like I was insane.

I would walk back and forth and say, "I'm no good. I can't do this. I always fail. I'm a terrible person," and on and on. I would not add anything to it, but just listen to what was coming out of me, hearing what the conditioning contained: memories and images, but it also contained self-invoked thoughts, reprimands, and all of that. I just wanted to get a sense of what was in there. I didn't want to reconfirm what was in there—I just wanted to let it out and air it.

I would just walk, back and forth, and let my mind move in whatever way, just accessing whatever was there, not adding anything to it. That was the most important thing. And I kept doing it until it was empty, until it was quiet, until it was flushed out.

Sometimes, later on, a new wave of judgment would crest. But when I found myself working with it in that way, it didn't last long. I did a few months of this kind of ranting and raving before it got quiet in there. And, having lived with this sense of unworthiness my whole life, I was amazed at how quickly it could dissipate.

To this day, if there's any kind of motion toward that self-negation, that self-reprimand, I'll just be quiet. That kind of thinking is like dust left in the corner. You've cleaned the room but there's still a little bit of dust in this corner or underneath the shade. I'm just interested in getting all of it clean—I actually look forward to doing more cleaning in that room.

I don't know where this sense of determination, this resolve, comes from. Those are kind of mysterious qualities but they've been extraordinarily important in my own development. You realize that you're alone in this process. I think, at first, we all try to hook up with the teacher of choice, the book that resonates with us, and we try to hover around there. But, somehow, I knew this was going to be up to me. I don't know where that knowledge came from, but it was so helpful.

It was helpful in dealing with situations in which, when the teacher's lecture would end or the energy would cease or the book would stop and I knew that there was more for me to do, there was a next step I knew I needed to take. I was just left on my own and I said, "Okay, so here I go. This is like diving off the deep end here."

I also knew that this is the way it had to be. I don't know how that came to me either, but I knew that it was a trip—a trip of each of our aloneness. And many times, people have asked me to join groups or to become part of this or that established sangha and I would back away from it—because I knew I would lose my own voice or I'd lose my own intention or I'd lose my own critical need to ask questions. So I have always stayed kind of remote for those reasons.

I think it's important to note that all structures have a lifespan. The path is moving beyond form, beyond seeing the world as self and other, me as formed object and the world as formed object. So much of our training is to see that form isn't going to satisfy, that it's impermanent, that it's not going to bring us happiness. We're moving somewhere else in this journey—we're moving outside of our relationship to, and investment in, form. I didn't have that direction when starting out. I didn't know the direction the journey was taking and didn't really understand how and where the spiritual movement was actually leading me. At one point, I had the feeling of "If only I can accumulate enough moments of stillness . . ."

Now, I want to shake myself and say, look how obvious it is. But I didn't have that then and somehow what was being communicated to me was that there was this moment in which, if I just kept being as mindful as I could be, everything would disappear and that would somehow allow other things to arise—including the absolute certainty of what Truth was. That's the kind of model I was working on.

But now I know that the harder you try in order to have that moment, the more you're interfering with that moment actually appearing. I had no idea that I was working against the stream of what I was trying to do. I think it would have been helpful to have known that!

This is a *realized* tradition. You can read and reading does provide a certain enjoyment and a certain satisfaction, but then you have to practice. You have to integrate what you've been reading in order to have it in your bones. It would have been helpful to have known that too.

THERE ARE three stages for me. There's reading and then there's practice and then there's full engagement and acting upon the insight you had. And I think, in our tradition particularly, that third stage of actually moving your insights into dynamic action hasn't been reinforced enough.

It's crucial for all of us going in to know that we are plagued in this culture with self-doubt. We try to balance our self-doubt with the assurance and confidence we have in our teachers or in our methods, but we don't really address the self-doubt. The self-doubt remains as another assumption about ourselves and keeps us dependent upon those methods and teachers. And that, ultimately, won't take us into freedom. You know, freedom is *freedom from conditions*—and if we are dependent upon any conditions, including the conditions of our practice, then the freedom is going to be incomplete.

I would suggest to people who are beginning to really look at their own sense of self-disappointment, what they don't feel they have in themselves, their self-diminishment, that they ask "What is it that you're lacking? What is it that, if you were to tell the most personal story about yourself, what would you say about yourself?" Then, start being conscious of those issues and bringing those issues up so that there can be this true independence of spirit that is so necessary in moving this thing to its completion.

It is very much about healing. Healing is needed to fulfill the spiritual journey. We all like to have mystical aspirations but really the most important moments are the ones that are right in front of us. The pain that I'm feeling in this moment, the contraction of my heart, the bitterness I'm feeling—all of that. That's really where we need to go. The more mystical implications of the journey will move us in accordance with how thoroughly we manage those issues that are directly in front of us. I think that's an important thing for practitioners to know.

THERE WAS A CRISIS in my time in Burma, where I realized I wasn't able to apply any more effort than I was already applying—and yet the teacher—whom I saw daily—would tell me to try harder. I knew I couldn't. I knew I just didn't have any more in me to give. There was so much physical and mental exertion being applied to trying to be continuously mindful that it somehow broke me open. I left Burma feeling broken, feeling very unaccomplished.

It was terrible—feeling that I had failed, that I wasn't going to be able to really access the fruit of the journey. And, so, somewhat dejectedly, I went to India as a monk. I went to Bombay, where I'd heard about Nisargadatta Maharaj, author of *I Am That*.

He was a beautiful being. And he shifted me completely. In essence, he said that I'd been wasting my time because all I was doing was chasing my own ideas about attainment and that, if I really wanted to know the truth, I'd have to stop that.

We usually have to be pushed to the point of utter hopelessness, complete disempowerment, and near-suicidal despair before we are willing to surrender our image. That is how much we value our thought-based life over reality.

After a while with him, probably two or three weeks, I went on to Thailand with the feeling that I had no compass anymore, that I needed to understand everything for myself, that I couldn't take anyone else's road map, anyone else's technique—no matter what.

I realized that everything that had ever come into me, that's all I had—other people's road maps. There was no knowledge of my own, no wisdom. It had been a completely self-centered practice in the sense that I was determining what I was going to do and I had my own ideas about where that would lead. It was all a self-determined concept of the path before me. And I realized that I had come to the end of what I could do for myself.

This evoked a crisis in me, a spiritual crisis in which I had no direction to take. I was at Ajahn Buddhadasa's monastery and he left me completely alone. He didn't ask for any ritual behavior from me. All he did was give me a little hut, a six-by-eight-foot hut—and I stayed there for three years.

During that time, I took the practice apart, questioning everything. I just laid it out in front of me. The practice that I had been taught was the Burmese, Mahasi-style meditation, which had a very linear approach to attainment, and a high focus on concentration.

There were certain experiences one had along the way, which confirmed a particular level of attainment and, then, at some point there was supposed to be this nonexperience where the sense of the subject and object vanished and one then became a "stream-enterer," in Buddhist terms.

My practice was all *me*. *I* was attaining. *I* was moving forward. It didn't have any mystery to it. It was all programmed out sequentially with the result and it was all due to hard work and effort.

I had no other frame of reference for it until I talked to Nisargadatta—and he had no frame of reference at all for it. His way was, "It's here . . . why don't you see it?" So, although it freed me of a particular way I was thinking about it, it didn't seem to get me any closer to the objective.

It did free me of the concepts of what I'd been carrying around about the practice and the fruit of the practice. I realized I had to discover this thing for myself.

It just wasn't clear yet.

Cynthia

I FOUND AND CONNECTED with the Catholic, Episcopalian, and Benedictine lineages in doses. It was a ten-year period of deeper and deeper immersion, which ended when I was baptized.

I began to study medieval literature as a graduate student, gravitating into medieval liturgy and the liturgical dramas and that brought me into proximity with the church. An Episcopalian priest was a mentor who led me into the church at the same time that I was discovering the great wealth of the Christian sacred traditions.

The real significant moments were Eucharistic. I just, totally fortuitously, began to have experiences with the bread and the wine of the living communion with Jesus. And it was just ineradicable and very, very profound and powerful. This went on and on over a period of five years, my experience of actually having met some reality that for me was not only familiar but normative. It just sealed the path.

It was all a pretty exciting time. I was married to my music teacher, and we were performing gorgeous music with professional choirs—and I was coming out into my own. I think the frustration was as I gradually realized that, even with my graduate degree, I was just going to have to bushwhack to find a place in the world.

I should say that the civil rights movement was, without doubt, the best thing that ever happened in my young life. The propulsion toward the black community as a sense of wholeness and an alternative vision to the 1950s white ghetto that I'd been trapped in up to that point just added heart and passion and compassion to what I was experiencing in my young awakening life. I worked with inner-city kids and saw the light in them.

I thought of the time as one of the happiest periods in my life and saw it as a time of metaphysical awakening. "Metaphysical awakening" was what I was working on in my little head because Christian Science is a very metaphysical religion. It's all about getting the map right and using it. And my father had gotten me interested in maps from a different perspective.

It was all about, "Is there a God?" That was the big first question, followed up by "How do I know?" and "What are the qualities?" and "How do you stake your life on something that's invisible?" Those are the issues I was working with.

If I were to do it now, I would simply know to look within me and see that the things being experienced in the heart were the eternal verities, but I didn't know that then and nobody told me that. I thought anything in the interior life was "subjective" and therefore not accurate. And I was also getting this great rush of existential philosophers—Sartre and Camus at the time—who were telling me "There ain't no map anyway. There ain't no reality."

The way I tried to work at the problem was just the way I'd learned from Christian Science, by simply stating in logical, even syllogistic, fashion what truths I could figure out to be objectively true. My process was to try to convert or translate interior verities into external, objectifiable philosophical truths. That was the only way of working I'd ever seen modeled: making something seem reasonable by wrestling it into the laws of logic and fitting it to the syllogism. I have journals and journals of a young girl trying to fit God into a syllogistic model. I later gave up in despair.

I remember a time when I had been reading the Existentialists, like Sartre, and was hearing them saying life is meaningless, there's no purpose, no reason for living. I stood in front of my third-floor bedroom window and thought to myself, "Well, okay—if life doesn't make any sense, if there's no purpose to this, if this consciousness that I'm feeling—the one that's waking up and wondering who I am—is such a heavy and intolerable burden, why not just jump out this window?"

I was actually on the ledge. I don't know whether I was serious or not—but just as I was sort of dangling with my feet over the edge, I thought, "Well, you know, life is no more *nonsensical* than death, so I might as well go on living." Looking back, I would call that a great day—and I do feel like I received some guidance in those moments.

If someone had just taught me meditation when I was fifteen, I would have known *exactly* how to proceed!

I WOULD SAY, taking the hard-nosed definition of spiritual practice, that it wasn't until I met Centering Prayer in 1987 that there was really something that could begin to put methodology into my journey. I was forty years old and I met Centering Prayer and the Gurdjieff work in the same year. Up to that point, I'd been working with the usual mix most Christians have of theology and devotional and liturgical practices and a lot of what Arthur Lovejoy calls "emotional pathos" as the chief form of logic.

The "usual mix" sustained my longing and my conviction that there was more, but I continued to want and to look for skillful guidance. I was hungry and I was yearning and I was throbbing and I was alive—but I was also unconscious. I was all bound up in *seeking*.

You create an image of yourself as the seeker, with characteristics and yearnings, and then you tell the story and you write the poems and you read the novels and you listen to the music that gets your system aching—and then you say, "Oh, I've got it!" It keeps the forward movement going—it did so for me—but it's only when the forward movement stops that you begin to see where you are.

In my thirties, I kind of muddled along with children, a new husband, an active family and community life, no longer acting as clergy, and piecing things together with part-time jobs. It was a life in which my spiritual yearnings had gone very, very much on the back burner.

And then right at forty, I was out for an early-morning walk on the beach by myself on the most remote of the remote islands of Maine. All of a sudden, something like a clarion call came out of the sunrise and the morning, reminding me visibly of this ache in my heart for spiritual practice. It was a rekindling of those kinds of mystical experiences that I had in my twenties but with quadruple the force, saying, "Get on with it, girl!"

I realized that I had been hiding. I realized that I had just been hanging out and running away and, as they say in Christian terminology, "hiding my light under a bushel."

I had given up trying to find the fulfillment I sought. I had the archetypal image in my head of a person who would be the spiritual teacher and the divine lover at the same time. I kept looking for that person and it kept blowing up in my face as I got these miserable divine lovers with clay feet. Nobody around me was interested in the church or what I brought; none of the currency of degrees or profession cut any kind of swath in the world I was living in. So I just sort of numbed it all out.

Along the way, there were little periodic wake-up calls, a chance meeting here and there, a few people—but those were few and far between, just enough to keep me from leaving the path entirely.

I lost my bearings. Like Dante says, "in the dark wood in the middle of the night," halfway in the journey. In retrospect, I can see that absolutely none of that era was to waste. I couldn't have moved on to the stuff I was finally to discover if I didn't have those years and years of lostness and difficulty under my belt to begin to rise to the next part. None of it was wasted—but it was a wasteland for a long, long time—the old light within gradually and slowly going out.

AFTER THAT, I came back and did a couple of things that were definably different. I reconnected with a monastery in Big Sur, the New Camaldoli Hermitage, with hermits with whom I'd spent some time a few years before. I committed myself to two annual retreats a year—and I rekindled the searching around the Gurdjieff work. I had been given a copy of *In Search of the Miraculous* in 1980, followed very quickly by Jacob Needleman's *Lost Christianity*. I contacted Needleman and made some initial efforts to try to find where the work was—but the classic way of the work was to make it hard for people to get in. So I got thrown back—and allowed myself to get thrown back.

But by 1987, I had gotten in and was assigned to a group. By the end of that year, I had my initial contacts with the work, and during one of the monastery stays I met a woman who introduced me to the practice of Centering Prayer.

It was a watershed year in my life, where I realized that the journey was going to be part of it from here on out. Within a couple of years, I was back in the saddle as a vicar at a local Episcopal church and was beginning to teach Centering Prayer to a growing group of people who were hungry for this sort of stuff. And of course I was practicing it myself.

The ten years I spent with the Gurdjieff work gave me the practice that I'd been missing before. I've always thought that Christianity and the Gurdjieff work fit together. They're a pyramid. The classic kind of theological training and devotional training form the top half and the Gurdjieff work forms the bottom half, the part that allowed you to actually see yourself—witnessing practice, nonidentification, being present with attention, living in a world beyond rhetoric and illusion.

I think in a deep way that there's some sort of direct relationship, some sort of direct line, in my sense of spiritual kinship with G. I. Gurdjieff himself. I like the guy.

Around this time, I began to work with Father Thomas Keating early on in the development of his training in Centering Prayer. I learned the "gesture of surrender"—the simple letting go of any thought or emotion or image that has snagged our attention. With practice, the gesture becomes ingrained and begins to arise for us spontaneously.

To put it in the shortest possible bottom line, Centering Prayer prepares the ground inwardly, steadily, gently, but inexorably for the establishment of a fairly stable nondual practice.

I think that you gradually change, by this repeated method of letting go, letting go, letting go.

We change in the repeated surrender.

Llewellyn

GRADUALLY my meditation deepened, the inner horizons expanded. At the same time, I began looking for a teacher, sensing that I could not go much further on my own. Inwardly, I knew that this initial "awakening" was only the beginning of a spiritual journey for which I would need a guide.

I met a number of teachers, including Krishnamurti, in whose presence I had a powerful experience of a reality of complete freedom. I experienced the space from which he was speaking, a space beyond the mind, beyond any seeking, a place of pure being, the pathless path.

I was trying to reach an invisible goal through too much effort, too much focus on the physical, through purification and intense practice. I was making myself quite unbalanced. I did not know the simple truth that Rumi explains: "Through our own effort we cannot even reach the first way station."

Then one day when I was nineteen years old, I was invited to a spiritual talk on mathematics. I found myself sitting behind an old lady with her white hair tied up in a bun. After the talk, I was introduced to her. She gave me one look from her piercing blue eyes. In that instant, I had the physical experience of becoming just a speck of dust on the ground. Then she turned and walked away and I was left empty and bewildered.

It was many years later that I read the Sufi saying that the disciple has to become "less than the dust at the feet of the teacher." I came with the arrogance and intensity of a young man who had some spiritual experiences. In her presence, something within me bowed down and despite my rebellious nature, I knew that I would do whatever I was told. When I looked in her eyes I knew that she knew, and I wanted what she had more than I had ever wanted anything in my life.

The next Tuesday afternoon, I attended her small meditation group. We meditated, had tea and cookies, and she spoke about her time with her teacher, a Sufi master in northern India, with whom she had been until he died in 1996. I felt completely at home. I had found the path to take me Home, a journey that would lead to deeper and deeper states of awakening, of immersion in a reality of divine love that I had not even imagined existed.

Through Irina Tweedie, I became connected to my *sheik*, my guru, my inner teacher with whom I felt a profound and, often, living inner presence. This connection with a teacher who no longer has a physical presence is known as *uwaysi* and is part of the Naqshbandi Sufi tradition.

In time, with healing and great transformative shifts, I came to realize that in the bond with my teacher there was only oneness and that if I trusted my inner teacher completely, then that teacher must trust me completely.

At that time, I believed in the journey as something to be accomplished, a journey with a destination.

The sense of a journey Home, the image of a journey Home, seemed to give me certain security and belonging, a sense of purpose. I traveled it with all my longings and struggles, only much later to have my images and my "journey" tossed aside. I had entered with the ignorance or innocence of youth, having no idea what it all might mean.

The real mystery is how the divine unveils Itself within us; how the Beloved makes Himself known to Himself in the fragile container of a human being.

I remained with Irina Tweedie, in a state of mind I describe as "innocence." The states of love and longing can last for years. The months and years passed. Awakening can be both a momentary happening and also a gradual process as one is inwardly prepared for an expansion of consciousness, which I now understand to be the nature of spiritual awakening.

My relationship with my inner teacher was one in which I was destroyed and remade. I was made soft by a very hard system.

MY NEXT EXPANSION of consciousness was dramatic. It was both terrifying and intoxicating. It began one summer afternoon in my early twenties. I was housesitting and had felt the need to be totally alone, to have no one intrude upon this space I had been given.

As the days began to unfold, I felt an intense introversion of my energy and focus take place. My attention was drawn more and more inward, deeper and deeper. There was a sense of uncovering a timeless, ancient part of myself and entering a world far away from the conventional world in which I was living.

Energies began to flow around my body, and my consciousness would follow this flow. Then the flow of energy that held my attention started to encounter psychological blocks and hidden pain. What had begun as a simple introversion of energy changed into the most painful and transformative two weeks I had ever known.

I felt a need, an intense drive, to stay with the energy as it uncovered these hidden layers of pain. I knew that my consciousness was vital to the process, that I had to willingly go into the agony that was being touched. But the nature of my attention was also important. I discovered that it was not enough just to be with the pain, just to experience the block.

Within the pain, within the block, I had to focus on the beyond, and throw myself, my whole being, into the emptiness of the mind and beyond myself. As I went deeper and deeper into myself, this required intense effort, a greater inner effort than I had ever experienced. Instinctively we avoid pain, but not only did I need to voluntarily experience the pain, I had to stay with the pain and then use every ounce of energy to take it into the beyond, to offer it up to His essential emptiness.

In each moment there were two alternatives: avoid the process or focus inwardly on the nothingness I instinctively knew was real. A combination of consciousness and an inner commitment drew me into this process and guided me along the maze of agony. There was no desire in me to realize or to reach anything, no feeling that I was doing this because it was spiritual.

A different process had taken over in which there was only the need of the moment, the call to exert myself more than I had ever believed possible. And as the days progressed, the process became more and more intense, more and more painful, more and more demanding. I stayed inside, often lying down for hours. And each hour I thought, "I can only manage it for a little bit longer. The end is just around the corner." And the next hour came, and the next.

The pain I felt was far deeper and more potent than any physical pain I have ever encountered. It seemed to belong to the very nerve of my psyche. This pain was not about something, about being rejected or abandoned. That would have made it easier. Instead, it was the essence of suffering, pure inner psychic pain. If I withdrew my consciousness, my inner effort, the pain stopped. I would focus on the beyond, on the inner goal, for as long as I could bear it, maybe thirty seconds, maybe a minute. Then I would retreat, and the whole psyche and also the body would be left quaking. But I knew with the knowledge that comes from somewhere, certainly not from the mind or ego, that I had to continue.

This process was more important than life itself. I didn't know why. I just felt that the whole dignity of myself demanded this work, this tremendous effort.

I would pause a little to eat and had a few hours of sleep each night. After about ten days, I felt that the process was reaching some point of completion, though what was completed I didn't know. The Sufis talk about the work of "polishing the mirror of the heart," cleansing the impurities of the lower self. Something was being cleansed, with pain and inner fire. Even while I cried out for release, there was a deeper and stronger calling to focus on the beyond, whatever it cost.

I do not remember any comforting presence, any inner reassurance. All that I was aware of was my own ruthless desire, relentless drive, that pushed me through every barrier. It was pain upon pain, not light upon light. There was no warmth of love, no taste of bliss. Sometimes, there were moments of inner space, a resting place. But then the drive to the beyond would push me out of this oasis into the desert and the burning.

The process intensified as it reached its culmination. In moments of despair, I cried out to my teacher. Every muscle, the whole of the fabric of my psyche, every cell of my being, was stretched. Then there were glimpses of something beyond this process, a peace that belonged to the other world. I began to feel the presence of my teacher, whom I loved and feared.

My teacher was suddenly in my heart and, in a moment of simple wonder, I was made conscious that *I am a soul*. This consciousness would stay with me for the rest of my life: the knowing that I am not just a physical, mental, or emotional being, bound by time and space, that my ego identity is just a small part of my whole being.

SPIRITUAL AWAKENINGS are so simple that there is little to say. But the wonder was beyond anything. Spiritual processes are like childbirth. The agony is often intense, but in the moment of birth the agony vanishes as the mother sees her new child. The intense two weeks of suffering left no trace, no residue. There was no resentment, only the wonder at what had been given, what had been revealed.

I had been thrown into a reality of bliss, intoxication, wonder. Here was a dimension of light and love, far beyond my ego self, beyond any thought or mental picture. In the weeks that followed, I was hardly present in my physical body and often had powerful visions and mystical states. I went to live with my mother, who was kind enough to look after me. She cooked me meals but I ate only a little, often sitting all day in the same place, because I was awake in a timeless inner reality. There was no need to meditate because I was where meditation was. I was completely alive, only not in this outer world.

As the months passed, I found myself more and more in states of bliss. Day followed day, wrapped in this state of bliss. Bliss is the sheath of the soul, *anandamaya kosha* in Sanskrit, and there I remained. It was a deeply healing period, without any conflict or problems. For five months I remained mostly in this state of bliss, a state softer than ecstasy and more enduring. It is a natural state of being, full of peace.

Gradually my mind began to return. My ego consciousness and sense of an individual self, which had been left behind in the state of bliss, began to reconstellate. But it was a different consciousness, no longer bounded by mind, but knowing another reality. I was awake in another world while at the same time present in this outer world.

Gradually, the longing no longer burned so fiercely. A soul quality of deep peace had been entered, one that I knew couldn't be taken away because it isn't of this world.

ONE DAY I had a dream in which I saw a coffin on which was written "spiritual aspirant." I knew that the stage of the journey in which I was a seeker was over.

Sherry

I DID PROSTRATIONS every day for the next seven years. At some points, I did a thousand a day. Sometimes five hundred a day. They were one of my greatest teachers.

I came to understand a lot from doing the prostrations. I was somebody who tried very hard. It was very difficult for me to see through my ordinary mind by only sitting still. Sitting still, I would get so tense. The prostrations were physical—they let me try hard. I had to stand up, do the prostration, stand up, do the prostration, over and over and over. There was something to do with my body.

I could see my mind and it was so amazing because it would tell me, "I can't do it today. I'm too tired. I'm too sick. My knees hurt. I'll probably hurt. I'll probably ruin my knees if I keep doing this."

The Zen master said to me, "Even if you die, you do your prostrations. If you die doing your prostrations, it's fine." So I really thought, "Okay—no problem. Even if I die, I'm doing the prostrations." And, then at the end of the prostrations, my mind—which had been trying to persuade me to stop with every single prostration—would come out and say: "Look what I did? Isn't that great!" And I would take credit for what I did.

The deviousness of my mind was so obvious you couldn't miss it.

I became sort of a prostration evangelist. When one of my friends would say that it seemed like I had a lot of calmness or a lot of steadiness and ask what was the secret, I would tell them all about the prostrations—but, of course, nobody wants to do prostrations. I really couldn't give the practice to anybody. Yet it was right for me. It gave me a chance to see how my own mind worked.

I was so oriented toward *doing*, believing that for anything that I really loved and cared about to happen, I had to do it. I just thought that's how you get anything in this life. Changing that way of thinking feels like the deepest thing I've ever had to do.

I'VE HAD to learn how to actually be interested in the truth of my own experience, the truth of what's actually here as opposed to the old way of thinking, where I believed I needed to change in order for something to be true.

In order to be clear, in order to be awakened, in order to be present, in order to be a friend, in order to be a lover . . . before I felt that I had to *do something to myself*, be responsible for changing something in myself in order to be the way I wanted to be or longed to be.

Prostrations were my doorway through that belief, the only doorway I could have come through because of that "doing" belief. The "doing" belief was very supported in my family's perspective. We were taught that you have to have effort, you have to try, you have to keep your eye on the goal, and you must never let down. I just carried that "doing" belief right into my spiritual path, like I did in all the rest of my life. It seemed to have worked fine up to that point.

I learned otherwise.

Prostrations were a wonderful entry for me to the spiritual path. The capacity to *be*, to actually care, and to be interested in my experience regardless of what it is—that's taken all the rest of my life to begin to do.

Prakash

—— ❦ ——

I HAD BEEN teaching out in the world and practicing Transcendental Meditation. The Transcendental Meditation felt like kind of a respite. It was a lulling, soothing, calming influence on my life. But I didn't have that deep *bhakti*, devotional love, connection with it since I still felt so wounded in my heart.

There was a period of time of deep despair arising from a painful relationship. It was a crushing blow. For a time I even felt suicidal—I was in so much pain. When the call of my inner voice came to go out into the world, I followed.

I went looking in Istanbul, went to Rumi's tomb, and all the different places in India. But I couldn't feel that dance of connection. I didn't feel it until I first connected with Osho in Australia when I was twenty-five.

I met a friend who'd just come back from India and she had some tapes of him speaking. And the first time I heard him speak, it was like this guy was speaking to my heart. Osho had a warm, enchanting, attracting way of speaking. I felt like he was speaking my own thoughts back to me.

This friend was offering Osho's meditations. So I started doing Dynamic Meditation, a breathing, whole-bodied, mindfulness practice. I had to do it for twenty-one days, every morning, and then she let me come out to the meditation center and listen to other tapes and meet Osho's followers, the *sannyasins*. The experience was intense and I realized that this is the way I wanted to live.

Osho's active meditations had a deeper and more transformative impact on my soul than Transcendental Meditation did. Doing Dynamic Meditation was powerful. It really freed the energy in the body. I started experiencing the emotional release it offered and that was bringing me back to a sense of freedom again. So I became a *sannyasin*, a follower of Osho. I went to his main center in India, in Poona, and lived there for three years.

Those three years were dedicated to practice, dedicated to awakening. At the time, I imagined that enlightenment was like a one-time shift and then we always remain in that transcendent state and that, in a sense, was what I was going for at the time.

Even so, there were powerful transformative shifts during that time, healing some of the most painful wounds, wounds very deep in my soul—lifetimes of healing.

I began feeling that I did have worth as a person. When I became a *sannyasin* with Osho, as he gave me a new name, he said, "Prakash. This is who you really are. You are blissful luminosity. So whenever you see light, know that that's who you are—not your history, not who you've taken yourself to be." I was learning to live into that.

MY TWELVE YEARS with Osho, living in the ashram in Poona and at the Ranch in Oregon, were a wild and deeply satisfying part of my journey. In India, our practices were *satsang,* the spiritual transmission of sitting in the presence of the teacher; *darshan,* sacred gathering for spiritual discourse or teachings; and meditation—and many different kinds of therapy groups. On the Ranch—it was work, all work. We felt we were building a city "to provoke God." That was our task.

The shift into living in the authority of my own realizations occurred for me in Poona, after I went there to really confront Osho about the whole devastation that happened at the Ranch, where there had been an explosive scandal.

I FELT DEVASTATED and very surprised to find myself back in the world after the dismantling of the Ranch—and a number of causes and conditions led me to turn to hospice work. In 1986, I read *How Can I Help?* by Ram Dass, which catalyzed my connecting with hospice work. The writings of Stephen Levine and Elizabeth Kübler-Ross were influential. I worked in hospice for a long time.

While engaged in working with AIDS patients, I found myself still struggling with my feelings about what had happened at the Ranch and my connection with Osho. I felt angry and full of doubt and was unable to get through it on my own. I felt that I had to deal with this directly at the source—so in 1989 I returned to India and worked directly with Osho to try to find some clarity. He was very supportive and helped me to come to terms with my confusion and mistrust, with my tremendous disillusionment. He told me the way I needed to move through was with the "Mystic Rose."

"Mystic Rose" is a twenty-one day meditation. The first seven days is three hours of laughter each day, and you're in a room with about a hundred and fifty people doing the same thing—and I wasn't in the slightest bit amused. I was amid so much hatred—at Osho—that I couldn't laugh.

I told him, "I can't move; I'm stuck." This time he suggested hypnosis. Through that, I saw a pattern—over lifetimes—of connecting with power and then giving up my power to someone else. And here it was again.

Osho told me to be free of this, I needed to cut through the cords of all of the fear, in all of those lifetimes. Through writing, and with his guidance, I did that. I was feeling more and more seated in my own sense of freedom, and it was stabilizing. After five days he told me I was on my own. "Let yourself just be with us," he said.

Previously, I would experience that stability in meditation—but it wouldn't last. Now I was able to integrate my split and hold the good, the bad, and the ugly—and once more feel my love and gratitude for all the teaching and guidance that I had received from him. I also had the clarity to see that it was time to move on and find a new path.

One day, I realized I didn't need to do anything to be in that state of freedom.

It just was my normal day-to-day experience.

That was different for me.

Ellen

I THINK THAT my sense of individuation, if you want to use that psychological term, was pretty limited. I didn't feel like I developed my own sense of personal identity and real strength until later in life.

I went from what seemed like one safe and secure thing to the next, to the next, to the next. I chose a safe marriage with a kind man. I was seeking a sense of security, a place to fit in, a place to belong. Going to church continued to be a part of our family.

It seemed like spirituality was there, but it wasn't coming from a very deep place inside me—and the depth didn't really begin until much later.

At one point, I decided to end the marriage that I'd been in for thirty-two years—nothing had changed in the marriage and nothing had changed in me. It was stagnant and I didn't have the skills to make changes and deepening happen. I'm not blaming my longing for the real experience of being on anyone—I'm just saying that I didn't have the skills to change myself or my marriage at that point. Maybe the person I am today would have found ways to do that regardless. But I didn't have those skills then.

To me, the only way that I could see that I could really be my own person and individuate was to be *apart*. I had never forsaken the spiritual life, but that's when my spiritual life began to grow by leaps and bounds.

I even went through a stage of involvement with the charismatic movement because it seemed that there was more of the life and fervor I was yearning for there. I found a real depth in my own longing for God. There was more of an experiential component to it.

I went back to school, got two advanced degrees, and started working. Even though a lot of it was academic, it felt like everything was just flooding open. I felt I was no longer the same person I'd been. I was free to really be who I was evolving to be.

At about that same time, I started my meditation practice, beginning with Centering Prayer. That was my first experience of depth. I'm not just talking about the experience of something that's beautiful, the beauty and the sacredness of just sacred spaces. Those are beautiful and there's something that's very transcendent about places like that. I'm talking about going much deeper within, beyond all the mind chatter.

Back then, I thought I was what I was thinking; whatever I was thinking was who I was. It wasn't until I began a meditative practice that I realized I was much more than what I was thinking. I felt the spiritual life I had had before that realization had been stunted—now I wanted to live the full experience.

I had never rejected the religion of my growing up because I was fortunate not to be in a religious environment that teaches anything but love and grace. I may not have bought all the doctrine and dogma, but what I took in was the teaching of love and grace. All is grace. All is love.

ABOUT THAT TIME I started going to India to visit a teacher there that my daughter had gone to first. My first visit there was partly to make sure my daughter was okay. Actually, I wanted to go for her and for me, for both of us, not just to protect her. She portrayed it as a very loving community where the desire of the teachers was to help each person grow and find their true selves.

The teachers were a German man, whom we called Appa, meaning Father, and his wife, Amma. I remember one day, Appa said to me, "Ellen, you're what we call a fast grower!" By that, I think he meant I was ready—ready to experience, to learn experientially.

Practicing there, I began dealing with what Thomas Keating would call your own "garbage" inside. I started dealing with those projections, those things I had that muddied the water, that made me not see clearly. I began to see from a much larger perspective, giving me much more personal spaciousness inside of me—which gave a place to work with the "garbage."

It was an explosive, transformative period—going out into the world on my own, going back to school, beginning Centering Prayer, and going to India.

I became aware of other faith traditions and started reading about so many of them: Buddhism, Hinduism, and all forms of Christian mysticism and Jewish mysticism. It wasn't until I really started to explore what you could call a more mystical path that things began to open up so much. Ramana Maharshi, the man who taught my teacher in India, taught that there are many, many paths to God. And I began to look a little more critically at the Christian traditions, recognizing what made sense to me and what didn't—but I never felt the need to cut myself off from that tradition, even though there are aspects I don't agree with. I still belong to an Episcopalian church community that presents the teachings of love and grace.

Everybody finds the way that their experience has taught them.

Reflections on the Second Quarter

─────────────── ⟨✺⟩ ───────────────

OUR LONGING IS a beacon in the fog. It guides us through our obscurations until we emerge in clear seeing—the end of seeking, longing fulfilled.

These awakening stories beautifully illustrate remarkably similar insights emerging in similar progression through stunningly varied paths.

The second quarter, as these stories highlight and as our own exploration of spiritual biography will reveal, carries us on the grace of our longing through profound transformative shifts. In this quarter, the journey moves from reaching out, to the gathering of teachings, to developing stages of practice, all the way through to the surrender of egoic effort. Images we hold about the path, the goal, striving, and the self are all dismantled.

Each of the practitioners who shared a story described opening to vulnerability. None could ignore the honest recognition of wounds that needed to be healed so that grace's longing for itself could be fulfilled. Engaging in a transformative practice, we inevitably recognize our wounds, many of which we kept long hidden or perhaps never even noticed. Our increased opening and willingness bring them forward, more into the light of day. We bump into the truth.

This confrontation with our woundedness, lack of understanding, and lack of compassion for ourselves seems to be the norm as we begin a spiritual path and commit ourselves to awakening. The work of healing is deep and requisite.

Many of us adopt a spiritual path with mixed motives. Authentic longing is tinged with the hope that our practice will fix all that we believe needs fixing, that it will serve as an over-the-counter Valium. Most of us prolong our stay in the beginning stages of practice with continued mixed motives, mistaken beliefs, and self-doubt. As we've seen, it leads to discouragement.

When we attempt to bypass our wounds, we're catering to self and strengthening it. We substitute the desire for comfort for the intention of awakening. Our unhealed wounds will always pull us back, in one way or another, to attend to them.

During much of the second quarter, we remain largely in survival mode. It is only as we realize the futility of self-driven striving that we can even begin to experience Being. Willful effort arises as a strategy of the self, the card we hope to play. Ultimately, we realize that it doesn't work. Entering a spiritual path—and staying with it—leaves us with nowhere to run. Surrender reveals itself as the only option.

Jeff Foster, a respected teacher of nondualism, calls surrender "the terrifying free fall into wonder." It is our entry into transformational energy. Cynthia speaks of surrender as allowing God's presence to be known to us. We align form's intention within the pull of formlessness. The surrender that signals the end of the second quarter is gradual for some—for others, sudden and dramatic. It makes way for the maturation and ripening to follow.

Although surrender in itself is profoundly healing—we leave so much old baggage behind in the leap—a critical measure of healing seems a necessary prerequisite for surrender. The wounds and fractures of our sense of self are our roadblocks until we address them. They will keep us from the leap. Later in our journey, we see all our moments of acknowledging our wounds and all our moments of healing them were actually the steppingstones of our path.

There comes a time in the second quarter when we begin to take deep, personal responsibility for exploring and healing our own minds. Practice needs to become very personal before we gain the liberative momentum needed to release our attachment to the personal. When we attend to the healing of our own wounds, we up the ante on our commitment. We move from outer transformations—of moral discipline and daily practice, for example—and into more inner and secret transformative shifts in our being.

We ask ourselves questions specific to our own experience: "Where am I blocked? Where am I resistant? Where am I afraid to look?" We explore—with commitment, curiosity, and compassion—where we are stuck in survival mode, in self. No longer blaming or rationalizing or making excuses, we heal the only mind we can heal. This is the point where our practice ceases being a meaningful part of our life and becomes indistinguishable from our life. It is a shift in the depth of our sincerity.

Healing occurs when courage and commitment meet with the unconditional love of formless awareness. With that clarity, we see deeply into the feeling state of the wound, the stories that support it, the moods it gives rise to, the self-assumption it produces, and the mindlessness that allows the thoughts to be believed. In Ephesians 5:14, we are reminded, "Anything exposed to light turns into light itself."

Both the process and the outcome of healing possess dynamic, liberating energy. Healed, the self's wounds no longer disenfranchise us from Being. We begin to recognize the unity of the longing and the longed for. Trust allows that recognition and deepens within it.

This "sincerity shift" signifies a pivotal transformation, an inner, energetic commitment to embody our direct experience. It gives rise to both humility and dignity. In humility, we open ourselves to the healing energy of grace. At the same time, we experience a growing sense of value and worthiness. Speaking and acting from our own realizations, our own truth, we begin to live in devotion, in authority, in trust.

With trust, we let go of our defendedness, and space opens within our being. We allow the creation of a container deep, spacious, and porous enough for Spirit to fill. Llewellyn, for example, viewed his dramatic experiences of "purification," fueled by the intensity of his longing, as opening up the space for Spirit within him.

Toward the end of the second quarter, we all empty the space of our being in real measure—letting go of mistaken beliefs, conceptualized spirituality, and many old wounds. Our grasping to a self diminishes, as does the self's interfering reign. We develop our finer qualities, such as kindness, love, and compassion, through intention and committed practice. Emptying and the work of *development*—the training of our heart and mind—allow *discovery* of our own essential nature.

Our own essential nature is so much more than we could ever have imagined at the beginning of our journey. With its discovery, we become increasingly able to embody grace—to consciously embody the formless within form.

We become transfigured.

THE THIRD QUARTER:
Healing into Maturity

Allow
what you have already been given
to blossom in you
and open
at greater and greater depths.

—SOGYAL RINPOCHE

Introduction

THE THIRD QUARTER of our spiritual journey—our spiritual maturation—is marked by a genuine diminution in our attachment to egoic
self. Having known greater Being, we recognize the universe of self
as tiny and limited, not at all at ease. Self's enticements no longer hold
such enchantment.

We find new ways of viewing the separate self-sense we had
assumed to be all there is. Individuality becomes appreciated but
not grasped. Nor is it elevated in importance above other individual
expressions of the sacred. Just as a path is cleared in the woods simply
by being used, there is a widened opening to Being mode as it is more
frequently accessed or allowed.

The operating system of the survival mode remains available for us
to function in daily life. We begin to trust it only for what it is meant
to do—to navigate the world and our interactions in the world. There
is a greater hesitance to place unexamined credence in the assumptions and beliefs of self. Self is no longer seen as our sole or even
primary operating system nor as a reliable refuge.

In Being mode, we come to intimately know the Three Jewels of
Refuge. The Buddha jewel—our own awakened essence—is grace.
The Dharma jewel—the path to that essence and the ultimate truth of
it—is grace in action, freely and benevolently gifting us. The Sangha
jewel—our utter interbeing with all that is—is grace's endless, intri-
cate offering.

The surrender that ended the second quarter of our journey allows entry into the third quarter and becomes imprinted. A deep preference arises for the simple act of letting go of what no longer serves us. "Allowing" becomes an increasingly familiar stance and we begin to rest in more ease.

During this quarter and on into the fourth quarter, we continue to face life's endless challenges—and often its most painful ones. We're aging. Our bodies sicken and fail. Our loved ones die. Life is not necessarily easier, but our relationship with it, as a consequence of our deepening spiritual maturation, is.

Our unhealed wounds and remaining issues are increasingly highlighted within the growing ease of the third quarter. Their psychological and physiological effects become more noticeable, more in jarring contrast to a growing field of equanimity. Our healing continues, as it must.

The third quarter is characterized by increasingly clear-eyed discernment—a readiness to recognize what leads toward awakening and what leads toward the old trance of unmindfulness. In the third quarter of maturation, decisions are made with increasing wisdom. In the fourth quarter, wise responses and decisions begin to arise spontaneously.

The term "dharma lag" is one I use to describe the time between the arising of the inclination to fall back into the universe of form only, self only, and the recognition of that inclination. As we mature spiritually, the dharma lag decreases. Once, it may have lasted for decades, years, or months. As we mature spiritually, our growing discernment, greatly honed mindfulness, and more heartfelt intention diminish the time of our dharma lags to days, hours, even minutes. Eventually, there is no dharma lag at all and we remain mindful and open to whatever is arising, without dwelling even for a moment in the reactivity of self-reference.

The integrative healing of shadow and persona takes place mostly in the second quarter of the spiritual journey. Through that healing, we come to honor our own value, the value of our particular individuality as an endearing and singular expression of the sacred. We see that our essential nature has a reality and depth that the fabricated egoic self never had. We come to live in humble appreciation.

As both the search and the seeker are surrendered, Presence arises. Presence is a force field of embodied, actualized realizations. It is authentic and dignified. Presence, the increasingly conscious merge of our realizations and our embodiment, of formless awareness and form, characterizes the third quarter.

As each of us moves into deeper spiritual maturity, we are graced with an unveiling of the higher-order capacities that both signal and benefit continued, continuous awakening. They arise naturally with maturation, as Spirit is increasingly able to shine through a particular, individual manifestation of Being, measurably less congested with clinging.

WHEN YOU EXPLORE the third quarter of your own spiritual biog raphy, questions will point you toward recollections of your own transformative shifts. The questions will help you recognize whatever challenges, unhealed wounds, and unconscious beliefs remain.

Here are some accounts of that period, the beautiful transformations of the third quarter of our spiritual journey—healing into maturity.

Rodney

SEEKING HAS A natural time and duration within most people's spiritual journey.

The beauty of Buddhism, as I understood it early on, was that it was moving me from the suffering I knew very well personally to the end of suffering, which I could only conceive but I knew wasn't there. I had a lot to do.

This directed me toward the suffering that was immediate, and its causes. It felt to me like a very practical, pragmatic, and personal exploration. I took the Buddha at his word: "This is to move me from suffering to the end of suffering." So, I asked myself, "What does that look like? Right now, I'm suffering. What is my suffering due to? What are the causes? What are the conditions? What am I saying to myself that creates the tension of the suffering?" It was a very personal and immediate path for me.

I really considered myself a beginning practitioner until I understood the nature of effort. Until then, it was all *me*. It was self-promoted practice, self-controlled practice—all coming from my own ideas of how to practice. To me, that's the definition of a beginner.

The dropping of effort was like a night-and-day experience. Once I really awoke to what I was doing to myself and my practice, then my practice changed. Then, truly, I stopped being a beginner. But that was years, really. It was years.

Once I got over the despair of not being able to turn to someone, it actually got very interesting and exciting. In the quiet of the monastery—and having the background of all those years of meditation—my mind was very quiet, very still, and I began to see what was in front of me.

I began to ask questions—and I learned the art of inquiry and investigation. The first question I asked myself was, "How can I do this?" and then "Can *I* do this?" This threw me back on the sense of "I" and what "I" was trying to do—and how did I know what to do and where I was going while I was doing it. Time and place and space and objective and mind involvement and effort—all of that was kind of grist for the mill during my three years at that monastery.

I just began asking the most meaningful questions and exploring the assumptions that underlay the questions. No one had taught me that practice—though since then, I have heard other people expounding on it and talking about investigation and inquiry. At the time, I saw it working for myself, in myself. I remember just posing myself any question, like "What is ignorance?" and then just being very patient with it. It felt very important for me to know. It had a kind of urgency to it but I wasn't going to look for it in books or ask a teacher. And then at some ripe moment, I would see what ignorance was. The question would come to fruition. And I would say, "Ah!"

Then I would ask a question from whatever arose from that question. And it was just a beautiful opening, a vista of observation into whatever I wanted to know. At some point, it became so rapid that it's like when you see these darkened football stadiums with flashbulbs going off—the rapidity of insight seemed like that to me. Wherever I turned my mind, I would have understanding, flashes of realization of what the question behind it was.

My practice took off from there. That was the major turning point away from self-reliance, self-effort, standard and formal techniques, maps of the terrain—I just threw all of that away. It didn't resonate with me anymore.

The aftereffect or the glow of realizing your own being is a confidence that's unshakeable. Literature just falls away. Even if the Buddha were to come down in some manifested form and say, "You've been doing it all wrong, Rodney," I would say, "Well, excuse me, Mr. Buddha, but if you get out of the way, I'll continue."

There's a subtle resonance that arises when we feel at home in our own path. It becomes a dynamic that can't be denied. Words that are in line with this felt sense move us when others do not. It is not arguable or transferable to another person. Each of us has it uniquely.

That's the confidence that is so empowering, because you see it, you know, and once you see it, it's like somebody trying to convince you that you don't have a maple tree in your yard when you know you do. You can't be persuaded against that.

Simplicity is also part of it. How complicated could it be? How far away is now? And how distant could that be? Whenever I would try to make it into a journey, I would stop and say, "How far is the journey to now?" Simplifying it this way reframed everything.

There's a positive and negative view to our qualities. Like the quality of effort—when you can concede that effort won't take you there, the energy of effort doesn't stop. It moves toward a resolve, a confidence, and a determination. It moves very strongly into a passion and an urgency. The ball isn't dropped because effort is released—the energy is translated into a different form that then becomes vital for liberation.

We all start out with capacity. All of us have capacities for awakening, but we just use them in service of our egoic identity. Once the egoic identity is seen through, then that energy doesn't stop. It keeps going now in the service of the unmanifest, of awareness, of liberation.

There was a lot of passion in me in those days, even though I felt that what I could do was limited in terms of an egoic sense of what I could do. But there was an awful lot of seeing, and there was a lot of passion and understanding in the seeing. I really reformulated the path in terms of moving toward something to being able to see things in depth and with depth.

WE'RE ALL VICTIMS of our understanding. We have to stay within our understanding until our understanding evolves us out of that particular frame of reference. For me, I had to stay within the field of my own efforts until effort broke me out of that understanding, until I couldn't do anymore. Then I had to see what I was doing wrong in order to understand what the next step was for me.

I realized I was to trying to live someone else's understanding. When I met Nisargadatta, he threw a completely different level of understanding on me, which I didn't have the capacity to hold. I knew it was true, so I had to let it sit and find its own way out of me—I couldn't just take his words and apply them, because I didn't have his understanding.

It's only through the wonders of wisdom that I was able to move at all. I suddenly understood what I didn't understand before—and all of the strategies that that particular level of understanding involved I could now undertake. It became a completely understandable course of action.

Wisdom is the key.

As I continue to mature in my own wisdom, I see that there are not two things at play here—wisdom and surrender. There's only one thing. There's life coming back for itself, to recover itself.

It's unrelenting—it's not going to let any of us forget that there's more to see because it keeps showing us, through its manifestation, that problems exist when we don't see. So it manifests as a problem, and then as the urgency to uncover and resolve that problem, and then as the energy to move forward toward full liberation. Life keeps manifesting in different ways to get our attention, to keep us moving forward so it can join us once and for all.

I made this discovery through obstructions, what I call "the counter-influences." These would arise because of how I held reality—and this is the trick, the paradox of it all—I began to learn that the problems didn't occur from reality. They came from my perception, my understanding, and how I was trying to use reality to move forward.

Reality is just there and it's waiting for you to drop into it—but I kept assuming that I was outside of it and I needed to get into it.

At some point, the tension between trying to get into something that already preexists started wearing me out. I realized that however

I perceive reality to be, I perceive it differently than the immediacy that it is. So in some ways I stopped fixing it as any particular form. I stopped creating it in such a way that it would be anything other than the complete surrender that receives it.

It was during the time in the retreat hut that all parts of myself came into view—all the ways that I used time to bypass and get over myself, and all the ways that I restructured my perceptions so that I could still maintain myself in walking through life in terms of goals, opportunities, and meaning.

I started seeing what was completely fictional in relationship to what reality actually offers, and yet I always had the option of being able to let go of the counterinfluences and sink back into the reality that is or to continue with the counterinfluences. Sometimes I would do one and sometimes the other—it would just depend on my level of understanding in that moment, concerning the strategies I was applying. I would still get caught up, but it was temporary.

That I was getting caught up couldn't stay hidden for too long. It was too obvious. I began to realize that most people interpret the spiritual traditions in terms of some "movement toward." And at some level of understanding, that works—it gets us off and running.

But then, it's essential that we turn back and ask the question of that very premise: "Is this a journey where I'm moving away toward something else, or is this the place that I'm moving into, in this very moment?"

This seems to be the only approach that works. We grow because we see the need to grow—and that's the only way it works spiritually, as well. We have to create an environment that allows both ourselves and others to see the need to grow, without any pressure.

After I left the hut, I realized that that phase of my practice was over. I could have stayed—it's an easy life, and it was a very smooth and abiding calm life as well. But I knew, intuitively, that that phase of my practice had ended.

DURING THIS TIME, I came upon a book that Stephen Levine had written, called *Who Dies?* I thought I'd really like to work with the dying.

This impulse didn't come only from some kind of compassionate need to help the dying. I realized that death was a part of life I didn't understand very well. It was much more an extension of what I'd already been doing than some sort of alternative way of working with the world and being compassionate. So I came back to the States and, after about six months of reorienting myself, I began my career in hospice care.

Returning to the States was the hardest six months, at that time, that I'd ever lived. Both my parents had died. I had no money and no place to go—yet I felt that the phase of my Asian practice was over, when I was focused on self-discovery and understanding. I came back to the meditation center that I had stayed in before I left and they allowed me to be on staff there for six months while I got my bearings and relearned how to do some of the daily activities of life in America.

People were suggesting that I start teaching and I knew I wasn't ready to. I deliberately wanted to get away from all of the influences that were telling me I should be someone, so I took a job in Texas where I knew no one. There, people would call me on my stuff and I couldn't get away with things. Everyone treated me like I was a normal person without any of the meditation, retreat, monk history.

I wanted to be a human being in the rawest form. So there I was, working in hospice care for my first job, right up against life in its rawest form.

It's so easy to use our spiritual journey as self-promotion, as a way to be recognized, or to gain that advantage. But I was onto that. Because of the questioning I had been giving myself, I wanted to start from the beginning. I wanted to work with death and dying, meet people, and reintroduce myself back to the culture after four years of being away.

At that point, I knew unequivocally that wherever I was and whatever I was doing, I had to mold my life to fit practice around my life. So here I was, with dying, and my life became about that central theme.

I brought the same power of questioning that I did in the hut to the death and dying that I was facing now. It was tremendously empowering. But also—I got caught up. I remember after about six months working in hospice care, I looked around and I couldn't believe it. It was Christmastime and I couldn't believe there was any life celebrating anything because I knew what was happening in all the darkened homes of people who were dying. My ego made an exaggerated significance out of death and dying, as it does when you first get involved in that.

I've since realized that until suffering is really brought into life as a complete, accepted component of living, as an extension of living, rather than this horrible thing that everybody envisions it to be, you never really settle with your life.

A WHOLE PIECE of life was missing in the hut—that discovery of life in its whole manifestation, life as it's being lived now, as it's aging. Each phase of life has its own empowerment, its own potential. Once I opened up to the entire range of what life is and offers, that was its fulfillment. I couldn't take it as just youth anymore, because I was losing my youth and seeing what happened when you turned away from death and dying. It really opened me, and was a very important piece of the completion of my own consciousness.

At one point in the hut I said to myself, "I'm willing to go through whatever experiences are necessary in order to wake up." I meant it. I consented to allow anything to happen to me, based on that intention.

That intention sent me home, sent me into working with death and dying. It wasn't always easy—in fact, it was very, very difficult. But every step I took there was something that I saw in retrospect that I absolutely needed in order for a part of my consciousness to heal.

We'd all like to bypass the hardship, but it just doesn't work. We all have to be willing, at some point, to admit this and say, "Okay, well, now I have to go into the hard stuff." This process is begrudged for all of us. None of us wants to take that on willingly, because it hurts to see it.

My determination to look arose from one part of me that has been matured for a long period of time, even from youth—the love of mystery, the love of wonder. I always had a sense that no matter where I turned, ultimately it would, through alchemy, change from something horrible to something wondrous, almost like Mara throwing spears at the Buddha and the spears changing to flowers in midflight.

I had a determination never to turn away from anything. I knew that whatever I was facing was really on my side and I just didn't see it from that vantage point, and that's why it hurt. All that I had to do was to watch it, to observe it sufficiently, and I would see that it was really a friend, rather than a foe. And that's proved to be true.

Cynthia

———— ⌒∞⌒ ————

"Working in the wonders" is a phrase from the seventeenth-century Christian mystic Jacob Boehme to describe how we continue to grow the soul by healing the dark parts and bringing to birth our untapped gifts. I felt the call to "become an unknown person" and knew that I had to drop my own weary self-reliance. That came to pass for me in a total self-abandonment in love.

In my experience with my spiritual teacher, the hermit monk Brother Rafael Robin, I felt that all was forgiven, understood, and poured out. I came to recognize that love's nature is that it evokes an increase in being. Where there is love, there is increase. I felt a total self-abandonment in love.

Essence—who we really are, the heart of our hearts—seems truly and mysteriously to be bound up with our hiddenness and pain. I found that in response to each significant descent into the ground of my woundedness, there is a parallel ascent in the form of inner freedom.

In the center of that moment—when the pain meets and is illuminated by unconditional love—there is a new creation. That instant itself is the dawn of the real *I*, the breakthrough of the majesty into the human realm.

The confluence of awareness and surrender basically imprints the default "letting go" attitude as the home of our witnessing presence. We begin to learn that that's what, in every situation, is going to work better—if we move into that initial relaxation and letting go rather than clenching and tightening inside.

The continuous practice of objectless awareness, as we draw our attention back from the ground of objects and begin to hold it in a different kind of form and vibrancy, allows us more easily to open to what you might call nondual revelation, inputs in vision—not so much visions like angels but just a sort of knowingness that comes from more than just the top down and the head out.

If your sense of self doesn't change as you age, you've missed the boat in some ways.

FOR THE FIRST HALF of my life, like so many spiritual seekers, I was just fascinated by my story. I thought my story had a plot and a drama and, like any good narrative, it had a beginning, a middle, and an end and interweaving themes.

I finally realized that this was all just the construction of the narrative line and that there's a whole huge world beyond it. As I began to learn to get comfortable in objectless awareness, I also got comfortable in point-less identity—to where I'm not always having to go and say, "Well, who was I?" The story of the young girl, Cynthia, is only tangentially related to this "I-ness" that I am now. Really, this could be anybody's story.

Now, in my sixties, I'm not succumbing constantly to what Gurd-jieff called "the disease of tomorrow"—the sense that you've got this endless canopy of time that you're going to paint your life on. I want to really become aware of the curves and the patterns and the shape and the trajectory, to sort out simply the unessential and the repetitive from the essential and the determinative for this stage.

It becomes very, very easy after you've reached a certain period in your life; you've built a certain reputation and you float on it. You have a certain sense of competence and you float on it, and you can float right downstream.

I had to learn to let go of all that kind of stuff and walk with begin-ner's mind into the next challenge. I realize that there's a tendency to keep on doing the things that I've done all along—just because I've done them and I'm good at them, and because they yield predictable results and keep my life comfortable.

I had to learn to take a deliberate turn in a different direction in order to open up, in order not to get trapped in the repetitive and mindless turning of the wheel but to turn toward what the next step is. That's what I find is on my plate at this time.

I would guess that, like most people in the world, I started out not being comfortable with surrender, because the way we use the term in the West has gotten so entangled with images. Its space is in the power world—where surrender means rolling over and playing dead. In that way, it seems to be on a collision course with what you really want to do—particularly when you're facing ultimate experiences like a fatal illness or something—when the impulse is to marshal your strength and fight.

I had to learn a gradual kind of humanization and expansion of my understanding of surrender. It moved from being immediately pegged as a gesture of weakness to being one of connecting with a deeper strength. It's basically gone along the route of realizing that surrendering really means to entrust myself.

To surrender means to hand yourself over and, in the classic spiritual sense of the word, it means to hand yourself back over into a higher intelligence or a higher guidance. Whether this is conceived as an inner wisdom deep within yourself or whether it's a God out there—the whole boundary is artificial—the field is Thou. The field is Love.

Surrender doesn't at all mean giving up. It means calling into play some higher possibilities that are blocked precisely by a too heavy-handed exercise of your will tied to your ego, to your willfulness. It makes room for the deeper dynamism of your being to emerge and take the driver's seat.

My learning curve has been a long one—learning that piece and then learning how to engage with it.

THE MOST POWERFUL EYE of the needle was when I began to seriously take up a practice of Centering Prayer. I tried many, many meditation paths that had a more concentrative nature, where you focused your attention and learned to hold it on a single desired focus, but I'd never gotten anywhere with them.

In Centering Prayer, the method is entirely surrender—understood as an interior gesture that gradually gets patterned into your being. In the actual language of Centering Prayer, they call it "consent to the presence and action of God."

This consent amounts to unclenching inside and letting go of whatever it is you're hanging on to. In Centering Prayer, that's whatever thought that comes into your head and begins to engage you—you learn to relax by letting go of your grip on the object. It's practiced as an inner gesture.

Consenting to the presence and action of God through the gesture of surrender was not difficult once I got started. When I approached it from the top down, from my mind, I could get all sorts of suspicious—thinking, "Well, what am I consenting to anyway?" That turns it back into a power structure. But when I did it as a gesture, it's obvious—consenting is the tag word they use to mean "let go of the thought when you realize you're stuck with it or interacting with it."

That much, I could do. It was only thirty minutes or so of working with just letting go of the object that my attention had gotten fixated on. I learned to do it bottom up rather than top down. Along the way, I discovered to my astonishment that this repeated imprinted pattern of consenting was building trust.

For the first time, I was able to distinguish trust from belief.

Belief was always presented to me as the way to get a doctrinal body of assertions that you agree with, while faith is the willingness to continue to agree with it when the chips are down. What I discovered in the practice of Centering Prayer was that, from a very relaxed way in my own body, my trust of life was beginning to increase just on its own.

I didn't have to cover control, I didn't have to drive, I didn't have to have a lesson plan in place for every next step. There was a sense that was opening up just because my somatic structure was learning how to relax into life through the practice itself. I began to see that I was really dancing with an invisible dancing partner, and I was held. I saw this would be true no matter how I named it, believed it, or had faith in it, because it was deeper than that.

It was a knowing deeper than words, much as Julian of Norwich knew, that "all is well."

I HAD A GROWING awareness of my bodily knowing, a trust that the inner gesture was leading me where I wanted. That had escaped me for all those years. And it's largely missing—this bodily knowing—even in the teaching of the prayer.

You learn to read the signals that are emerging from deeper within you, from the inner energetic living being within your body that really knows, and that somehow is keeper of the roadmap of your own evolution toward the fullness of what you are intended to be.

Centering Prayer actually began to bridge the gap between the whole body of doctrines that I believed in and my ability to walk a single one of them. Centering Prayer just patiently patterned and repatterned my breathing, to the point where my default position would be to, in any kind of moment, relax and ease into it rather than brace and defend myself.

That came really, really slowly. It is a reinforcing circle, because once I had the physiological capacity to breathe through the practice, then the attitudes begin to flow, and then experience. As I reached out to life in slightly different ways, I begin to get different feedback.

I began to develop a body of inner information that allows me to trust when I'm listening to signals reliably. This began to teach me to be aware of "the angle of deflection" that will always be there when our small self and our fearful self and our willful self gets ahold of us and it starts running in its own direction again.

Mostly I just hold "the angle of deflection" of the egoic self the way you hold a child who's having a temper tantrum. What really comes to pass in Centering Prayer—basically, in any form of meditation regardless of method—is more and more surely your sense of selfhood comes to repose in what the Eastern traditions would call your witnessing presence. From there, you can turn on your ego operator to do actions that need to be done in the world—but you don't get confused that that's you. You have a different plank to stand on as you watch things so that you don't immediately have to react to everything from the egoic point of view—you can come back to that observing position.

We don't always have the inner strength to stand up against the ego when it acts out. Sometimes you just have to live in the gap between what you see and what you're able to enact. But the ego lives under your roof too, and I don't think real spiritual progress is made by throwing out any of the inhabitants of your house.

Reality, or enlightenment as I've come to understand it, is being able to be okay in any state and to flow with things, so that there's no need to reject or exclude or bend yourself to some model that you have intellectually agreed is the way things should go.

In terms of outer actions, I'm still bound by what I understand of the Ten Commandments, Jesus's teachings, and that Wiccan precept: "An' that it harm no one, do as you please." There's a fundamental obligation not to harm or cheat other human beings and that's non-negotiable in any tradition. But beyond that, states come and go. Some days you're good, some days you're bad—but there's always that capacity to be present to what is without getting caught up in it. This takes the self-judgment and the striving out of practice.

SURRENDER HAS TAUGHT me over the years. I've learned to recognize, from the bodily aspect of it, that surrender is nonconstriction and nonconstricting. As I let go, there's an opening. When I experience any constriction in my being, any kind of clamping down, any kind of defendedness or clingingness, even if it's theoretically for a very high cause or ideal, that's when I realize I'm off the mark. I've learned to take this gesture of surrender as a very good marker of my capacity to stay aligned with what I really know is the liberating truth.

I know the truth of the situation is that when you go into constriction or contraction this is a clear sign that your ego is trying to grab the steering wheel.

Pain or any of those other states that we would identify as obstacles lock us into judgment and defensive behaviors. Unconditional love, physiologically, is the capacity to stay open, yielded, softened, and embracing of whatever is. That activates a whole different neu-rological circuitry and releases all the energy that's otherwise tied up in what Gurdjieff's work calls "identification"—attachment to your own identity.

It seems like we human beings waste more of our potential being energy in that particular kind of attachment than almost any other. It's the great energy leak of the human condition.

Self-healing and self-transcendence occur simultaneously. I learned that by loving my teacher. He was very keen on helping me to spot when I was creating unnecessary dramas—whether by an attitude, an agenda, or an emotional acting out that, again, came from my small self. He would teach me by simply leaving whenever I got in one of those states. When I got myself out of it, when I shifted the self, then he'd be right back—he could read it in the air.

I gradually came to realize that we're held in a deeper love—and that love, that deeper field, holds the whole of our small self in its sheltering embrace. As we let go into that we begin to get the con-firmation that there is Something that stands behind us, deeper than making people behave the way you want them to.

I first felt that "Something" when I first received Communion. There was something really quiet when I made my way back from Communion, that instantaneously in my body—in my inner body, not just the natural wisdom of the physical body—recognized the encounter and began to yearn for it. I'd seen more of the picture. Over time, I didn't want to be in a town where there's a Mass going on and not be there. There was just that sense of a recognition of a whole different dimension of reality.

I knew that the Divine Field had a heft to it; it wasn't just an idea. I was never taken in by the proposition that silence was emptiness or that the apophatic path—a form of contemplative prayer that is nonverbal, that rests in undefinable Presence—was simply about wor-shipping nothing. I knew that there was an invisible heft that was not discernible by the physical senses or the mind, but could certainly be picked up by this other interior homing beacon.

I didn't have the language at the time—but as I now say it, it's because the Divine Field has an energetic field, directly readable by a heart that is beginning to be attuned to it.

I DON'T SEE conceptual mind as something to be excluded from spiritual practice. It is a very useful tool in the egoic tool kit, and it's helped me be able to reframe and make maps that speak to other people. You have to have some view or another to begin to move forward on a path.

The conceptual mind can still come into a momentary interaction where it's unnecessary—this happens all the time. I think that as you move more into witnessing presence as the default place you live from, you recognize it as a dimension of the vibrancy of the field.

The conceptual mind is peering at things through a thick piece of glass that's a little bit filmed over. You notice that when you begin to become attuned to the signals that come from the subtle body, things are veiled, just like smog in the air. It's a different atmosphere. After trial and error, you begin to realize that in the moments when you're breathing that smoggy atmosphere of conceptualizing your way through life, that you're not really breathing. It's oxygen deprivation.

I think of my heart as "a vessel for listening presence." It's an organ of spiritual perception. That's a classic teaching in the Western mystical tradition—it's come from a long lineage. The locus of my identity has become my heart. I keep coming back to it.

Habitual patterns are largely unconscious, so you don't see them—we usually work with what comes to our attention and consciousness. As soon as it pops the surface I can begin to see and work with it. But I know I trudge through life—as I think most of us do—on automatic pilot.

There are lots of things that other people may notice before you do, recurrent patterns that are so much part of your own inner landscape that you don't even see them as causing the landscape until someone points them out. It's an ongoing thing.

But the way I picture it is that it's the human condition that we're falling asleep continually. We want to stay awake, we want to stay in the larger consciousness, but we keep falling back to sleep. We can say, "This is a problem. I've got to set lots of alarm clocks so I don't stay asleep." Oftentimes people understand spiritual practice in that regard, as setting alarm clocks. Certainly Gurdjieff did.

The other thing to look at is the amazing thing that sometimes wakes us up. All you have to do is, in some semi-lucid moment, sit on your porch deck and say, "I want to be more awake today"—somehow something reminds you that you're falling asleep again and right then you catch yourself.

All you have to do in Centering Prayer is sit there and say, "Okay, I'm going to sit here and do this for twenty minutes." You catch yourself thinking, you let the thought go. And something out of the depths calls it to your attention when you've gotten tangled up in a thought.

I've come to find this more and more remarkable, that there's a who or a what or a something out there that calls us back. It's so important to ease into that and begin to trust that dance, that I don't think someone's out there with a scorecard giving me a demerit every time I fall asleep.

It's more important that in these times when we're reminded of the greater possibility, we can awaken to a renewed sense of gratitude. This is an absolute moment in itself, not just a way station toward some unattainable higher place.

Practice for me is not a means to an end, but it's an expression of that gratitude for any given moment in my life. Surrender is the full expression of everything.

Like many other people, when I first started on this path in Christianity that had that big name, "contemplative," on it, I thought it was all about silence and about maintaining a state of being very, very quiet because God could only be heard in the quiet. I associated contemplative Christianity with a lifestyle.

Then I began to see—and I'd actually had some models in my data bank well before it—that it really is the contemplative practice of a presence that allows you to be present with enlightened action in every moment.

One of the most powerful examples of that enlightened action occurred very early on in my life. In the early '70s, I heard Brother Roger of Taizé speak. He kept saying, in his sort of broken English, "it is the springtime of the Church, it is the springtime of the Church." I was drawn like a bee to honey to the goodness and radiance of his personality—so much so that I did something completely uncharacteristic and went up and stood in a long, long line to meet him afterward. When I finally got up to him, I was terrified and thought, "What am I going to do? Tell him how important I am? Or ask what he wants with me?"

There was something absolutely remarkable about what he did. He wasn't looking over my shoulder to see how much longer the crowd was—he wasn't restless or acting as though he was being put upon. He just looked out to me and enfolded me in his field and asked me my name. I told him, and he said it was a lovely name. He looked straight at me with his radiant eyes and I realized that, for the first time in my life, I was in the midst of unconditional love. I finally knew what it meant. His love wasn't conditioned for my behavior, by my performing well or making a place for myself.

I was just blown away by the quality of this presence that could be completely whole in the infinite, in the middle of this long, impossible situation in time.

This seized me early on as a kind of icon of what the attained contemplative practice is all about. It's not about going off to holy places and mastering teachings and accessing states. It's being able, in the absolute inspiration of any moment, to be oneself—the gap between intention and manifestation gone by knowing how to be skillfully present. That's what contemplation is and, without that, it is simply another pious activity.

ANOTHER VERY IMPORTANT TIP I got from a wise teacher in the Gurdjieff works was that contemplation doesn't happen in the emotions.

It happens in the moving center. It's not about having loving thoughts about people or any kind of a heart scenario, which is another kind of conceptualization of how love ought to feel. The body is a lot more alert than the head or the emotions, and the emotions tend to get self-preoccupied pretty quickly. The body is alert to what really needs to happen in the moment.

At one work session, we had a hundred people for a week in this very small meeting house. And we had to use the room for multiple purposes—I was on the dishwashing team and had to quickly clean up the dishes from lunch and get the room set so they could have a movements class next. I was scurrying back, rattling and clattering with a tray full of cups, trying to get rid of them as fast as I could, all about my self-importance, and—*BOOM!* I bump into the woman who was receiving these cups and placing them on the shelves. She's moving on a Gurdjieff creep where every moment is "I am being aware of myself moving the cups."

She was in her own head, with no sense of time, no sense that the movements class was starting in ten minutes. In between us, as a third force, was the movements teacher—a wise, wonderful old woman. She looked at the situation and did something completely astonishing to me.

She didn't turn to the slow mover and say, "Hurry up, don't you see you're detaining the whole group?" and she didn't turn to me and say, "Slow down, there's people trying to be conscious here." Rather, she instantaneously matched my speed to take the cups off my tray, and then adjusted her speed in midair to place them carefully on the other woman's tray so that she could continue to put them on the shelf undisturbed.

In a completely nonjudgmental way, working entirely in the alertness of her own body in the moment, she was able to harmonize and bring the situation together without judgment or separation. I was halfway back to the kitchen before I realized I had witnessed a miracle.

Learning how to be there in the moment, physically, for me has been "where the rubber meets the road" in contemplative engagement.

I CHANT THE PSALMS and do Centering Prayer, and try as much as I can to be present and not get taken by automatic conditioned programs. I feel experienced enough that I suppose I'm practicing a good deal of my time, but I wouldn't call most of it practice. It's just the lifestyle that flows out of doing the things that are based in devotion and adoration and a lineage of practice, which is my own Christian lineage.

I think it's ultimately very difficult to be spiritual but not religious, because the deeper waters of transformation all flow through the deep lineages of the specific traditions. It's very hard to go through that ego boundary, to really get through it, without actually bowing the knee and the heart to a lineage and a teaching and a teacher. That brings the heart dimension in, in a powerful and traditional way.

Llewellyn

—— ❧ ——

MY TWO INITIAL EXPERIENCES of awakening created the landscape of my initial years on the path. At sixteen, I was awakened to the existence of an inner world and the beauty and sparkling light of the outer world. At twenty-three I was made fully conscious on the plane of the Self, that dimension of pure light, love, and bliss that is present within each of us, but veiled by the ego and our patterns of conditioning.

The next thirty years of spiritual life were a time to live this reality in the midst of everyday life, having a family, working first as a schoolteacher, and then writing and lecturing, first on psychology and then on Sufism. Deepening was more gradual during this period.

Although I was not inclined to teach initially, I was requested to do so by Irina Tweedie and my inner teacher. I felt some fear as I came to the United States to begin sharing Sufi teachings and to begin sharing myself, *as* a teacher—a role I took in a deeply meaningful way. My fears were allayed with a vision during which my teacher came to me and said, "The grace of the guru is in your heart. This is all you need to know."

During this time, there were other less dramatic, more gradual awakenings. When I was thirty-eight, I moved from London to a small town on the coast of California with my family to start a Sufi center. In London, we had been living in a house with forty or fifty people coming each day to meditate. Now, suddenly, we were alone on a hillside beside the ocean.

IN THIS UNEXPECTED SOLITUDE I spent my time writing, meditating, and walking. In the midst of this aloneness, nature opened her hidden self. The physical world became a part of my spiritual path in a way that I never expected. Among the trees and on the beaches, I found a oneness revealing itself in the outer world.

In meditation, I have at times glimpsed the oneness behind creation, the oneness that contains everything and mirrors divine oneness. But now I was experiencing this oneness *in full consciousness*. Wherever I was walking, looking at the multiplicity of nature—the different leaves, trees, rocks washed by the waves—oneness was visibly present. This oneness was so natural, so much a part of what I saw and felt.

It had always been there, but now I was seeing it for the first time.

Nature revealed something so wonderful that I still look in awe. At the beginning, I was just fascinated, expecting this oneness to be a passing mystical state. But gradually I sensed its permanence. An inner eye had opened in which place and state of being were united— the inner and outer oneness mirrored each other.

At first I thought that this outer oneness was only to be found in nature. But as the months passed, what I had found in nature permeated all of my life. I discovered that, whenever I stopped for a moment in the midst of outer activities, I could feel the underlying unity. Interacting with people, or just being immersed in everyday activities, my consciousness would necessarily be caught in multiplicities and the duality of the mind.

But I came to know that, behind this activity, a oneness is always present—a consciousness with which I could attune myself more and more easily. Gradually this dual consciousness became so much a part of my everyday life that I would have to try to remember what it was like to live without it, to live solely in the isolated consciousness of the ego.

This oneness was not static, not just a single state, but would deepen, as if I would be immersed deeper and deeper in states of oneness. And together with oneness came love. The mystical path awakened me to a very different love, the love that underlies and permeates everything. It was present within my heart, sometimes in states of tenderness and softness, sometimes in a power that evoked awe, that made me tremble and inwardly bow down.

My Beloved had come alive within my heart and within my life. When evening came, and the children were in bed with their homework done, I would lie on my bed with my face turned to the wall and merge into this love within the heart, the love to which I belonged.

There is no end to the states of love, to the awakening of the heart. The spiritual path had taken me to the shores of love where, like footsteps in the sand when the tide comes, one begins to get lost in an ocean too vast to name. What can be said of this journey within the heart, of this awakening to what is Real?

SOMETIMES I WAS LOST in states of nothingness, a bewildering and intoxicating emptiness that drowns one deeper and deeper. Here there is no mind, hardly even a fragment of consciousness to remember where one was taken.

One just comes to know that there is a reality behind and within the outer world, a reality both empty and full, devastating, bewildering, and deeply meaningful. This reality is the home of the mystic, one who has been lost and found and lost again, been taken by love to love. I found comfort in the words of one Christian mystic, John Ruysbroeck, who speaks of "the dark silence in which all lovers lose themselves."

The journey continues, the journey will always continue. In my experience, "awakening" means an expansion of consciousness, and once we merge with our divine nature there are no limits because the divine has no limits. On the mystical path some expansions may be reflected in the outer world, as for example when I was sixteen and suddenly saw light I had never seen—as if I had moved from a world of gray to one of color.

When I was awakening to the oneness that is within all of life, I had the joy of seeing this oneness in the outer world—in the trees, the birds, the clouds. But because the vaster horizons are within us, on the mystical journey the most intense awakenings are in the inner worlds, as for example when my consciousness experienced the primal emptiness that underlies all of creation or the currents of love that flow between the worlds.

These experiences are always an act of grace. We need to do the work that struggles with our lower self, the purification. We suffer the heartache and the longing and pain that burns away the veils that separate us from our true nature. The path and its practices are necessary preparation to enable us to contain these higher states of consciousness without being overwhelmed by them, without being shattered by a light so bright. But we are always given more than we believe is possible.

THE QUESTION then remains, who or what awakens? In my experience, it is not me, not "Llewellyn" who awoke. Part of me may have had a glimpse of a reality of love and light, of a oneness that encompasses all the worlds. But the real awakening happens deep within the plane of the soul. It is the soul or Self that awakens, and the joy we feel is the joy of its awakening.

This is the real miracle we are allowed to witness, the divine birth at which we are privileged to be present. What remains of "Llewellyn" after all these years on the path seems less and less, hardly a fragment of the intense young man reading a Zen koan on the London subway.

And yet there is a presence within me that has tasted a truth far greater than anything "I" can know or understand, knowing a Reality that is all that exists.

Sherry

THERE'S SUCH A HOPE and a tendency, at least in the West, to imagine that our path or our journey should be continuously upward or progressing or maturing. It's easy to trust the guidance or the longing when it's really evident. But what about when that goes away—when you feel lost? Can you trust then? That question was very alive for me over my time of unfolding.

The word "unfolding" suggests letting go of the obstacles in the way of what you already are—as opposed to achieving something, attaining something, or scaling the great mountain. I think of it as a process—more of a descent than an ascent, if it's anything. One of my greatest learnings was to trust the lostness, to trust the not knowing—but even deeper than that—to learn to trust what's happening now.

It includes everything, even not knowing whether to follow what your teacher says or not—and to trust that this is the truth of the moment.

I WAS A VERY RIGID PERSON. I did those prostrations every day for seven years, out of a sense of relief to feel I found something real and there was a path I could follow. I had nothing like that before. But somewhere toward the end of those seven years, during the time I was the head teacher at the Ontario Zen Center, I began to notice there seemed to be something wrong with my practice. All I could see and feel was about death.

I was doing very intense practice, living in the Zen center, and I would look at my former friends who would be going to dinner parties and celebrating birthdays and think, "Don't they realize how short life is? They seem so unconscious, so heedless." Everywhere I went I would see people who seemed to not know that we're going to die soon and that this life is so short. I felt like I was seeing things clearly. My Zen master had said, "Soon you die. When will you wake up?"

I took that in. Everywhere I went I could see the surface of things—people laughing and having a good time—yet all I could feel was this profound black emptiness and death. The black emptiness felt so deep and so real compared to all of the surface fluff. I couldn't see why anybody would engage in that, and this feeling got stronger and stronger for me and I felt more and more deeply alone. I didn't know what to do.

I remember seeing pictures of the Zen masters of old laughing and I thought, "They laughed—I'm missing something." I wrote my Zen master and told him this. He said, "More hard training is needed. You have to do more of what you're already doing."

I thought, no, I don't think so. Whatever it is I was already doing was intense. I thought something was missing but I didn't know what it was.

I was still head of the Zen center for some time more—maybe a year or longer—still doing all the practices and leading the retreats while feeling like death was this immediate reality. I had a daytime radio show, interviewing wise people and spiritual teachers. My friend suggested that I interview a doctor who wrote about enlightenment and had some enlightenment experiences. My first thought was, "Oh no, I don't want to interview him." But my friend nudged me and I did.

At the end of the interview, we were chatting and I was telling him about what was happening in my life. He said, "Why don't you come on a retreat with me to Southern California? We're doing a seven-day retreat in the mountains and maybe you will be able to see something about where you are." I remember the fear that I felt because, even though what I was doing wasn't working, I had had this great relief of certainty for seven years and I was afraid to spend seven days away from my practice.

I did it because I was desperate. He was not in any tradition—he was an energy master who worked with the energies of the land and of the human heart. He taught others meditation and how to work with embodied energies.

During the retreat a lot of blocks were broken open. At one point he said to me, "Why are you still wearing your robes?" I thought, "What a jerk! I'm not wearing my robes. I'm in my shorts and T-shirt." But then I realized he was right—I was still holding on to the shell of my identity. And it cracked.

I could perceive that everything was light, and there was a freedom there. But then I came home and I felt totally lost because I had no tether left, no anchor.

I remember my husband saying to me, "What is the matter with you? Why can't you just have a good time?" I didn't know what was the matter with me—everything felt fake about the world. The only people I could bear to be with were children, because that felt genuine and open. Other than spending time with kids and hosting the daily radio show, I just didn't know what to do. I would just walk on the beach and feel completely lost. I would still go through the forms at the Zen center, but inside there was nothing there. That went on for several months.

There was some kind of rigid shell around me in the Zen center that I didn't have when I was just walking on the beach. I didn't know how to not be fake there. I felt like I had to let go of it and I felt like a great failure. But what could I do? I ended up leaving the Zen center.

MY HUSBAND SAID, "Let's just see what's there for us—see what's open." So when someone invited us to live in the mountains with them and their spiritual teacher, the same teacher I had met in the radio interview, we moved to the Sierras in California and lived there for a few years.

I felt open and lost and still like I was some failure on the spiritual path—but it wasn't horrible. I didn't feel depressed about it. *Lost* was the label I used for the feeling then, but my label for it now is *not know-*

ing. I wasn't quite okay with not knowing—it wasn't an experience of openness—but it was right next to openness. It was as close to openness as I could do at the time.

I started having some really remarkable dreams that didn't fit anything that I knew before. In one dream about the feminine, after going through a series of doors into a temple, I'm initiated by these dancing patriarchs wearing traditional Hasidic clothes. I recognized them as King David, King Solomon, Abraham, Isaac, and Jacob—the great patriarchs of the Jewish tradition, which is my background.

In the dream, they initiate me and I say, "You're initiating me? I'm a woman." And they say that they no longer know the way and that many women all over the world are coming in to find a new way, now, for our time and the times ahead. One said, "Will you help us?"

When I woke up, I thought, "What am I going to do with this? This is not just for me." When I would walk in the mountains, I started hearing this word that I had never heard before, but I could tell it was probably a Hebrew word—*Shekina*.

I kept asking everyone if they knew the word. Nobody had until one day a friend came in with a book on Tarot and Judaism. We opened the book to the index where it said that *Shekina*, in Judaism, is the feminine face of God. I never heard there was even such a thing. My friend and I started to meditate together, and in doing so we got guidance to start doing groups for women to discover what this means—to discover a new way, a way for our time. We would say in our meditations that we didn't know how to lead a group for women, and their guidance would say, "You don't need to. That's the point. The women together will discover what their truth is now and what's needed."

We began to ask our friends to host gatherings in their living rooms of women who would be interested in these expressions. We held meetings like this for a couple of years when a Quaker friend and I realized that we should write a book about the feminine face of God.

We wanted to talk to ordinary women who were really living their spirituality—women who got divorced, women who had kids, and women who lived in the world. We meditated often for guidance and followed the leads of people who knew women with real spiritual presence. It took seven years to finish the book.

We spent about a year or two traveling around and giving talks and workshops based on the idea of the book—then it felt like it was complete. After that, again, I didn't know what to do next. I felt very strongly that I wanted to go deeper and offer the deepest, realest thing that I could.

Prakash

⸺ ∞ ⸺

I EXPERIENCED a transformative shift that I describe as a stabilization in freedom through my healing work with Osho. Then I discovered that the ego echoes with all its old habit patterns, wishing to re-form.

My work matured with the Diamond Approach. I had been introduced to Hameed Ali, the teacher, and felt very drawn to the teachings. The precision and clarity of the teachings spoke to my soul and gave me a very different understanding of what realization and enlightenment was. It wasn't this big, grand opening in the way that Osho described his awakening.

This work has been a grounding in the totality of one's experience. There's a shift out of earlier idealization of teachers and "the way" into an ever-deeper owning of our own way.

I once talked with a young student about returning from a retreat, where newer students were fawning over the charismatic teacher. It was interesting to see how in this generation coming up there is the need for that idealization and the shattering of it—both. And, then, we need to be able to heal the split and hold both.

My work with Hameed is challenging because it is humbling and very much an ego reduction. I began to train as a teacher within the Diamond Approach. I thought I was the one who was going to be the teacher—when I realized I was being erased and Being is the teacher.

It was a difficult challenge for a while to feel as though I was being used by Being. I felt like an instrument that Reality was using and that it didn't matter what I felt or did. What was coming through was what needed to happen, and I was not able to take any sense of personal accomplishment from that.

There was still very much a duality where I wasn't feeling that one-ness with Being. I had resentment and a lot of anger, in a way. Thank-fully, I'm not in that place now.

AFTER MANY YEARS of training for ordination within this lineage, Hameed told me that he was not going to ordain me. We were in the final period of ordination and I felt devastated. But it created this resolve in me that no matter what it would take, I was going to com-plete the ordination.

Three months later, Hameed came back and said he would ordain me. I asked him what changed and he said, "I don't know, but I know that I had to do it." But in that three-month period, I was helpless and confused and didn't know what to do.

It was very painful—I cried a lot. But really, it forged my practice—it was like the warrior in me came forth to do whatever it would take to complete my ordination.

That was the completion of a ten-year training. To actually come into the body of teachers was a very joyful experience. Now, once a year I have a retreat with my teacher and I enjoy being in his presence and receiving his teaching.

OVER THE YEARS, I have been very involved in hospice work. I began working with HIV-positive patients, in the years before much was known about it and it was considered a death sentence. It was a time of fear and I had a great deal of fear, too. But somehow I found a way to hold my fear so that I didn't bring it into the patient's room with me. I felt a "calling." I wanted to lessen fear.

One time, three people died on the same day and it felt like a war zone—I felt that I just couldn't keep doing this work. I read Ram Dass's *How Can I Help?* and it had a powerful impact on me. I felt that I wanted to give my time in service. I wanted to connect with the dying, with something bigger than myself. I wanted to bring presence to these patients and not shut down with the fear. I wanted to be with the dying—not in a role, but in full personhood.

I did a retreat on *Being with Dying* and felt the burden of my emotions case. I felt myself lighten and that I no longer needed to be so *responsible* for the way people died. I had been caught in what Ram Dass calls "the helper's prison," trapped in the "I have to fix it" mind. I found I could surrender to something bigger.

In that surrender, I found that I could be even more intimate with patients by being not so self-referential. I felt more present when "I" was not present. I found that I had stopped trying to manipulate the experience for myself or for the dying person. Something integrated inside me. Before I had felt that my spiritual path was separate from the world, from the life I was living—that stopped.

IN 2009, I was given a cancer diagnosis and was told I had three to six months to live. I thought I was relaxed about death, but my reaction to the diagnosis was total terror. I went into a self-referential, freeze response—the animal body's instinct. After that, I decided I would explore more about my medical condition, eventually coming to find that it was a misdiagnosis.

The whole experience was a gift. It was humbling and I was no longer so complacent. It deepened my practice because I saw I had more work to do.

I had a fear of being unlovable and my first reaction, when I still thought I had cancer, was that I did not want to let people know because of that fear. But friends challenged me to reach out and the incredible support I received challenged the belief about being unlovable. I let myself feel loved for the first time—I couldn't deny it anymore. I really took it in.

There was nothing I could do when the shock shattered my defense. When my armor was gone, love was able to penetrate and really change me.

Ellen

I REALLY THINK the call was always for something transcendent. I've learned, too, that it's immanent.

I've come to a place where I know I don't have to believe. I don't think everybody has to believe the same thing anymore, the way I used to.

Old habits still arise. A friend died of glioblastoma. His wife called me and asked if I would offer a reflection at his funeral. I was in a state about that—I was so blown away. I felt intimidated that there would be clergy there at the church funeral, but his wife said, "You understood his journey."

And I did. We both had cancer. Our eyes would connect sometimes at our meditation group and we would just silently grin at each other. We *knew*. I wanted to give a reflection that came from a place that wasn't my mind or what my mind wanted to say about it. I wanted my reflection to come from that place really deep within me, the place that my friend and I connected with and connected about.

It was mind-boggling to me. But I decided to say yes and I decided to trust.

I decided to trust that it's all part of the opening, the continuing, to the oneness that's each of us. That's what he and I knew. We knew it was much deeper than that he had cancer and I had cancer. We had touched something so far beneath that—where it didn't matter whether we had cancer or not.

IN THINKING about spiritual biography, my call was always for meaningful and deep connections that I had not experienced in normal relationships.

Maybe because of that, I have such a yearning for meaningful, real connection. I'm glad that I looked for it. There are a lot of places people look for that—such as in relationships or drugs, so many ways. I was graced in the way I looked for transcendence—through the texts and scriptures that were always meaningful to me, Centering Prayer, and going to India. I always looked for help when I felt alone or when I felt separate or overcome.

The way that I thought about transcendence changed over time. It was always changing. I looked first in a narrowly confined way to tradition. I looked within my own tradition and then within certain narrow expressions of it. I experimented a little bit with the charismatic movement, then with Bible studies that were more literal with an Evangelical approach. And then, slowly, things broadened. It all opened up—and the more it opened, the more there was.

I started with Centering Prayer in 1992. I saw that Basil Pennington, who was sort of a forerunner to Thomas Keating and the Centering Prayer movement, was coming to one of the churches in town. I went to his presentation and from that day forward, I have used Centering Prayer almost every day.

When I first tried meditation, I was so overwhelmed with monkey mind—it was hard. I thought I'd never make any progress with this huge monkey mind!

But I knew that it was a matter of discipline and grace. I knew that the more you meditated, the easier it became. And that's exactly how it is—it's like bending to touch your toes. You can't do it the first time, but if you try every day, eventually you can touch your toes.

I resonated with what Basil Pennington had to say and was drawn to the idea of contemplative practice. At that time all I knew about Centering Prayer was that it was one form of silent prayer beyond words. That's all I knew—but it called me.

When it's right, it's like you hear an inner call and can say, "Yes, that's for me." You just know—there's something that says, "This is for you to do."

I HAD THAT SAME resonance when my daughter invited me to India.

The very first time I went to be with my teacher Appa, I was carrying such deep grief and loss. I had decided that the marriage I was in was just not going to change and there was a four-year period after the divorce when I was in a deep, deep grief over all that had been lost, the dreams that were never realized. Often, during those years, I would sit down to meditate and I would just cry. That's all—I would cry. I realized that those tears were the grief of many years being shed.

Healing was definitely part of the process. It was about everything. I had a deep well of grief, but I had survived as a fairly strong person because I often disassociated from it. Meditation was a way to reconnect.

When I was home from India I was working, but I was single and had a lot of time to myself. I would sit to meditate every morning before I went to work and every evening when I got home. I cried often in those times; I just shed the grief—I let it go. Gradually, that heavy grief subsided and I was in a different place.

Connecting with the buried grief and allowing it to heal was a huge part of my journey. My whole journey has been toward wholeness—trying to be more whole and less separate, less divided. That was my search for meaning, transformation, and change.

FOR ME, change has always been exciting, wonderful, and something to be thankful for and hoped for. It's a flow—a spirit flow.

I'm seventy now and that's a lot of years. I've had a slow process toward inner healing and wholeness—trying to grasp what life really is and what it's not. I became absorbed in that flow.

Human beings are what they are—at the core, every ego is the same. Everybody has the same issues across the human spectrum. In India, where I used to go twice every year, after we meditated together there would be a question-and-answer session with the teacher in a large group. Appa's comments might be aimed at one particular issue or person but they applied to everybody. I learned a lot in that environment.

Meditation time, sitting, was your own internal process with Appa—he did not give a great deal of instruction. We had to sit with whatever arose. Sometimes at the beginning, we would sit for almost three hours. That's tough—a lot comes up, a lot of fear and anxiety. I took on meditation as a part of my journey toward the inner process of healing—an unloading of what Thomas Keating calls "personal garbage." If ever I got stuck in my meditation and needed to talk, I could. But the time was about sitting with myself, unloading all of that personal garbage, and then going deeper and deeper. It was experiential.

Things you didn't know, that you couldn't even recognize, were healed just by sitting with whatever arose. I learned to trust myself.

Though I didn't have a dependent relationship with Appa, I have to admit that there were times when I perceived him as an authority. Since I'd struggled with my father as an authority figure, I sometimes struggled with him in this way. But over time I became more and more able trust my inner self.

Amma would always say: "The true guru is within." It's not outside of you—the guru is wherever you are because it's within you. This helped me become aware that I could trust myself and my journey.

I BEGAN TO READ widely in other traditions and appreciate the wisdom I found in them. I had never heard the word *awakening* before— I'd heard *enlightenment* used, but it seemed like such a far-reaching thing, I couldn't think about it.

Over time the terms *awakening* and *awareness* became much more apparent to me—I began to realize that's what was happening in my journey. I was waking up, aware of what was in my mind in any moment. I was waking up to the reality of grace.

The point of my practice was to become aware, and then go where I was able to go with that awareness, and then practice some more. Slowly the distance shortened between my awareness of what I was thinking and feeling and how I was able to respond to it.

Practice is as much off the cushion as on the cushion. While I have established a practice on the cushion, it's important for me to stay in awareness when I'm not on the cushion—to watch. If all of a sudden I become reactive or angry, now I'm aware that something else is going on.

The homily I gave for my friend who died from cancer is a good example. At first, I was thrown back into the old bodily memories, my old reactions and fears. I talked with a few spiritual friends about this. One reminded me that my body holds all these memories; it is imprinted with them.

Healing occurs when our bodies are relieved from these fearful memories. The more we think about it, the worse it gets. Instead, we fall back into presence, into the body—which is where presence is in your form. When we can do this we're released from the mind that's fearful, self-doubting, and afraid of failing. This helped me on the day of my friend's funeral—it was my natural and not my contracted body that was present during the homily.

There are many words you can use, but everything is grace—absolutely everything. My own particular journey has been completely toward grace. I don't know how or why it happens this way, but I trust this grace.

Reflections on the Third Quarter

ONCE AGAIN, we see remarkable differences in the outer circumstances of each who shared as well as differences in language and views describing inner and secret processes of transformation. Each worked with what resonated with him or her.

All authentic paths lead home. The stories shared also illustrate the remarkable similarities of realizations and shifts in both identity and cognition as these teachers and practitioners emerged into spiritual maturity.

The energetic shifts of transformative processes drop us out of conceptuality, allowing our attention to rest increasingly in our hearts. We come to know love. Love calls us, heals us, and makes it safe for us to be who we are. We change our place of reference from ego to essence. Essence, as nondual teacher Adyashanti notes, "means the truth of you as opposed to the untruth of you." It is neither complicated nor inaccessible.

Further healing, growing equanimity, and a more pervasive embodiment and actualization of realizations characterize this third quarter in each person's spiritual biography.

For a time, spiritual idealization can move us further toward that which we idealize. Eventually, though, such idealization has to shatter. As it shatters, "complexity" vanishes and the path is revealed in its simplicity and profound fulfillment. No longer seeking, we simply see.

Eighteenth-century Zen master Hakuin reminds us, "Not knowing how near Truth is, people seek it far away." In the third quarter of a spiritual journey, we begin to live in truth. We begin to join Hakuin in his recognition that "all beings are, from the very beginning, buddhas."

Jacob Boehme, as Cynthia reminds us, calls this quarter of anyone's awakening journey "working in the wonders." There's no room for cosmologies or theologies. There is simply, moment by moment, the next wonder of bare experience. Surrender—of cosmologies, theologies, mistaken beliefs, and our tendency to cling to self and conceptual mind—gives rise to wonder. Wonder is alive and exhilarating. We surf the waves of Presence, the wind blowing through us.

The path becomes more filled with ease, an awakened stance more ordinary. This sense of ordinariness arises within spiritual maturity. We simply *experience*, rather than searching for an "experience" we deem suitably "spiritual."

With so many habit patterns and mistaken beliefs cleared by grace from the space of our attention, we follow wisdom's lead in more and more of our lives, enter ever more deeply into Being. Rodney Smith notes, "Life turns around to meet itself and pull us through the ignorance that our minds have created."

Thomas Keating calls the transformative energy of grace "divine therapy." On this endless journey of illumination, as we allow that transformative energy to work upon us, we become able to receive and bear and integrate increasing levels of grace's unfathomable majesty.

During this time of maturation, we respond to our inner and outer challenges—those waves are never going to stop—with more mindfulness. There is more compassion in our responses, more willingness to accept that there is a measure of suffering—predictable suffering—to bear in every human life. In this quarter of ripening, we honor our own painful challenges while maintaining a sense of perspective in this suffering world.

We entered into a new sense of *value* with the healing work of the second and third quarters. Delivered to a new and deep integration of shadow and persona, a greater lightness hovers about the quirks of our individuality, an acceptance of the limps that remain even after the fractures have healed. We surrender to who we are and experience the great liberation of ordinariness.

Presence, the capacity to *be* present, arises in the third quarter. Healing continues during our time of spiritual maturation as we approach the bedrock of our wounds. As this healing ensues, we integrate body and mind in self-forgetfulness. Presence manifests naturally when the divine flow is no longer blocked by self's interference, when there are only remaining wisps of self-reference, when we show up fully and undefended with all our scars.

In Japan, there is an old and beautiful aesthetic of repairing broken ceramic pieces with gold. Rather than trying to repair the cracks by matching the original color, trying to mask the repair, the cracks are filled with gold and become visibly highlighted. The process is called *kintsugi* and it yields its own "survivor" beauty. The experience of *value* is the experience of our own survivor beauty. It is not easy to be a person.

THE FOURTH QUARTER:
Ripening

Hope starts the journey.
Faith sustains it.
But it ends beyond both hope and faith.

—RAM DASS

Introduction

⸻⸻⸻⸻⸻⸻ ⟨∞⟩ ⸻⸻⸻⸻⸻⸻

THE FOURTH QUARTER of each of our journeys is a time of ripening. Outwardly and expressively, it may look quite different for each of us. The ripening pours through our unique individuality. Inwardly, in inner and secret ways, the realized awareness of ripening is of the same taste—liberation.

Some people attain renown and deep respect, sharing their wisdom with others who are also walking a spiritual path. Some are utterly unsung except by those fortunate enough to be in their close karmic circle. Some quietly and continuously practice the Four Immeasurables—Buddhist practices of love, compassion, joy, and equanimity—while others walk by us through airports and the grocery store silently sending blessings.

I think of many others who have returned to their own playfulness, their own original ease. When we deeply realize our commonality, our individuality comes out to play.

In the fourth quarter of a spiritual journey, trust is alive and well in us. Trust permeates us when we cease believing in the frightening illusions of separation.

As we ripen, we find ourselves increasingly unwilling to remain confined within survival mode only. The call of the self is heard more mindfully and less seductively. The siren song is seen for what it is. The confluence of surrender and awareness makes its beneficial appearance over and over, with growing effortlessness.

Ripening, we come to fruition. We embody our deepest realizations, allowing the sacred formless to shine through the form that we are—that form not other than the sacred formless. We rest in that immeasurable refuge. We become illuminated. There arises a deep recognition that there is no difference, save what the mind imputes, between transcendence and immanence, between sacred and mundane, between self and other. We rest at the zero point, the locus of a liberated life.

In Being, we are increasingly luminous in the essence of our individuality. Our very body becomes a vehicle of spirit. We know ourselves as grace—an ancient truth newly known to us and, through us, newly available to all we meet.

Buddhism speaks of a ripened being as a *bodhisattva*, one who has embodied *bodhichitta*—a mind wishing to discard self-reference, enter Being, and serve all other beings. In Tibetan Buddhism, a tradition of many lists, there is a list of the benefits of bodhichitta. One of the benefits is "all beings will bow before you." I used to wonder why anyone would want others to bow before them. One day I realized that bodhichitta was such a profound attainment—the most beautiful and meaningful use of a human life—that anyone would be stirred to bow before it.

We all need to honor our own bodhichitta, perhaps only as tiny as an apple seed now, but here and growing nonetheless.

A heart of bodhichitta is the ripened fruit of a spiritual journey.

The fruit is shared in communion.

Rodney

WORKING WITH THE DYING was a healing process for me. It wasn't only about coming to terms with death and dying for myself, but also about the interpersonal aspect of being with very, very sick people.

I knew I had to stay working in hospice even though my temptation was to buckle at the knees around people who were that infirm. I learned how to work with the heart, in a refreshing kind of way, so that I could stay present with each patient and also release their suffering when I went on to visit the next person.

I learned that I could not be there for the next person if I was still ruminating about the last one.

I would sit there in front of a family that had different emotions coming up, depending upon the patient—how old they were and what their relationships were. As the social worker I was working often with the emotional reactivity of a family that was never going to be the same.

I could feel the impact of having worked with those family members in their pain. But since my job covered a whole sector, I worked with about twenty-five patients and their families at any given time. I would have to get in my car after one visit, knowing that the next family I was going to see needed me to be present with them in exactly the same way that the previous family had. Unless I learned to release what had just happened, I couldn't be there for the next person.

That drive between homes became a time for me to learn what love, real compassion, is about. Generally, we like to draw it out—to think about it, reflect upon it, ponder over the misery we have seen, and somehow that gives us a sense of having been in touch with sorrow.

But that's not real compassion. Compassion isn't in the reflective mode, it's in the immediate connection. And that immediate connection needs to be refreshed. As I was driving from one home to the next, I was essentially learning how to drop the first home so that I could be present, with my heart fully attuned to the second home, and on and on.

The impulse to turn away from such suffering is almost genetic. My interest in the subject of death and dying was my salvation. I couldn't turn away from a subject I was interested in, even though everything inside of me wanted to at first.

I learned to find some equanimity in my car as I drove from home to home. I was learning to open my heart—but only for as long as I was with a hospice family. It didn't last all day.

I would come home and be irritated and annoyed. I was missing the opportunity to step over the boundary of hospice care and bring compassion and equanimity into everyday interactions. I thought my "real" attention needed to be with the hospice family, not with the rest of the world. Well, that's not true, and as I learned how to do that, everything came into focus.

MY NEXT STEP was opening my heart. I call it "the full engagement of insight."

In the heart, all the qualities come together. In the heart there's spaciousness—none of the walls or boundaries that I lived with for much of the time.

There are times when I get lost, just as anyone else does. But the sense of limitation and confinement that I felt as a young person isn't there anymore. I don't live with a sense of personal limitation, because where the person used to be, now there's just vastness.

This doesn't mean I'm special in any way—it's no different for anyone else. This vastness is universally shared—and into that vastness comes the response of the heart. You might say the response of the heart *is* that vastness.

Opening the heart also brings us into an immediacy, because the vastness is lost when we start talking in terms of past and future. We lose ourselves in the designation of words when we identify things and fixate based on those words. There's a quiet and stillness in consciousness that has uprooted the limitations of self—which is the same as nonseparation.

When we open the door of stillness, all these things come in at once. They're not separately attained.

My teaching now is focused on how to perceive interconnection or, said differently, nonseparation, rather than to keep applying the laws from the paradigm of separation in order to get to nonseparation. There's a whole set of rules and intentions that must be present in order to step out of that existing conventional paradigm of separation into the stillness of just being.

Those two paradigms coexist quite nicely together—they are actually inseparable. Taught together, there is less conflict and struggle. This works well within the world of form, even though much of the time spent in meditation is in kind of a formless awareness.

Formlessness doesn't interfere with form—form conflicts with form. If I'm "me," I have a lot of problems with other people and objects around "me." But if I don't manifest as an individual "separate from," then there isn't any conflict with other people or objects.

With formlessness, there's a peacefulness and an ease that's hard to speak about.

THERE HAVE BEEN some significant turning points in my maturation. I had invitations to continue on the circuit of retreat teaching, but that's not where my understanding is anymore.

My understanding is not that we need special environments in order to mature, although at some points special environments are very helpful. I want to stand in the declaration of the proximity of our full engagement of life. One thing I do know without any question is that freedom is here and now. It's not something to be attained. That takes a different way of teaching.

In some ways, I've kind of grown into what Nisargadatta was telling me thirty years ago.

I make a special effort not to complicate this. How complicated is seeing? We're letting the seeing move us into deeper levels of understanding and wisdom. There's nothing complex about it.

What's complex is being willing to see. That's where skillful means come in, and all of the other methods and techniques. Once we've established the need and the intention to see, we then ask questions about what it is that we're not seeing and what we want to see. Seeing itself is the whole basis of spiritual unfolding.

I deeply honor people's skillful means, their methods, because that's their expression of their understanding. Skillful means are ways to settle us down sufficiently so that we're willing to see. If we have a lot of self-hatred, for instance, we're not going to want to look at who we are or at our emotional life—we think all it will do is confirm our worst fears that we're as bad as we think we are.

Most of us journey forward by using skillful means to dampen that reactivity. That way we are willing to look into areas that had up until then been too frightening.

At some point, maturity does not move *from* anything. That's a crucial time in our practice—when we realize that whatever state of mind is arising within us we can't move from, because as soon as we do, we've made it into something other than the illusion of what we believe it to be.

When I sit, I'll have a state of mind come up and I can see my tendency to start moving from that state of mind. I'll catch myself and say, "Okay, let the stillness do the action." I have to see through the transparency of the state of mind.

That state of mind is the acknowledgment of the form as it's arising. If I invest into that with any reactivity, the state of mind becomes something very personal and I then act out a narrative around what that state of mind is telling me. But if I arrest that movement and fall into stillness, the state of mind has no traction to continue. It dissipates so I can move forward from the quiet rather than from what I have believed about myself.

Seeing is a multipurpose tool. I've learned that it allows release and healing, and needs to be reinforced again and again. My own tendency was to not just see but want to do something about what I saw. I thought I needed to take some action, to search it out. I needed to justify it even being in my consciousness—and I think that's the way we all think.

But it all goes back to the true nature of reality—that whatever we're seeing has come from, and been a projection from, the consciousness, the seer. If I do something about the thing I'm seeing, perhaps an emotion or a person, any object outside of myself, I'm actually tampering with my own consciousness. I'm trying to reestablish some sense of steadiness within my consciousness so that I can see this thing in the way I want to see it.

There's self again. We learn to be quiet with things and therefore our consciousness becomes quiet with things—so that our consciousness and the thing merge together in nonseparation and are no longer at odds. Real healing ultimately arises from stillness, rather than from acting out and from the self.

Awakening teachings need to be elegantly simple. We need to understand awakening with the metaphors of our time associated with it. I think what's happened in my tradition is, with twenty-five hundred years of editorializing and commentary, I just don't know whose opinion I'm getting anymore. I knew that I had to discover it completely independent of the *suttas*—Buddha's teachings, recorded three hundred years after they were given.

At different times, the need or the urgency to be free creates the projection of freedom onto something that might be a catharsis, or just an emotional high.

A lot of energy comes through us in meditation. As we begin to release some of the blockages and begin to heal, that trapped energy comes out and sometimes it fools us completely as to what is happening within us. Many times in my own practice, I thought, "This is a liberating moment," because I was extraordinarily high from some insight that I was having or some passion I was feeling, or even the energy that was being released.

Some people are difficult to redirect at these times, but I sensed that this was not the end. No matter what came up, I had the feeling that it was merely an experience. I knew that if this was true, then two things were happening here: me, and the experience I was having. That wasn't the end—so I kept marching forward. But I saw many people, including teachers, get sidetracked with these false nirvanas.

Many of us work with the mistaken idea that awakening is a place to land. But there *is* no place to land—the very place of landing is itself conventional reality. We always try to land somewhere firm and stable so that nothing changes, but that's the definition of ignorance.

When we get sidetracked like this and we have a lot of emotions pent up, we can get the sense of renewal. Often, false nirvanas are renewing. I'm not in any way criticizing them—they're part of everyone's practice and path. They can be important when they release a certain energy that has built up and created a false boundary in ourselves.

When that false boundary breaks, we feel healing and reconnectedness—that something is coming together that wasn't there before. The heart elevates. We feel the real joy of practice—becoming more conscious. Those are tremendously important times. We just need to remember that we must still keep walking.

WE PRACTICE to ensure we have an appropriate container for realizations. There are energetic changes that come with awakening.

One of the ways I conceive of the journey is as a movement from form—the designation and specificity of phenomena, even "me"—to formlessness, the abiding grace of presence.

Everything is arising from the same *is*-ness, you might say. As we shift our energy out of designation and specificity, calling something "something" and fixating our life upon it, when we release the need to arrest ourselves upon particular points in our chronological history, we effortlessly move toward the formless. We don't invest our energy in the form anymore because we've seen the limitation and the pain associated with that investment.

This doesn't take effort. Our energy automatically retracts itself from constant form formation and goes to the only place it can—the formless. We start seeing things coming together in ways that we never could when we were invested only in form.

This energy is heart energy—the energy of all the *paramis*, the Ten Perfections, or qualities leading to enlightenment.

Formless awareness carries all of the things we've ever wanted: patience, love, compassion, and joy. But if we haven't completely seen the end of form, form will then come back in and claim a personal identification with that arising.

When we grasp onto formless arising, we'll think, "Oh, I'm joyous! I'm more loving!" We try to arrest ourselves upon this new plateau, this false but pleasant nirvana. Not until we see through this as a limitation, just as we have all the other false summits, are we free to move on.

Ours is a natural unfolding, but it's one that never stops. It's not as if we can say, "Now I can start seeing in form again." Instead, form and formlessness begin to coincide. It's as if you want to know how to get back to your car—the memory is there. You know which car is yours, where it is parked, and how to drive it. All the mechanics—the designations—are there. Yet you don't need to fixate on your mind so that it becomes the officiator of what you do.

Form rests within the formless. It's never singly determined to be "something"—there's always a mystery associated with the object. We can see an object, but it isn't just what our mind says it is any longer. Form has a glow of mystery as well.

LIKE ANYONE, I've lost significant people throughout my life and unsettling things have happened. I know I'm going to die. I don't live under the illusion that I'm somehow saved from any catastrophe.

I no longer think, "Why is this happening to me?" I don't say that. Things happen, and "the happening" can be hard. I still face challenging times, but it's no longer tragic and conflicted somehow. I don't feel the wish for life to be different than it is or long for a different time in my life.

But I do feel all the emotions of life—of loss and grief—in the losing.

Openhearted contact with life is going to move us into tender areas—like grief. Some emotions don't arise as strongly in me anymore—those emotions of separation, based upon conflict. But I don't see that emotions that come from tenderness, like grief, are any limitation on me at all.

In fact, any time I pull back from the tender areas, what I'm doing is pulling back into thought. That's the only place we can pull back into. I'll then reflect upon life in some kind of objective way, thinking, "Oh, if my life were just better than it is now." That brings me into sorrow and conflict. Then jealousy, anger, and resentment—all of these separate emotions—come into play. Since I don't often try to pull back from tenderness, that doesn't happen very much for me anymore.

The biggest forgiveness work I had to do was with myself. It's a skillful means that I've certainly used many times in my life. I have many occasions in my life when I look back and think, "What was going on in me in that moment to have me act in that way?" Those occasions become tethers, decade-long tie-ins to a particular thing I did that becomes rigidly defined.

I work with these moments differently now. I hold the situation, along with grief or sorrow or shame about it, and let that memory just sit in my consciousness without trying to adapt a new story to identify with.

This can be unpleasant—I wiggle a lot—but the steam comes off of it. I've noticed over time that if I don't move from that memory, somehow my consciousness starts accommodating the circumstances around it to the point that awareness and wisdom come through. I see that I couldn't have acted any differently, that I was stuck somewhere when I did that particular thing. I can finally forgive myself because I acted the only way I could, even if it was troublesome at the time.

When we forgive ourselves like this, we're really forgiving a different person—the person we used to be. We're no longer that person. We would act differently now.

This process is refreshing. Now I look for anything in consciousness that still needs that kind of attention and complete ease, because now I'm fully confident that it's only stillness and quiet that allow full healing to take place.

As things come into consciousness that I feel are not adapting, I certainly turn my attention to them. I no longer feel the conflict I used to. There's a lot more stillness. The way I perceive the world is different.

While everything has changed, I still move through the world the same as I always have. With this practice you don't lose your personal memory. The mind doesn't go blank, but I don't think people realize that. Some people feel like they're going to have to give up a lot, even their memory, but that's still in place. Those memories just don't define where I stand any longer—they're about my formation but not about my formlessness. My formlessness has never changed, really. It hasn't altered one bit in the course of my lifetime. I just grew into understanding it and then relaxed with it.

AWAKENING IS a shift in identity. I designate two things. First, there's the journey of awakening we're all on, toward something that we may not have very clear reference to, or understanding of, exactly how we're going to get there. There's something pulling us out of ourselves into a different orientation to the world. In this way the spiritual path, if it is authentic, is a path of awakening.

Second, there are awakened moments within that path—when the veil of life is so thin there's a tear between one paradigm and another. This happens to everyone—and it happens with sincerity. You can't decide when it's going to happen, but our practice creates a fertile ground for these moments.

In these awakened moments the heart has gotten so close, it doesn't put any distractions between itself and the quiet that's there. The veil gets thin and, at some point, it ruptures. When it ruptures the first time, everything turns upside down. There's a shift of identity outside of the egoic sense of "me" and we see the seat of where all life comes from. We see that that all life comes from the unconditioned, and you see it birthing "me" and everyone.

That sight—that moment—throws everything into question. Once you've seen yourself flipped 180 degrees, you can never come back and fully believe the way you used to relate to yourself.

This awakening speeds up the journey. Now there's no questioning where you're going and how to get there.

Often what happens to me, after a tear like that, is that the tear closes back up and I find myself back in the conventional paradigm, doing pretty much what I always did—except with a memory of what occurred. I can't settle back into things in the same way. It's more than a memory—something shifted energetically.

Then I find I can't take life as seriously anymore—not in the way most people do. Then I work diligently and linearly to open up an abiding presence to that shift in paradigms. I meet everything with stillness, because I've realized that that other paradigm exists in stillness. I use the only tool I know from that new paradigm—which is stillness and quiet—to meet everything.

I don't want anyone to feel as if they're missing something—everything in our own spiritual journey is what it looks like to awaken. We all have to go through a lot of different experiences, turmoil, and judgment. In its completion, that's what awakening looks like. We'll have moments within that process when the journey gets very interesting, one of those being the shift of paradigms.

No one should get upset about where they are in the spiritual journey. If we each apply our own understanding to what's in front of us and are willing to see what's there, our consciousness will mature all along the way. And that's all there is.

Cynthia

WHILE I WOULDN'T SAY that suffering causes the path, I think it's a way in which the thing begins to get set in motion. The cover, our boredom or smugness with the status quo, gets ripped away. A. H. Almaas speaks about "the enlightenment drive" in each one of us. I 100 percent agree with him.

This drive is as fierce as crabgrass pushing through the tarmac. It's there because each of us is coming from God from the start. We are a little slice of Divine Purpose wanting to find and express itself in form. This drive is as deeply rooted inside us as our breathing and our heart pumping.

We get out of touch with this by the way our life tends to be set up by the circumstances that we live in. This is the natural journey of developing this ego consciousness, which we need to navigate here. We forget the divine enlightenment drive—so we tend to get lost, floating on the river of space-time, and we buy into what Madison Avenue or the internet or anything tells us is the meaning of human life. The depth dimension gets moved right out.

Suffering is often exactly what makes it impossible to float along in the pretense anymore. Very few people wake up when they're comfortable.

I would say that most of my suffering is what Gurdjieff would call "stupid suffering" or what Helen Luke would call "neurotic suffering." It's the kind of suffering that gets induced in your life, the kind of drama when your little ego self, your agendas and emotional programs for happiness, gets in the driver's seat. Of course, they bring you into a headlong crash with life.

A lot of the suffering I experienced as drama for the first forty-five years of my life stemmed from my immature and distorted visions of what true love was, and from unaddressed business about self-esteem and affection. I just kept making mistakes. One of my Buddhist friends says it's like squeezing the cactus.

When that kind of stupid or neurotic suffering combines with the enlightenment drive that's always there underneath the surface, then it is possible to use the disruption—what calls us to attention through the suffering—to refocus. Then we come deeply in touch with that sense that's carrying us and has been carrying us all along.

Suffering has always been the ground in which awakening happens—as it certainly was in my life.

IN MY RELATIONSHIP with my teacher, I found that he had no patience with my false self's distorted visions of what true love meant. Yet he was committed to me, so I began to feel an intuitive trust.

I could relax into our relationship and drop the defenses that John Welwood, in his wonderful book *Toward a Psychology of Awakening*, calls our "soul cages"—the primordial postures that we adopt to get through life with all our brokenness. These cages can only be thawed by love—either a love drawn on directly from the Cosmos as we gradually awaken, or the guiding love of another human being that springs us free. My life has been fortunate to have been blessed with both types of grace.

When I go back and look at the narrative of my childhood, I felt that sense of unconditional love lacking. I never felt that it was truly there, or that my parents were able to be comfortable in their own skins around me or even fully there in their being.

I experienced a love that was contingent upon performance—like so many kids—and never felt safe. I had a strong spiritual drive from the time I was a kid. I coped with this in the only way I could figure out how—by becoming strong in myself.

The downside of that posture, of course, is that I was unable to fully enter into giving and receiving—which is the rhythm of a healed and whole life. That had to break down. It happens that way for everybody. We all draw a different set of deformity cards and then we have to play our hands. It's not the question of "if" we'll get a card, but rather which ones we got. Although we don't get instructions for the game, after a while we begin to recognize the cards that are not serving us well and begin to improve our hand.

MY DAUGHTERS UNDERSTAND me only too well—though in the same way that people say it's amazing how much your parents grow up when you're between the ages of eighteen and twenty-one. Well, it's amazing how much your daughters grow up when you're between the ages of fifty and sixty. We all seem to have a kind of myopia—we understand and we don't understand. We tend, particularly when we're young, to come up against each other as friction points.

My daughters know the depth of me. But this is difficult for all parent-child relationships because for them to know the depth of me I also acknowledge the depth of them. At this particular stage of their life's journey, where each is very much engaged in making a successful marriage and raising children, sometimes you have to put the siren call on hold.

Because I wouldn't put the siren call on hold—I accepted the universe as untidy and chaotic—their lives have been, in a kind of funny way, about picking up the pieces of my own life. I caused a lot of damage as I bounced around early in life—but I kept striving toward what it was that was striving to be born inside.

Just as I got my agenda from my mother—I reacted against her Christian Science and social convention and conformism—my daughters got their agendas from me.

My own reactive and freewheeling life created some pain for my daughters. They tried to hold the line and not be chaotic and self-indulgent. They've given themselves to a path that requires a certain distancing from what has been at the heart of my own journey.

It all comes around. I reinterpret old Saint Augustine's unpopular doctrine of original sin as simply the web of woundedness. Then it makes perfect sense. As we grow in love, we move toward forgiveness.

There's no human being on the planet who doesn't carry some piece of woundedness—it's not a matter of my daughters, my mother, or me being defective or failing to do something. Original sin—our web of woundedness—simply refers to how we all have to peck our way out of the eggshells by whatever means.

THE EXPERIENCE of being in community with others has been grace—absolute grace. Some of the huge turning points in my life have occurred in connection, when I've stood in the presence of a person who looked through the surface and saw the depth, and then loved me at that depth and called that depth into being, into accountability.

Of the many encounters I have had like this, one was with a woman who saw my depth when everyone else only saw my surface manifestations. She saw I had a real yearning that she could work with, so she took me under her wing as a student. Of course more than anyone else, my beloved teacher Rafe, whom I write about in *Love Is Stronger Than Death*, saw me at that depth.

These people have created in their lives a space where depth isn't scary—it's the familiar ground where people meet. I think those people are like an invisible underground river through which we all are swept along toward our full fruition.

While of course sangha, our spiritual community, is important, I also think that your path will come to you. A lot of people read books and say, "I've got to find a sangha." Immediately, an urgency and constriction drops down that gets deflected. As soon as anything is done with a sense of "I need" or "I have to have," it's going to be distorted by the ego.

I found it most useful to say, "Well, God is with you, because God is at the helm and in the energy of this whole transformation." If we can simply do what's on our plate and trust in the goodness of the unfolding of the Cosmos, what we need will be there. It may shock us and come in untextbook forms, but we won't be left high and dry as long as we keep listening.

To learn to do this through repeated practice allows us a sense of ease. Here, in our own ground, we're connected with everything. We must discover that in our own being. That's our life's purpose.

I've HAD MY TIMES of discouragement along with everyone else—what the Christian journey calls the "dark night of the soul." These times are purifying. During the years after my beloved teacher's death, I developed a deep, protracted discouragement. I had to move away from the monastery where I'd lived nearby him and take off to a different land—to British Columbia, where I lived and worked with a wonderful group of people called the Contemplative Society.

I knew I had to break the mold. It was an inner imperative that kept pushing me back on course. I knew that if I had stayed at the side of the monastery, sifting through the ashes of my teacher's earthly life, I'd have been on a path to death.

To actually choose to leave—to pack up my belongings into the car and start over on a shoestring in a new country—was more than I bargained for. The seven years I spent in British Columbia were some of the most beautiful learning years of my life. The path I'm walking now was tried in the fire there.

For most of those years, I didn't feel I was in a compatible environment—everything was just a little bit off, slightly out of tune with the way my own system was tuned. My friendships were formal and not close. I was living in this edgy space where I knew I had to be, but it was discouraging in the classic meaning of the word—with *coeur* meaning the heart.

This period did not involve obvious heart-beating for me. My weary self-reliance came back again. It was like a long winter in some ways, which is a classic feature of the spiritual journey. It's not *if* this dark night is going to happen—it's *how* it will come into your life.

This helped me discover what it means to surrender. I was moving away from my old attachment to trying to find meaning in relationships. That serial monogamy finally died.

This period marked the beginning of my ability to actually occupy a post and teach with authority, as I learned how to draw from deeper resources—unimaginable resources—to be able to know what I knew. It was a time of yielding, of tremendous creativity, as I learned to draw on the energy of that larger life, the energy of prayer and attention and boundaryless love. I felt the objective love from my teacher's continued presence, rather than looking for codependent, dramatic relationships, sentiment, or romance. Basically, I grew up.

There's a wonderful quote from Rene Doumal, in the Gurdjieff tradition: "The path to our heart's desire often lies through the undesirable." I found that so true! Although this period was emotionally difficult, I never for an instant doubted its coherence. I understood clearly that to bolt back to the monastery where I had lived with my teacher would be spiritual death. Although it was trying in the desert, I never came up against that most fundamental trying-ness of it not making sense. It always made excruciating sense.

A sense of inner coherence guided me along. I put up with the abrasions and the wounds of the surface because I knew they were moving me along in the only way they could.

My time in the desert was good for me. I entered it a cosmic orphan and I came back a hermit.

FOR ME, the stunning discovery was that I had to stop listening with my mind—even with my emotions. I had to start listening through my body. By the body, I don't mean just the natural, organic health of this physical body, I mean the inner body inside you that's already there.

Before we can listen with this second body, we have to develop the capacity to do so physiologically, by means of a neurological rewiring. Until then, we live in conceptualization and drama—period. We think our heart is about feelings—which are really our stuck emotions. We think they're reliable, when in reality our mind is spinning out scenarios one after another, confusing meaning with logical outcome.

But our body—once we've learned to tune into it—can discern if we're listening with a constricting or nonconstricting ego, if we're listening with coherence or noncoherence. Once we've learned how to do that, then the inner listening follows automatically because when we're not living in the ego constriction that throws us back into story, we find that our heart is always broadcasting true and clear. It's a holograph of the Divine Heart.

I come back to what is simple—using meditation practice as the beginning of learning how to embody awareness.

I call this embodied awareness "majesty"—it is a measure of our actualized essence, the path actually traveled. It is created by awakening to self, playing out the hand dealt by essence. Embodied awareness is brought about by engaging life fully—with all our skill and courage—in order to draw forth the great secrets of God hidden in the potentiality of our human form. With it, we have the power of actualization, "the conscious shaping of the vessel that bears the light of Christ."

In my life it has been important to understand what it means—what it feels like—to conceptualize and live in my head. This was an early defense for me, but during those early years of practicing, in the Gurdjieff work, discovering a new body of information changed my life. I remember positing great ideas as we sat in group circle only to be asked quite simply, "Where are your feet when you're doing that?"

I used to get angry because I thought I was putting forth these great ideas and their questions seemed rude. It took me years to realize that I was using—like so many of us in Western culture—these great edifices of mental and emotional construction and calling that reality.

I finally learned simple embodiment—how to use my whole being to orient myself to a world of truth. I anguish so much for people who've grown up in authoritarian church structures and others who've been taught to distrust their own spiritual authority.

Theology has made it complicated to trust your own spiritual authority—we're told that until we go to seminary and get a degree, we can't possibly understand these truths. Because we're told "Father knows best," I've watched people with deep spiritual wisdom not be able to trust or even recognize what gifts they have. They have been programmed to disenfranchise their own wisdom in favor of intellectual and theological mazes.

I want to encourage people to trust their own authority, to enjoy their own maps, to allow God to unfold them as God is unfolding them and not to worry about whether they're following an external template correctly.

I think of spiritual maturation and ripening as "the reconciliation of pure interiority with the conscious exercise of our gifts."

This means we must not be afraid to make mistakes. Our mistakes become grist for the mill—even the worst acting out, the howlers, the choices that you look back on in your life and say, "Oh my God, how could I do that?" I remember seeing an epitaph on an old lady's grave in Boston. It said, "Here lies the grave of Miss Effie Jones. / For her, hell held no terrors, / Born a virgin, died one, too, / No hits, no runs, no errors." We have to step up to the plate, even if we strike out.

AGING PRESENTS an interesting new curve ball. At this point, I'm the same age as my beloved teacher, Rafe, was when I first met him. He loved Helen Luke's book *Old Age*, and he borrowed her phrase "growing into age." I realized that his real challenge was to let go of a self-image based on bodily ruggedness, based on another time of his life. He liked to be the cowboy, yet all his habits of wary independence were dependent on a certain physical well-being that was fading. Now here I am twenty years later watching that process in myself.

I never saw that when I could count on my physical vitality as part of who I was. I've realized that we unconsciously construct our identity based on temporality. That's the great gift that aging can unmask.

The cosmic cowboy Rafe finally had to ask for help. By doing so he began to discover his gifts for gentleness and nurturance. I can see already how I'm developing much in same way. Many of my habits and even the great privileges of my being are not at all who I am. They're an easy kind of collusion with my nature. As I age I know a further unmasking will occur.

I live alone out on a beautiful island. I have to be strong enough to carry water even when it's frozen much of the year. I have to be able to chop wood, keep my firewood in order, and navigate around. I realize that if my physical strength were to fall below a certain threshold, I couldn't continue to live on the island anymore.

For a person whose spiritual life has always been based on being in my own space as a hermit, that's a wildcard.

There are some stern imperatives and invitations in old age—if you're willing to step up to the plate. Aging is the ultimate unmasking if you have the stomach to see it for what it is. Everything you thought you were, you see you aren't. It pulls you more directly into the question, "Well, who am I then? What *does* sustain underneath the flow of time?" When we find that, we can zoom out and see what was always there under the seasons of our life. But we won't find it until everything else is taken away.

We can step beyond all the ravages of time into the eternal presence that is love. Something else remembers us and holds us.

Llewellyn

I DID NOT KNOW anything when the journey began, I only had the intense longing of a young man. Now, after almost fifty years, I hardly know more. Maybe I have experienced a little of the grace of God and know that we are taken to God by God, taken to love by love, rather than through our own effort.

But at the beginning, I had no sense of God and no experience of love, so these words would have meant nothing. I know now that it is important to stay true to our desire for God, for Truth, knowing that this desire belongs to God, to Truth.

This is for me the great mystery of the path—that our longing is His longing, our desire for Truth is Truth's desire for us. From Rumi: "Sultan, saint, pickpocket; love has everyone by the ear dragging us back to God in secret ways. I never knew that God, too, desires us."

Few words can be said about this deeper journey, the real birth. Our language, our images, even our feelings belong to the ego and its relationship to the world. They help us understand *our* place in the world and *our* life's journey. The divine, that eternal presence that is always here and yet continually reveals Itself anew, is a mystery beyond words, something that can be hinted at but hardly told. But looking back on this story I have told of my journey, I feel more clearly the presence of love, I sense its light behind the incidents and happenings of the way, how it was pushing me to make itself known.

THERE IS A DEEP and profound relationship between our individual journey and global transformation. Our individual journey is part of a greater journey—the evolution of the whole. Nothing is separate.

The soul of the seeker and the soul of the world are being drawn together more closely: a global oneness is coming nearer to our consciousness.

The planet is a living spiritual being of which we are a part. We cannot abuse it anymore. We were asked to be guardians of the planet and we need to step into that relationship. This will mean something different to each of us, yet each of us needs an attitude of respect for both the planet and ourself. There is a spiritual light within human beings that can speak to the light in the world.

Real mysticism is practical. The question to ask ourselves is "How can I be in service to God and to the world?" We need to listen to life's wisdom, to be present, attentive, aware, discovering our own unique connection to life's sacred dimension.

There is something profoundly beautiful about the part we play in the process of God making Himself known to Himself in the fragile container of the human being—the human side of the divine drama.

I had hoped that the human being, the "I," would dissolve completely. Although there have been inner experiences of completely dissolving, being lost so completely that it would appear that nothing could ever be found again, each time there has been a return to something essentially human, some segment of self.

My person is very different from the fragmented human being who began the journey those years ago, and yet at the same time there is an essential similarity. The meaning of this return, the part the human plays in this divine unfolding, seems to be one of the great mysteries.

I return over and over to the question of what the human secrets reveal. We mix the endlessness of love with the ordinariness of life. I would like to say that this is all of the story, this return to the simplicity of our self. It has the quality of a return to Eden, recapturing the innocence of a childhood we may have never had. But what of the person who has made the journey? Does anything remain of the traveler?

I have come to believe that even when every image of ourself has dissolved, there is still a story that has a meaning and a purpose. Love's journey brings many scars, often scars in the heart, and they do not all fade away even if their drama has lessened. They tell us something about what it means to be human. They are an essential part of our human mystical experience, our deepest knowing of our self.

For so long I tried to leave myself behind, but always something remained, calling me back. Again and again, I tried to avoid it, tried to purify it with love, dissolve it with light. Yet it still remained, as if its story needed to be told, its meaning uncovered.

THIS IS WHERE I AM at the moment, with wonder and sadness—I know that there is part of my own story that is still waiting. Who is this person who is present at this place, whose light is part of the light of God even as I need to live it in my own small life?

For me, to live this love between human and Divine is the love story of the Beloved. For me, to live this love story is to be present "where the two seas meet," to hold this tension, this paradox. Here, in this meeting of the infinite ocean of divine love with the frailty of my human self, in my own heart and mind and body, His love story is being told—told to me, for me, and through me. What can I continue to do with my life but live this love story of my Beloved?

Sherry

AGAIN, I FOUND MYSELF in a situation where I didn't know what to do next. One day I heard about a teaching from a school called the Diamond Approach and my guidance said, "Go and find out more about this," so I went. I had my usual reaction when something is actually going to become my path—I hated it. I disliked everything the teacher said—it was so different from my experience working with feminine spirituality, which was wide open and free. I kept trying but didn't want to go back. I felt like I couldn't.

After a year of this, I noticed that a friend of mine who was part of that school was becoming deeper and more mature. She was working with a private teacher and I started to work with that woman, too. I became interested to the point I thought I'd like to come into the program, but as there were no openings, I had to wait another year or two until they started a new program.

When I went to the first meeting, I had my familiar reaction—I hated it. It was all wrong, at least from the rigidity of my perspective. I remember thinking, "They're doing it wrong, they're all sitting in chairs, and people stand up in the front of the room and talk. I know what real spirituality is—it looks like a Zen center."

Yet there were marvelous questions. At the end of the talk we'd be given one or two questions to discuss in groups of two or three. I didn't know how to answer them. Here I was with a PhD in psychology, and they're asking questions about our own experience—about ourselves—I didn't know how to answer. I didn't know these things about myself.

I was intrigued. The teacher said if I wanted to be part of the program I would have to agree to stay for one year. I thought, "Well, I'm

not going to do that, but I'll stay as long as the questions intrigue me."
Now twenty-five years later I'm still with the school.

I became a teacher in the Diamond Approach fifteen years ago. My
primary practice is called open-ended inquiry. I work with questions.
My soul loves this.

The questions explore. In *East Coker*, T. S. Eliot says all people must
become explorers. When we explore, there's a discovery. What's
thrilling about that is each discovery is grounds for more exploring.
The process of exploration is delightful. It changes too—it gets more
and more subtle over time. If you think, "Oh, okay, now I know"—
which of course is my tendency—you'll get stuck. Then you explore
what it's like to be stuck.

My path of questioning is not for everybody. It's not a *bhakti* path
of love and devotion. I sometimes wonder why I didn't go to that kind
of path—but my particular being likes this kind of path. It's what lets
me open.

Prakash

———————— ⟨∞⟩ ————————

NOW I FEEL like I am a container, in that I have a greater capacity to contain my reactivity. I still get snagged by my reactions but not as often. When I do, I let myself be with the pain of it. Last time I got snagged was because I didn't get what I was hoping for for my birthday. There was a lot of pain in this because it echoed the pain of my childhood. I grew up poor and birthdays were horrible events. In the past when I have been reactive, I didn't know what was going on, but now I have more clarity. I no longer act out my disappointment but rather work with that disappointed part of myself inside.

Going straight into the hurt is what Gurdjieff called "conscious suffering." That's how I deal with difficult feelings that still snag me—I let myself have the feelings without either dodging them or indulging them.

IN A WAY, my path has been a maturational path. I've experienced the ripening of my soul through the work and through the teaching I've received.

One of the most profound things I learned years ago was to let myself be where I was. All my life, the place I was trying to get to was ahead of me.

During a teaching with Hameed eight years ago, I felt a change— "Duh!? Where you are is right here!" To settle into that has been a profound liberation.

This particular teaching is called *The Journey of Descent*. It's about bringing the Absolute into the world—as embodiment, as the actualization of our realization and our illumination. I've found this is what this time in my life is about.

Soon I'll be going back to review the teaching with Hameed, to see if I understand it any more clearly from where I am now. I'm a completely different being, so it will be at a whole new level of depth and understanding.

MY SENSE of the journey has shifted over all these years—shifted into becoming ordinary.

That's not to say that I don't experience incredible depths of awareness and being. But now, I'm focused on integrating those states into drinking a cup of tea, or making contact with another being—the intimacy with myself and with another.

I learned this by working with the dying. The intimacy that I shared with someone at the end of life was what I was yearning for in my day-to-day life, but felt so cut off from. I didn't trust people. That's since changed.

I love the experience of actually being ordinary and not trying to be special. For so many years, I felt I was trying to be special as a spiritual person, a meditator. I was living in another dimension—some god realm—apart from the guy at the cash register in the supermarket.

I love coming back to earth in a grounded, embodied way. This has been my return to the simplicity of being. The integration of my spirituality into my day-to-day life has been the greatest thing that these transformative shifts have brought me. My spiritual life is not separate from my everyday life.

I began this journey with the feeling that everyone else had something that I didn't have and that I couldn't get. I put this judgment onto those I idealized, thinking they had something exalted that was out of my reach. I wish I had listened to my grandmother. She told me the truth when I was a kid—"We're all God's children. No one's better than anyone else."

I feel a tremendous gratitude to have come to where I am now. I feel so much gratitude to the teachers who have guided me on the path.

Ellen

I AM GRATEFUL for the inner sense that's always guided me from one step to the next. The steps I took were the steps that a lot of people take at different stages of their life—just like James Fowler outlines in his book *Stages of Faith*. I know some of those stages to be true.

Most people look at God differently when they're eight than they do when they're older. Some of my progress along the path was slower than other people's. I didn't have the confidence to individuate in a way that was true to myself. I had detached to protect myself. It probably took me longer to get where I am now, but it still happened.

I feel like my own children are much further ahead on this journey than I was at the same age. But that's the way it is if you believe human beings evolve their understanding over generations.

I've had my own times feeling that I had to apply effort or "do better." There are some people who are gifted with extraordinary experiences, who haven't cared a bit about spirituality. It just happens, for whatever reason. As a disciplined person I had a commitment to practice. I tried as hard as I could to give my heart to it—not in the sense of striving so much as developing a strong intention.

What's different for me now is that I know *I* don't do the transforming anyway. To go back to the example of giving the homily at my friend's funeral—my friend and his wife were clergy, as were many of the guests, and two were even bishops. I remember thinking, "Oh my God, I'm getting up here? Oh my heavenly days!" But it was okay—I knew that I wasn't really doing it.

Of course, I have a body and mind, but I also have this grace within, this energy that animates the body and the mind, that makes this body move through this life. I knew that if I would just allow it, this grace would deliver the homily.

My Buddhist meditation teacher says: "Go back into the space and the energy of your body, away from this mind, and just let it happen." And it does!

I've been letting "it"—meaning grace or presence—just be there. Grace works. I'm less striving now than I used to be.

My deepest moments of understanding have had to do with trust. I've learned to trust whatever this is that guides—to go ahead and do what needs to be done, because our mind can certainly have us in a state.

When I go into that spaciousness of presence, I am certainly aware that I have a self and a body, but I'm no longer self-conscious. Within that spaciousness there's really no "within" or "without." Because we're in a body it feels within—but it's really everywhere.

THE LATEST LESSON on my journey has been about awareness. Every now and then I read something that I read six years ago and I think, "I missed that entirely!"

Now I more readily accept the fact that every human being's ego basically works the same, though each has different issues and agendas and is trying to protect itself. But beneath that, in everybody, is this energy—this healing, animating energy that doesn't judge anything, that comes and just *is*.

When someone says or does something that I find either obnoxious or unattractive—anything that my ego uses to separate myself from others—if I'm aware of that then I'll just soften my eyes and fall back into that "something else." That something else is what does the transforming—it is the grace that makes it work. My only effort is to be aware enough to realize what's happening. The moment of realizing is actually, in itself, a form of healing.

The moment I see that and am willing to fall back into grace, then there's a possibility for something different to happen within myself. I have a tendency to judge and separate, likely because of my genetics and because I grew up in a critical and judgmental household. I've worked on that for a long time. I have worked at that because you do have to be willing.

Instead of judging an experience—which makes more separation—I can fall back into letting the universe handle it. This is a gift that's quite freeing.

LIVING WITH CANCER has deepened my understanding. I have thought about mortality because of my friend who died. He was sick for just six months, whereas I've been sick almost seven years.

He had to come to terms with death very quickly while I've had to do it slowly.

I've looked deeply at Teilhard de Chardin's concept of the grace in diminishment. The idea is that the things we're letting go of or that are falling away are only the trappings of our ego. Grace in diminishment means letting go of the roles we play, the functions we have, and all the adjectives, descriptions, or costumes we've had to wear. It even means letting go of our physical activities and things that seem unimportant—but are symbolic—like our hair.

I've had to be willing to let go of these things with each round of chemo. Then when the treatment doesn't work and we start again, that's another form of letting go. Sometimes I feel like I'm disappearing. I'm not—but because I'm down to a very small size now it feels like everything is falling away.

This has been one of the greatest gifts of cancer. My friend who died said so, too. He had played a lot of very important roles in life and suddenly found them gone—he was just lying there. He was so within himself as he approached death that he was nothing but just there, just being. You practice grace in diminishment when you have cancer over a long period of time. I feel like I've had practice in it.

Piece by piece, this process has felt like disappearing. I am left with a sense of just being. You won't feel this unless you've let go of every attachment.

My friend and I bonded over the fact that he, also, was so totally shocked and surprised by grace. As he was dying he felt a joyous trust and peace. He kept saying over and over, "I feel such peace, I feel such peace."

Peace is what's left when everything else is stripped away. It's joy, too—a hard kind of joy, but that is what's left. This doesn't mean that some days aren't hard, though—because when your body feels bad, this can be hard to get beyond because it is so distracting.

When I don't feel great, I practice sinking into that place of presence and grace to find that I can be held in that peace without the pain getting in the way. My friend was fortunate in that way—with glioblastoma there isn't pain. Who knows why? Everyone experiences illness differently.

I have peace, too. I take chemo one day at a time. If it doesn't work, then the medical people try another treatment. But now I'm getting to the end of the barrel—there are some options left but they're not easy. I ask, "Do I want to spend the next four months of my life totally miserable only to have them say, 'Well, that didn't work either'?"

I'm trusting that as each day unfolds, I'll have a peace about what is the right thing to do. The voice in my heart has never led me in the wrong direction—and I trust it even more now. I'm more aware of it. I know that I need to listen to what my intuition inside is leading me to do, not my thinking mind.

It is pure grace that I've been given these seven years to learn all this. This has been a tremendous gift. I know I have a lot more to learn. I'm hoping to learn just to "be" more. Everybody talks about being and doing, but the being I'm talking about is beyond that—it's about just being in this place, being a part of something that's actually whole. It is hard for us to see that in some peculiar way we're one huge organism. That's why there's no judging of right or wrong or what seems good and evil, because we're all really part of the whole.

I may have a tiny understanding of that, but I yearn the most to truly feel a sense of oneness. This oneness is a knowing—not a mental knowing, though—it is something you can only experience. I long for that most of all—a true experience of oneness, such a deep experience that allows you to live more in it and not forget it.

Maybe we don't do that until we die. Maybe that's the great gift of death. We can't begin to understand with our minds.

Reflections on the Fourth Quarter

<hr>

As you can see from the stories here, each person who shared his or her awakening story is an utterly unique, utterly endearing being. No individuality is lost as self-reference is shed. Each entered the path through a different gate. Inquiry, the impulse toward freedom, love, suffering, grief, aging, and illness can be the organizing principles that pull us to depth. The number of gates is boundless.

Along with the stunning display of unique differences in temperament and circumstances and path, we also, once again, find beautiful similarities. The similarities have to do with the fruits of the path. We see, in each person who shared a growing simplicity, ease, gratitude. Freedom, the capacity to love, wisdom, and a quiet and enduring trust emerge.

Each practitioner sharing had a season of development—moral discipline, committed practice, the holy work of healing—and a season of discovery. These seasons allow and amplify each other.

Paths of development and paths of discovery are both offered as spiritual teachings. Both are necessary. May we not get needlessly caught in the path of development—working away to be "spiritual enough"—and miss the opportunity grace offers us in each moment for the discovery of our essential nature, the holiness of our individuality.

Each practitioner came to know that once self-driven effort is surrendered, that long-held energy is released into wonder. Each describes energetic shifts as form—freed from congested self-reference—

became more and more enlivened by the formless. Llewellyn speaks of the humility of ripening and the simplicity of service. We experience a deep fulfillment in embodying the mystery of oneness.

No matter the name given to the continuum of our journey—from suffering to the end of suffering, from confinement to freedom, from defendedness to love, for example—each of us lands in vast, unfathomable Being and comes to embody the qualities of the sacred.

Disenchantment with beliefs, limitations, conventional seductions and a growing longing for more than a meaningless life led each person to begin the Great Search. Recognizing the suffering inherent in separation, in survival mode only, leads us to a willingness to surrender ego and its effortful strategies in the second quarter. The end of seeking, marked by that surrender, liberates previously entrapped energy into Being.

In the third quarter of maturation, we recognize that the only spiritual practice is to be present in and with each freshly arising moment. We stop trying to use the strategies of survival mode and self to "catapult" us beyond self. Disenchantment with all of that grows as striving shifts to deepening intention and trust. Conceptual understanding begins to shift to embodied realization. Development transforms into discovery, determination into wonder, and strategy into surrender.

During the fourth quarter, the quarter of ripening, there occurs a merging of the wisdom of transcendence—the blissful highs of transformative practice and ego-shattering insight—with the wisdom of immanence. As Kabir, the fifteenth-century Sufi mystic and poet, puts it: "Everyone knows the drop merges into the ocean, but few know the ocean merges into the drop." It is all grace, all sacred.

Each practitioner shares recollections of bringing that peacefulness and the wisdom and compassion that co-arise with it to the daily tasks of human life. We see it in the sharings—one teaching classes, one chopping wood on her island, one addressing our planet's need for protection, one leading others to endless inquiry, another having a cup of tea, another finding grace in diminishment.

The questions of wisdom-seeking inevitably bring us to the answer of love.

There is a beautiful ordinariness, an embodied and humble dignity, in spiritual ripening. The emotions, trials, and realizations do not cease. Awakening isn't static. It has nothing to do with getting to the end of an imagined journey and everything to do with being deeply and fully present exactly where we are—as Being reveals as much of its majesty as we can bear in that moment.

It is a never-ending journey.

PART THREE
Recognizing Grace in Your Life

---— ∞ ———

Don't be satisfied with stories,
how things have gone with others.
Unfold your own myth . . .

—RUMI

The Exercise of Spiritual Biography

—— ✧ ——

How did the rose ever open its heart
and give to the world
all its beauty?
It felt the encouragement of light
against its being.

—HAFIZ

THE FIRST PART OF *The Grace in Living* investigates the nature and purpose of spiritual biography, placing this exercise in a context of spiritual unfolding. The second part holds the stories of awakening of teachers and other sincere practitioners. This third part, looking at *your* life through the lens of awakening—except for a few pages of instructions and contemplative questions—is yours to complete. Each one of you will have an utterly unique third part.

This is an opportunity to look at your own unfolding, to notice "the encouragement of light" that has always been present in your life. This is the transformative fulcrum of the work of spiritual biography. It can provide a release from discouragement and lead to a growing sense of gratitude for your own journey.

You might begin to experience trust and confidence in the grace that is always extending itself in response to your heart's yearning. You might begin to recognize that your heart's yearning is itself grace.

The exercise of spiritual biography is a meditative contemplation, a recollection, a remembrance. Be very clear about this: this is a biography not of self but of movement into Being, beyond self.

The contemplative questions evoke recollection. Allow time, per-haps a couple of weeks or a month, to hold these contemplations in your heart—front and center in mindfulness. It isn't possible, and cer-tainly would not be of much benefit, to do the exercise in a single sit-ting. The questions would be overwhelming and the answers would probably be shallow. You need the resonant authenticity of deep and honest reflection.

It is important to sit in meditation as you begin and, again, as you return each time to contemplate the questions of the exercise. Hold your intention full-heartedly and you will deepen your understanding of the unfolding process of your own awakening. You will come to honor it.

The questions of spiritual biography are proposed in order to highlight your experience of each of the quarters of your journey. As you trace your journey right up to the present moment, vignettes, "memory bubbles," will arise in response to the questions. Allow them. Notice them. This is recollection. And notate them on your time line.

Stay with the exercise for as long as it is beneficial for you, until you've wrung the benefit from it. Most people do one question at a time, maybe two, and return to the exercise of spiritual biography almost every day. They often find memories arising one day from a contemplation days earlier.

The first time you engage in the exercise, it seems best to go slowly through the questions of all four quarters first. After that, it can be beneficial to sweep through the questions of each quarter several times. Doing so will engage a deeper looking and a progressively deeper understanding. Doing so serves to awaken the eye of contem-plation, capable of embracing the memory at outer, inner, and secret levels of depth. You will come to deeper understanding of the exqui-sitely calibrated dynamic between the form of our manifestation and the sacred formlessness manifesting it.

In each of the four quarters, there are two overarching questions.

- *What prompted you to turn toward Being, toward awakening and liberation?*
- *What inclined you back into the limitations of survival mode?*

All the other questions, although incredibly beneficial to contemplate, are subsidiary to these two primary questions. The two overarching questions are designed to highlight an important realization.

When your spiritual biography is complete, constellated with the notations of your recollections, you will notice patterns that can deepen your trust in grace and serve as powerful encouragement. You'll see that, in our committed journey, every time we returned back to self, we returned to patterns that needed to be brought into the light of consciousness along with the unhealed wounds that fueled them. Both the turning toward Being and the turning back to self have purpose and necessity—a perfection. You'll see in your recollections how your karmic imprints were transformed, how you healed, how you were transfigured in your journey of awakening. You'll see it all as grace.

Of the many other contemplative questions offered for the exercise of spiritual biography, use the ones that resonate with you. Resonance indicates attunement with our own understanding, our own realizations and dawning insights—our own path.

Many people find it helpful to do the exercise with a spiritual friend. There can also be great benefit in doing it in small groups of like-minded fellow travelers. Do whatever works best for you.

I suggest you spend half an hour or so at a time with the exercise. As you return to it with rhythmic regularity, you will notice that the investigation and the reflection begin to seep into your daily consciousness. You'll have "aha" moments as a memory suddenly reveals itself with startling clarity. As you go through your day, you'll witness more and more awakening moments, attention's movement into Being.

After completing the exercise of spiritual biography once, you might want to revisit it from time to time. You'll note your own growing illumination and freedom with gratitude.

As you engage with the exercise, don't judge yourself. Don't compare yourself with others. Just note the movement of grace in your life.

Watch out for false humility or false pride. The journey of awakening has little to do with the "who" you believe yourself to be. Awakened awareness—and you will notice that it has been present at many points in your life—isn't personal. Paradoxically, as we awaken increasingly into freedom, you will note that your individuality is more freely enjoyed, employed, and offered.

Watch out for whatever beliefs you have concerning what awakening "should" look like. Our conceptual mind doesn't know anything about awakening. Stay in the heart, which knows with deep gratitude that *we are, in this moment, awakening beings*—each of us following the path of our own utterly unique homing device, our longing for the sacred.

Keep in mind that the "progress" we make on our spiritual journeys generally proceeds in an order, but the individual way that it proceeds for each of us is hardly orderly. It's rarely a straight or linear journey. We usually take the scenic route.

For example, we don't usually eliminate a habit pattern or a negative self-judgment along with its stories and justifications in one fell swoop. Usually we spiral around it many times, each time lessening the intensity of its unconscious pull. Each time we return to confront it or it returns to confront us, we are a different person—in many ways a more spacious person with more wisdom, able to contain more of the jagged energy within equanimity.

I think of the circling-over dynamic as being like a backstitch. This is a sewing technique where, with each new stitch of the needle, we move a little farther along in the line of our sewing, and then backtrack to the middle of the last stitch. We move forward again in our sewing and backtrack again to the middle of the last stitch. Pioneer women used this stitch to make work clothes for their families, as it is the strongest stitch there is. In the same way, the backtracking we do as we tend repeatedly to remnants of an original wound makes for the strongest healing.

THE EXERCISE OF SPIRITUAL BIOGRAPHY will highlight for you that you're on the only path you can take. You're in the only place you can be. There are no alternatives. Relax into trust and gratitude. Once your yearning has entered the stream of awakening, grace will carry you along in your own unique pilgrimage.

Engaging in this exercise calls forth our honest self-reflection. It may well be that our journey has not yet led us through all four quarters. Although we can trust that ultimately we will come to our own spiritual maturity and ripening, it is good to recognize where we're at. It's the only place where transformation can occur.

If we recognize our path as one characterized by longing that is, as yet, unengaged with a transformative practice, we know ourselves to be in the first quarter of the journey. We can add momentum by repeatedly contemplating the impermanence of all phenomena, including the self. We can acknowledge the suffering—the lack of ease and connection we experience in the living of our lives. We can focus on discriminating between thoughts and actions that mire us more deeply in that suffering and thoughts and actions that allow us to embody greater ease and kindness.

We want to stoke our longing and deepen the clarity and thoroughness of our intention to awaken. We can invoke grace—although be forewarned! "To summon grace," as Anne Lamott reminds us, "say 'help.' And then buckle up."

If you are actively engaged in a transformative practice—however old or new that engagement—and find yourself frustrated, caught in your own beliefs of unworthiness, and vacillating between striving and discouragement, your journey has landed you in the typically extended, rough passage of the second quarter.

For most people, the second quarter lasts for a long time. It is the quarter where much of the work is done, where much of the healing is effected, where many of the confusions about the spiritual path and our goals for our spiritual path are clarified.

It is helpful to go slowly through our exploration of the second quarter. More questions are offered for contemplation in this quarter than in the other quarters. They're meant to provide multiple avenues or angles of access into clarity about our own unfolding during this pivotal part of the awakening journey.

The second quarter is the quarter of the self's stark realizations of the extent of its limitations. Although there are certainly people whose word we can trust when they declare that striving, strategizing, and trying to "figure out" awakening are hopeless ploys, most of us have to go through the process of checking all that off on our own list—so that we know their limitations for ourselves before we are able to surrender them.

If, indeed, you find yourself in the second quarter of your own awakening journey, stay open to the possibilities of each moment as it presents itself to you—exactly where you are and without judgment. Stay mindfully attentive to whatever mistaken beliefs are obstructions to the ease of grace. Heal your wounds with tenderness, with growing wisdom and compassion. Stay present and familiarize yourself with the spacious clarity of Being, beyond self. Look for grace—it's always here. Cultivate trust.

The second quarter is the time where longing begins to be fulfilled and seeking ceases. It ceases as our confidence in our capacity to enter Being grows and as our trust grows in Being's ever-present welcome. Practice in the recognition that all practice is preparation for the surrender that will carry you on your journey into the third quarter. As we surrender both the searching and the seeker, we come to know the exhilarating beauty and freedom of liberation.

If grace has carried you into the third quarter of your path of awakening, simply stay in trust. Healing into maturity can be a long period of gradual, further development leading to ever-greater discovery of essence, meaning, truth. Simply continue with the work of healing and releasing. Surrender is renunciation. It clears out the space in our being that attachment and aversion had occupied for so long. It allows us to approach, bear, and embody the sacred at ever-deepening, ever-more-inclusive levels. It becomes a joy to let go of the burden of self and enter into the vast dimension of Being.

IN THE EXERCISE of spiritual biography, we make use of a time line of our life. You can create one for yourself by simply drawing a line —a series of dashes—on a blank piece of paper, or a few pieces taped together, in a landscape orientation, marking the quarters one through four. The time line, as we use it, extends from our earliest memories, at the left, to the very moment in which pen hits paper to engage in this exercise, at the right.

We begin with just this simple line of dashes tracing the footsteps of our journey. Each gap between the dashes is a *bodhimandala*, a gateway into the vastness of Being, bearing witness to the ever-presence of grace. Each gap holds the "sacrament of the present" and allows each dash to consciously participate in the sacred.

— — — — — — — — — — — — — — — — — — — —

The only demarcations would be the recognition of entry into a new quarter of your journey. In a foreshortened, "telescoped" way, that would look like this:

```
     1         2         3         4
— — — — | — — — — | — — — — | — — — — | — —
```

With a quieted, undistracted mind, ask yourself the questions. They will evoke your recollections. Notate your responses to each of the questions in approximately chronological order, the "river of time" we typically impute. Memories won't necessarily present themselves in chronological order, so you want to leave space between notations for memories yet to arise. Think of the way, on a street blossoming with new houses, house numbers aren't assigned consecutively at first. Some numbers are skipped to allow for new houses to arise between the ones already built.

Our memories arise as they will. We hold our intention for them to reveal what they have to reveal. And, as they arise and as we reflect upon them, our understanding of our transformative shifts becomes deeper—as does our recognition that grace has never, not once, been absent. Such recollection has great value.

Some transformative shifts occur in a moment. As you explore these shifts, it can be of benefit to stay with the specific memory of that moment. Other transformative shifts are more gradual. We may notice that a shift has occurred after the fact, when we are beyond the causes and conditions that allowed and held the trans- formation, and we have the vantage point of looking back on it. In this case, we explore the memories of that period, that chrysalis time.

Along your time line, notate each newly emerging memory of a moment or a chapter in your life as it arises in response to the ques- tion you're reflecting upon. Remember it's helpful to use a single word or catchphrase as we notate significant moments in our journey on the time line.

For example, one of the most meaningful turning points that set me out on a spiritual search occurred almost imperceptibly on a hill in the Connecticut countryside. I was sitting on the soft, green grass of New England on the top of a hill. The sky was the brilliant blue of autumn. The valley below and the surrounding hills were ablaze with fall's colors. My experience was of going into silence—everything around me going into silence. There was a beautiful, complete stilling, a deep and prolonged pause of absolute peace and ease and joy. I had no idea how long it lasted but it resonated profoundly within me. I knew that this wasn't the typical way in which I spent my days and I knew that I wanted more of this deep peace.

The memory is one at the very edge of the first quarter of my jour- ney, one of the moments that nudged me into seeking in earnest. So,

I would place it near the end of the time line of the first quarter and simply notate it as "hill."

```
        HILL  1            2            3            4
        — — — | — | — — — — | — — — — | — — — — | — —
```

EMPLOYING BOTH your longing and your sincerity, open to the great benefit this exercise holds for you. You will discover, as Hafiz assured us all centuries ago, "the astonishing light of your own being." You are charting the sparkling points of your own growing illumination as you enter, embody, and radiate that astonishing light of awakened presence and share it ever more inclusively with a suffering world.

THE FIRST QUARTER:
From Tasting to Hunger

Two overarching questions:

What were the moments that led you to search for greater being, for Spirit?

What were the moments that called you away, back to limitation in survival mode?

What were your deepest moments of understanding or of vastness / unity / presence?

What were your conceptions of yourself?

What were your ideas about the sacred?

What was the nature of your relationship with others?

What were the moments in which you felt wounded?

What conclusions did you come to about yourself and about the world?

What were your challenges?

What gave you strength?

What beneficial qualities did you develop?

What negative beliefs about yourself did you develop?

What did you learn from the spiritual mentors or "teachers of goodness" you might have had?

What rules for living did you come to hold? Which of these remain? Which have you discarded?

What are your legacies from your family of origin?

What were the moments when you experienced a shift in the way you saw yourself?

What were the moments when you experienced a shift in the way you experienced the sacred?

When did spiritual hunger or curiosity begin to awaken in you?

THE SECOND QUARTER:
From Seeking to the End of Seeking

Two overarching questions:

What turned you toward spirit?

What turned you back toward the separate sense of self?

When did you first reach out to find a spiritual path?

What instigated the beginning of active searching?

What teachers or teachings resonated with you?

What shifts occurred in you in response to the resonance?

As you began seeking, what were your ideas about the spiritual path and spiritual "goals?"

What healing did you find to be necessary in order to continue?

How did you tend to the healing that was needed?

What shifts have there been in your self-concept and sense of worth as a result of whatever healing has taken place?

What inner obstructions did you bring to the journey, and what has been the changing nature of your relationship with them?

What challenges were you facing in your life at this time?

What challenges were you facing in your practice?

What has been the changing nature of your relationship with emotional reactivity?

What practices did you engage in during this second quarter, and what was your experience of them?

What were the changing ideas you had about these practices—what did you believe would happen as you practiced?

What was the nature of your effort and striving during this time?

What were the shifts in your understanding of the spiritual path?

What was your spiritual goal initially? How has that shifted?

Were there periods of disappointment in terms of the goals you set for your practice and your journey? What did you learn from these disappointments?

How has your practice shifted over time?

What do you consider to be the awakening benefits of the different practices you've engaged in?

What have been the shifts in your changing relationships with family and loved ones?

Were there moments of spiritual crisis?

What were your deepest moments of understanding?

What have been the shifts in your capacity to love and compassionately care?

What have been the shifts in your relationship with conceptual mind?

What turning points allowed you to surrender?

What growing disenchantment with seductions and distractions have you noticed?

When did you assume responsibility for your own spiritual path and began to give authority to your own direct experience?

What has been the changing nature of your spiritual confidence?

What were the moments when you most felt the presence of Spirit?

What has "rearranged" in you on an energetic level?

At what point(s) did you come to hold yourself accountable for your realizations and understand that they're meant to be embodied?

What has been the changing nature of your relationship with faith and confidence? With trust in grace?

What are the moments during this time for which you are most grateful?

THE THIRD QUARTER:
Healing into Maturity

Two overarching questions:

What inclined you more deeply into awakening?

What drew you back into a separate sense of self?

What healing was necessary?

What practices and experiences have brought you more deeply into your heart?

How have you reduced the distance between your realizations and your embodiment of them in everyday life?

What has been the changing nature of your practice?

What shifts have there been in your understanding of the spiritual path? Of awakening?

What shifts have there been in your understanding of the self?

What would be the name of your continuum?

The Fourth Quarter:
Ripening

Two overarching questions:

What inclines you more deeply into Being?

What can pull you back into the reactivity of a separate sense of self?

Have you had times where you felt, "This is it!
This is enlightenment!"? What did you learn?

What is your practice now?

What do you offer the world?

What are you grateful for?

About the Contributors

RODNEY SMITH. Rodney is a retired Guiding Teacher for the Insight Meditation Center and the founding teacher of the Seattle Insight Meditation Society. This year will end a phased-in retirement where he is cutting back on his formal teaching and devoting himself to personal reflection and writing. Previously, he served as the director of the Hospice of Seattle, as well as having spent a number of years as a Buddhist monk. He has always taught the immediacy of the Dharma that, without qualifications, is forever accessible regardless of conditions. Rodney says, "This is the great Lion's Roar of the Buddha: it is here, it is now, it is forever." His books include *Lessons from the Dying*; *Stepping Out of Self-Deception*; and *Awakening: A Paradigm Shift of the Heart*.

CYNTHIA BOURGEAULT. A modern-day mystic, Episcopal priest, writer, and internationally known retreat leader, Cynthia balances her time between solitude at her seaside hermitage in Maine and a demanding schedule teaching and spreading the recovery of the Christian contemplative and Wisdom path.

She has been a longtime practitioner of the meditative practice of Centering Prayer and is a prolific writer, always encouraging contemplative practice.

Her books include *Mystical Hope*; *The Wisdom Way of Knowing*; *Centering Prayer and Inner Awakening*; and *The Meaning of Mary Magdalene*.

LLEWELLYN VAUGHAN-LEE. Llewellyn is a Sufi teacher and author. Born in London in 1953, he has followed the Sufi path since he was 19. In 1991 he moved with his family to California to found the Golden Sufi Center. In recent years the focus of his writing and teaching has been on spiritual responsibilty at a time of global crisis and the emerging subject of spiritual ecology.

His books include two spiritual autobiographies: *A Face Before I Was Born* and *Fragments of a Love Story: Reflections on the Life of a Mystic*.

SHERRY RUTH ANDERSON. Sherry is a psychologist, author, former Zen teacher, and present teacher of the Diamond Approach to Spiritual Development. Her path is one of inquiry. She writes and teaches about spiritual development with a particular emphasis on women's spirituality and on aging as awakening.

Her books include *The Feminine Face of God* (coauthored with Patricia Hopkins); *The Cultural Creatives* (coauthored with Paul Ray); and *Ripening Time: Inside Stories for Aging with Grace*.

PRAKASH MACKAY. Prakash has lived in Maui for thirty years. He began meditating at the age of seventeen and has remained a dedicated practitioner since that time. He has worked at Hospice Maui since 1992, serving as Spiritual Care and Bereavement Coordinator, and still facilitates grief support groups there. He is a Diamond Approach teacher, working in both Maui and the United Kingdom.

ELLEN KYMPTON. Ellen lived in Virginia her whole life. She was greatly supported by her husband and three children and all of her family, as well as by a group of friends both old and new and by teachers and communities in Virginia and India. She continued to "sit" almost daily as she lived with metastatic cancer. Bluebirds appeared often in her garden. She said they taught her how to just "be" as part of her practice. Ellen died on January 2, 2016.

Acknowledgments

DEEP BOWS OF RESPECT and gratitude to Llewellyn Vaughan-Lee and Cynthia Bourgeault, and to Rodney Smith—one of my own most precious teachers. Deep bows, also, to Sherry Anderson, Prakash Mackay, and Ellen Kympton, longtime practitioners who also shared their spiritual biographies.

Thanks also to the dear and helping heart and mind of Sarah Burrowes and to the support and encouragement that I receive so often from friends, including Mark Brady, David Colin Carr, Frank Ostaseski, and Rose Mary Dougherty. The readers of my books humble me with their thanks and I am very grateful for their kindness and inspiration.

Again, as always, I thank my children: Colin, Megan, Valley, and Bethany; their spouses/partners: Meagan, David, Kent, and Keith; and my brothers: Ted and Michael. My grandchildren are all endearing in their support as well. So, thanks, too: Patrick, Hannah, Blake, Kalie, Emily, Aidan, Alyssa, Cory, Dustin, Bailey, Kerin, and Abbey.

I'm appreciative of the careful reading and all the thoughtful, nuanced suggestions offered by Arnie Kotler. There were many.

Wisdom Publications is a wonderful group with which to work. I thank them there for helping to bring this book into the world.

A SMALL PORTION of the chapter "The Journey" is adapted from "Full Circle: The Evidence of Love," which appeared in *Oneing: Evidence* (volume 1, issue 2), published by the Center for Action and Contemplation.

About the Author

KATHLEEN DOWLING SINGH is a Dharma practitioner and in-demand speaker and teacher. She is the author of *The Grace in Dying: How We Are Transformed Spiritually as We Die* and *The Grace in Aging: Awaken as You Grow Older*. Kathleen lives in Sarasota, Florida. She maintains a website at kathleendowlingsingh.com.

What to Read Next
from Wisdom Publications

The Grace in Aging
Awaken as You Grow Older
Kathleen Dowling Singh

"Don't grow old without it."
—Rachel Naomi Remen, MD, author of *Kitchen Table Wisdom*

Living and Dying with Confidence
A Day-by-Day Guide
Anyen Rinpoche and Allison Choying Zangmo
Foreword by Kathleen Dowling Singh

This guide provides a daily companion to help readers prepare for death intellectually, emotionally, and spiritually.

Living Mindfully
At Home, at Work, and in the World
Deborah Schoeberlein David, MEd
with David Panakkal, MD

"Simple, direct, and full of real-world wisdom, Deborah's excellent new book is for everyone interested in bringing mindful awareness into their daily lives."
—Susan Kaiser Greenland, author of *The Mindful Child*

How to Wake Up
A Buddhist-Inspired Guide to Navigating Joy and Sorrow
Toni Bernhard

"This is a book for everyone."
—Alida Brill, author of *Dancing at the River's Edge*

If You're Lucky, Your Heart Will Break
Field Notes from a Zen Life
James Ishmael Ford

"A valuable companion filled with encouragement for beginners and experienced meditators alike."
—Diane Eshin Rizzetto, author of *Waking Up to What You Do*

About Wisdom Publications

Wisdom Publications is the leading publisher of classic and contemporary Buddhist books and practical works on mindfulness. To learn more about us or to explore our other books, please visit our website at wisdompubs.org or contact us at the address below.

Wisdom Publications
199 Elm Street
Somerville, MA 02144 USA

We are a 501(c)(3) organization, and donations in support of our mission are tax deductible.

Wisdom Publications is affiliated with the Foundation for the Preservation of the Mahayana Tradition (FPMT).